THE FORGOTTEN PRINCE

By Monika Mangal

Text Copyright © 2016 Monika Mangal

All rights reserved

Prologue

The silence was unbearable. It weighed upon him like a rock threatening to crush him. Only every now and then was it broken by the soft dripping of a waterclock.
Siamun had been listening intently to the intermittent sound, which had somehow been comforting at first - something to hold on to. But with every drip it became louder and grew in intensity until his head eventually began to reverberate with it. Siamun wondered how a sound that went almost unnoticed during the day could make such a noise at night. It must be down to the immense strain he felt that put him so on edge. In this last night before his departure his mind was in turmoil. Having abandoned any thought of sleep he sat up and ran his fingers through his short, black hair. A close look at the waterclock told him that daybreak was not far off.
The past hours had been crawling by, stretching out almost endlessly. Time went by agonizingly slowly and yet far too quickly for his liking, which struck him as odd. Until now he hadn't realized that this was even possible. Surely only someone longing for something to happen and dreading it at the same time could feel this way. Just like he could hardly await his departure and yet would rather not leave at all, because he wasn't sure if he had made the right choice.
Nonsense, he told himself. What could possibly go wrong? Like so many other young men before him he was only trying to make things happen, to succeed in life. He was both intelligent and gifted. His talents would be wasted if he didn't dare make

this move. But try as he might, he didn't quite manage to silence the doubtful voice of his heart.

Slowly letting out a deep breath, Siamun rose and walked up to the window overlooking the extensive garden. Leaning his shoulder against the wall, he took in the familiar sight of the bushes and trees outlined by the pale moonlight, but his mind refused to be put at rest.

It wasn't that easy. He had to contend with difficulties others were spared. Nobody was to know his true identity. But even though he had taken great care to conceal it, it was by no means certain that his secret could never be uncovered.

But then perhaps the greatest danger lurked within his own heart. What if he was ever tempted to reach out for what was rightfully his, yet belonged to another? What if in doing so he brought death and destruction about and plunged scores of people into ruin, perhaps including himself?

Deeply engrossed in his gloomy thoughts as he was, Siamun had lost any sense of time. He was surprised to see a faint sliver of light just above the horizon. Glad that the wait was finally over, he turned away.

There was no going back.

Chapter One

"Are you sure you haven't forgotten anything?" Meritamun asked, not for the first time.

"Yes, mother," Siamun replied patiently. "I'm absolutely sure."

"Hearing you talk like that one might think that we are about to march across scorching deserts," Panakht cut in, "when we're actually only going to cross the river in slightly southerly direction, so to speak."

"But still it's almost a whole day's journey," Meresankh pointed out.

"Of course it is, my dear," Panakht said. "Though it should be noted that much of the time is taken up by embarking and mooring the ship. And afterwards," he added with a meaningful lifting of his eyebrows, "all the amenities that a great city like Mennefer has to offer will be at our disposal."

"Which you will be craving in vain soon enough," Meresankh shot back.

Panakht grinned roguishly and raised his hands in mock surrender. "All right, I admit defeat! You're really never lost for words, are you?"

Meritamun gave Siamun a worried look. "Wouldn't it be better if you took on a different name from now on?"

It hit him hard to see her troubled face. Her hand shook slightly as she smoothed a strand of her greying hair back. He thought of the many times Meritamun had heaped reproaches on herself for not having changed his name while the time had been right. He knew that she wouldn't have dared, anyway. Too much had she feared to incur the wrath of the gods, or that of his deceased father, who after all hadn't been just anybody.

"That's really not necessary," Siamun said cheerfully. "My name isn't quite as uncommon as you might think. Besides, it has to match this one here."

He patted his broad green sash, from which the upper end of a scroll stuck out. Her slight nod confirmed that his foster mother had understood his allusion to the letter of recommendation given to him by the high priest of Ra, in order to facilitate his prospective career as an architect in His Majesty's service, which was all he hoped for.

"Uncle, are you sure you won't forget to bring something back for me?"

Siamun's glance passed to his little nephew Ranefer who was tugging hard at his sleeve.

"You meant to say for *us*, didn't you?" Ranefer's younger brother Amunmesse butted in at once.

Siamun smiled at them both. "Of course you two will get something nice once I'm back."

"And when will you be back?" chorused the boys.

"Soon, I hope."

One glance at the billowing sail of the ship told him that it was ready to go. The two young men hurriedly embraced everyone in turn. At last a young woman who had been standing there in silence for the whole time stepped forward. She was strikingly beautiful with her large almond-shaped eyes and delicate nose, and Siamun hadn't failed to notice the glances of plain admiration she attracted from all sides. Even the somewhat sullen expression on her pretty face didn't hamper her good looks.

Apart from the shape of his eyes and the bold arch of his brows Siamun bore a strong resemblance to the young woman who could easily be recognized to be his sister.

He gave her a quick hug. "Take good care of yourself, Satet," he told her.

"Yes, and please do behave yourself, will you?" Panakht shouted back over his shoulder while he strode briskly towards the landing stage.

Before Siamun turned to go, he saw how a reluctant smile spread across Satet's face.

"You'd better watch out for yourselves!" she called out in a good-natured tone of voice.

In passing Siamun patted his young nephews' heads one last time before he too made for the ship.

No sooner had Siamun's feet touched the planks of the deck than the ship cast off. The journey had begun.

He found Panakht standing at the rail waving frantically. Then he stopped to cup his hands around his mouth. "Give Taneferet my regards when she comes!" he shouted.

When he turned round to face Siamun his eyes were glistening with tears. Quickly he pulled his sleeve across.

"I hate this kind of thing," he muttered bashfully.

"Don't worry, it's the same with me," Siamun admitted. "I'm glad it's over and done with. Come on, let's find ourselves somewhere to sit down. I don't want to grow roots standing here."

They strolled across the deck towards the stern. There, in the shadow cast by the great sail, they came across a number of folding chairs.

"Just what we needed," Siamun sighed contentedly as he lowered himself onto one of them.

The ship on which they travelled was no fancy affair but rather a robust freighter purpose built for the transport of heavy cargo. It was part of a small fleet that belonged to Siamun's brother-in-law, Meresankh's husband Kenamun who was trading quite successfully with precious woods. As every so often he was on his way northwards in order to acquire another load of the especially coveted cedar wood from the city of Byblos. Sometimes his business trips took longer than expected, and the family often jested about his wife's at times sharp tongue being the true reason behind his extended stays. Panakht had assumed a very relaxed pose indeed with his long legs stretched out in front of him and his hands clasped behind his neck. The muscular shape of his limbs could only be guessed under his ankle-length sleeved robe. Siamun was dressed in a similar way, perhaps a bit more lavishly with his broad colourful collar and the decorated sash. Despite the still prevailing heat of the last month of Shemu, the harvest season, his elaborate garment didn't bother him. Quite on the contrary, the smooth linen lay cool on his skin and screened it from the rays of the blazing sun. However, for reasons of comfort he had refrained from wearing a wig. This kind of formality could wait. After all, he didn't have to impress anyone just yet.

Siamun was first to break the silence. "I'm worried about Satet," he said in a low voice.

"Why?" Panakht asked lazily. "Because she still hasn't found herself a husband?"

"Rather because she doesn't want to find herself one," Siamun pointed out. "And it's not just that. I haven't told you yet that she asked me to take her with me to Mennefer."

Panakht grinned. "She asked? Are you sure she didn't more like demand it?"

Siamun gave a slight shrug. "Well, you know what she's like. Anyway, she was adamant that I let her come with us. I had a hard time talking her out of it. It was only when I told her that rather than attending lavish banquets I was going to crawl about dusty construction sites that she finally left me alone."

"Then I take it all is well," Panakht said with unnerving calm.
"No, it's not!" Siamun insisted. "Haven't you noticed the sullen look on Satet's face? Honestly, I fear she might be up to something really stupid."
"What could she be up to? You think she's going to run away?"
Siamun shrugged helplessly. "Maybe."
Panakht shook his head. "I can't imagine her doing that. Satet might have her bad ways, but I'm sure she wouldn't go that far. She'll keep on sulking some more, then she'll forget all about it, you'll see."
Siamun said no more. He hoped fervently that Panakht was right.

The hours passed by pleasantly enough, and when they felt hungry they tucked heartily into the delicious cold duck roast and fresh bread Meritamun had packed them along with figs and the nuts of the dom-palm. It was late afternoon when they reached the plateau of the Great Pyramids. They stood near the prow, watching in silence as they moved along the awe-inspiring giants.
"And?" Panakht cast a curious look at his friend. "Doesn't the heart of the aspiring architect beat faster at the mere sight of such majesty?"
Siamun laughed amiably. "It sure does."
"It's a pity that nowadays they don't build the like anymore," Panakht said quietly.
"To be honest, I don't regret it," Siamun replied. "I mean, pyramids are most impressive buildings, particularly those of a certain size, but to me they are not challenging enough. All that has to be done is to work out the dimensions of the base along with the correct angle of inclination for the desired height and to calculate the number of stone blocks needed to build it.

Everything else is a given. I tend to prefer more demanding projects which require a whole lot of imagination."

"Now, listen to this," Panakht said, lifting a brow. "Someone's having grand plans here!"

Siamun laughed, hoping that it didn't sound quite as nervous as he felt. "I know that I'm probably only fooling myself. If I'm going to be accepted at all I'll most likely be nothing more than the underling of some other underling and spend my time going on errands and carrying out orders."

Panakht's face took on an unusually serious expression. "I don't think so," he said slowly. "Knowing you as I do, I guess you'll be right at the top in no time at all."

Right at the top...

In Siamun's mind these words suddenly assumed a different, more sinister meaning. Desperately he tried to rid himself of this forbidden thought.

Panakht must have sensed his uneasiness, for he looked rather sheepish and carefully avoided Siamun's eyes for the next few moments.

"I believe we've already reached the outskirts of Mennefer!" he suddenly exclaimed with obvious relief.

He was right. The first houses belonging to the grand capital had come into view, and so had the moored ships which were gently bobbing on the waves. The further they proceeded, the denser the tangle of ships and boats of all kinds grew. Soon there were no more free berths to be seen at all. They had arrived at Perunefer, Mennefer's busy harbour with its extensive docks. How different it was from the much smaller port of Iunu which they had just left behind! Here there were ships as far as the eye could see, occupying not only one, but both riverbanks, and in addition to them many more boats and skiffs were passing by, weaving their way skilfully in between the throng of hulks.

Siamun doubted that they were ever going to succeed in finding themselves a mooring place, but the experienced captain spotted one soon enough and -aided by a few strong men on the quay who pulled hard at the ropes- even managed to squeeze his freighter into the tight space.

The sun was about to set when the two friends disembarked. While they were waiting for the man who was supposed to carry part of their luggage, Siamun realized for the first time how soon he and Panakht would have to part.
"I can hardly believe that you'll be off to the far north in a matter of days," Siamun said. "And only the gods know where I am going to end up."
"It's not that bad, you know," Panakht replied with a wry smile, adjusting the bundle with his own belongings which he had slung over his shoulder. "The new military base is situated close to Avaris, and therefore it shouldn't be too far off the beaten track. I have heard it said that they keep great numbers of horses and chariots there. Just the way I like it."
Siamun smiled at him affectionately. He knew his friend's fondness for horses and animals in general, and he also knew how apt he was at riding the chariot and handling weapons. Without any doubt Panakht would make a fine soldier and charioteer.
Siamun felt that the time was right to say their good-byes. He closed the distance between them and the two young men embraced each other warmly.
"May the gods protect you," Siamun muttered. "When do you think we will meet again?"
Panakht shrugged. "I don't know. It's quite possible that we'll return from our base before embarking on our first campaign, but then I can't be sure about that. Besides, it is open to

question if you will be around then."

Siamun nodded slowly. "We'll see about that."

Just then he caught sight of his porter who was approaching them, loaded with two small chests.

"There he is, finally. Let's go!"

They set off, forcing their way through the throng of people consisting of yelling and cursing sailors and porters, shouting merchants and wide-eyed newcomers. The air was filled with various smells mingling into an overwhelming mixture from which only the stenches of sweat and raw fish stood out. They were roughly pushed and barged into more than once before they eventually emerged from the chaos.

In front of an extensive single-storey building bare of any decoration they came to a halt. The seemingly only entrance was flanked by two scribes sitting on folding chairs, their writing equipment at the ready. It was plain to see that this place was a military barrack, temporary home to new recruits like Panakht. Although he had already served as a common soldier for several months, he had to register anew before he could join the royal chariotry.

The scribes cast expectant glances at the new arrival. Before he walked up to them, Panakht nodded one last time in Siamun's direction, his eyes gleaming with excitement.

Siamun turned and hurriedly followed the porter who had already continued on his way. They had to cross a canal in order to get to the southern district where most impressive villas surrounded by extensive gardens bordered the broad streets, screened from view by gleaming white walls. Clearly this part of the city was home to the more illustrious members of society like high dignitaries and wealthy courtiers. Even a small royal palace was said to be among the exclusive properties, whereas the great ancient palace which had served almost all the kings since Thutmose Aakheperkare as residence lay beyond the grand temple of Ptah, the city centre proper. Siamun had trouble to keep up with his porter who seemingly couldn't wait to get rid of his burden. But it was something else that caused his growing uneasiness. It couldn't be long now that he reached his destination, the house of the royal architects. He had been informed that it adjoined the estate of the venerable Nebamun, who held not only the office of the northern vizier but also that of the overseer of all royal works in the Place of Truth. Therefore it was only natural that he wanted to have his subordinates close by.

Eventually the porter made for the entrance of a large building and put Siamun's chests down. Siamun rewarded his efforts with a small piece of copper worth a deben, and the man took himself off.

Upon entering Siamun was stopped by one of the doorkeepers. He explained that he had come to join the royal architects, and the man scuttled off without making it clear whether Siamun had been expected or not. He reappeared soon after with a young fellow in his wake who greeted Siamun, indicating with a slight jerk of his head that he should follow him. The young man led him through a columned hallway at the far end of which lay a number of chambers. He opened one of the doors which had been left ajar and motioned Siamun to enter.

The room was illuminated by the light of several oil lamps. Siamun found himself standing opposite a large desk which was covered with scrolls. A middle-aged man was sitting behind it, hardly raising his eyes to glance briefly at the new arrival before he carried on scrutinizing the papyrus in front of him.

Siamun's companion had left the room. Since the man had failed to offer Siamun a seat, he just stood where he was, trying hard not to show his growing annoyance at the other's indifference. Eventually the man put the scroll away and addressed him.

"Any recommendations?" he asked, not wasting his time on greeting or polite conversation.

Siamun produced the scroll from his sash and handed it over without saying a word, seeing no need to be overly courteous either. With an expression that could best be described as bored the man broke the seal and unfolded the document. Then he held it so close to the lamp next to him that Siamun feared it might catch fire at any moment. Clearly, his eyesight left a great deal to be desired. With his shaven head he looked like a priest, but judging by his demeanour he had to be one of the higher-ranking architects.

While the man skimmed through the text his eyes widened considerably. Once or twice he nodded approvingly.

"So you are Siamun, son of Neferibre?" he eventually asked without taking his eyes off the scroll.

Siamun confirmed his question.

"And your father was an architect before you? Which projects has he been working on?"

"He was mainly occupied with designing tombs for the wealthy," Siamun explained.

"Hm." The man stroked his chin while he thought hard. "Never heard of him before," was his devastating verdict.

"My father died almost seventeen years ago, shortly before the birth of my younger brother."

The other didn't show if he saw this as an acceptable excuse.

"How old are you?" he only asked.

"I'm nineteen."

"You look older than that."

Siamun smiled amiably. "I hear that quite often."

"Which position did you hold in the temple of Iunu?"

"At first I was a wab-priest. Then I rose through the ranks until I became a lecture priest in my third and final year."

The man leaned back and folded his arms across his chest, watching as the papyrus rolled itself up. If he was impressed by what he had read, he hid it very well.

"Your credentials are excellent."

Siamun was quite baffled at hearing such a positive remark.

"The high priest of Ra is full of praise for you. But," the man continued with an air of importance, "you will surely understand that we need to form our own opinion before taking you on as an apprentice. Therefore you will be subjected to a written examination first thing in the morning which will comprise all the theoretical knowledge you have allegedly acquired during your three years at the temple. It is quite possible that there will also be additional, more challenging tasks to test your abilities to the full. Should you pass this test, you will have to demonstrate your practical skills as well. That's all for now. You may leave."

He clapped his hands twice, and the young fellow Siamun had seen before appeared at once. He must have been waiting close by all the time.

"Nebnefer, show him to his room!"

With a slight bow Siamun took his leave and followed Nebnefer.

"Have you been here for long?" he asked the young man, who could not be much older than himself.

"A few months," Nebnefer replied. "What's your name?"

Siamun told him. "And with whom did I have the pleasure just now?"

Nebnefer grinned. "Has he forgotten again to introduce himself? That's just like him. His name is Wenamun, and it is one of his duties to recruit and train promising new architects. In case you stay with us, you will soon find out that he is not as bad a chap as he seems to be."

Siamun had his doubts, but he didn't voice them. "How long will I be allowed to live here?"

"Should you be accepted, you can stay as long as you want, or until you find yourself something more suitable. Your living costs will be deducted straight from your wages."

They had reached a small room which was sparsely furnished, but at least it looked clean.

"This is yours for the time being," Nebnefer explained. "Make yourself at home. Tomorrow we will surely meet again. Do you want me to bring you something to eat?"

Siamun declined, and the young man left him alone.

Siamun's gaze swept the room. His two chests had already been placed along the far wall. Apart from them there was only a table, a chair and a low bed for which he headed straight away.

Deeply grateful he flung himself on its woven mattress. Then he clasped his hands behind his head and stared at the ceiling. Even in the dim light of the only lamp he could see that it was in some need of attention, but such little shortcomings couldn't bother him right now. His sense of relief was far too great for that.

He had made it. That was all that counted. He hadn't passed his examination yet, but Siamun was so overjoyed already as if he had just been made overseer of all royal building works. He had overcome the first, all important obstacle. Wenamun hadn't got the faintest idea that he had been fooled. Siamun had told him blatant lies, and that conceited fellow hadn't become in the least suspicious.

There was nothing wrong with Siamun's credentials. But his father's name was not Neferibre, and he hadn't been architect either. Siamun had no younger brother, and he wasn't nineteen. His true age was twenty-three, but for reasons he couldn't share with anybody he had to stick to these wrong details, both now and forever more.

Not a single moment did he worry about the imminent examination. He had always felt at home with numbers; he loved their versatility and reliability. There was nothing he couldn't do with them. He felt sure he'd pass the test with ease. Little by little the immense pressure that had weighed on him all day long wore off. His empty stomach was rumbling, but it didn't bother him. His eyes grew heavy, and when he finally closed them he drifted immediately into a deep refreshing sleep.

****

"How much longer are you going to wait, I wonder?"

Tuya helped herself to one of the appetizing slices of honeyed cake that were arranged on the table in front of her. She looked at it enquiringly as if willing it to provide her with an answer before taking a large bite.

Seti, at whom her question had been addressed, stifled a groan. His wife just wouldn't give up.

"You know well that the time isn't right," he said. "As soon as we're back in Mennefer I'll have to set off on an inspection of all my building projects, and afterwards it'll be high time for me to embark on my next campaign."

He could see from her dismissive wave that Tuya was not impressed. "These things can wait. What could possibly be more important than Ramses' official appointment as heir apparent? Besides, it only takes a simple ceremony which won't keep you long."

Seti knew that it wouldn't be that simple. Apart from the lack of time he just wasn't prepared to comply with her wish, and that for good reasons.

"It's not only that," he explained, eyeing his wife warily. "In my opinion it is still too early. Ramses is only fourteen years old. I would like to give him at least another two years. By then he will be mature enough to take on the responsibilities that come with this office. Besides, why the hurry? His position as future heir apparent is undisputed. After all, you are my Great Royal Wife, and he is my only son."

"Are you sure about that?" Tuya asked while she vigorously brushed a few crumbs off her ample lap. "About the fact that Ramses' position is undisputed, I meant to say," she added quickly when she saw the puzzled look on her husband's face. "I have heard that at Ipet-Sut you've had your friend Mehy depicted right behind your chariot. This is an extraordinary honour, and it is far more than usually befits mere commoners."

Once again Seti was taken aback by the derogative way in which his wife referred to those who were of non-royal descent. Prior to his coronation more than two years ago both he and Tuya had been just that –mere commoners without so much as a single drop of royal blood running through their veins. The haughty demeanour which she had adopted ever since becoming Great Royal Wife increasingly displeased him. And as was her habit she had put on far too much make-up for his liking.

"As you know Mehy has shown exceeding bravery during the recent campaign," he reminded her. "Therefore the honour he received was only his due."

Tuya regarded him out of fixed eyes. "I am sure that Ramses, too, would excel in battle if only you gave him the chance. But this is not my only concern. Sometimes I do fear that you might even consider appointing this Mehy crown prince instead of your own son."

Seti decided to ignore the reproach in her voice. At the moment he wasn't keen on a proper argument. For the same reason he also swallowed the barbed remark which had just been on the tip of his tongue.

"Why would I want to do that?" he asked, trying to conceal his growing impatience. "My father was only designated heir apparent because King Horemheb lacked a son of his own. I have succeeded my father on the throne, and Ramses will follow me in due course."

"Good," Tuya said with the air of a teacher who has finally managed to extract a satisfying answer from his slow-witted pupil. "With your permission I would now like to retire to my room. I am in sore need of a nap."

Seti nodded. The submissive tone of her voice didn't fool him into believing that this was a genuine request. As usual he couldn't fight the feeling that she was only mocking him.

For someone of her girth, Tuya rose surprisingly deftly from her cushioned chair. With a slight, almost condescending nod at Seti she rushed off, the jingling of her bangles ringing in his ears long after she had gone.

Seti didn't move. Shrouded in the swaths of her perfume he sat motionlessly. He, too, longed for a little rest, but he doubted that he would be able to sleep. Therefore he didn't even bother to try, but rose instead to walk up to the roofed porch leading into the lush garden. He leaned himself against one of the columns and marvelled at the peaceful atmosphere that lay over the whole complex. Nothing indicated the presence of the new military base which was situated nearby and sported not only extensive exercise grounds, stables and barracks but also workshops dedicated to the manufacture of chariots and weapons. Seti could almost delude himself that he was staying at his old ancestral home which was also close by. He might have just begun to relax, far away from the royal court and the responsibilities of kingship as he was, had it not been for the familiar bulky shape his eye had just caught sight of.

Tuya had emerged from a grove of acacia trees, with Ramses by her side. As they were slowly walking up the path, she talked to him in a most animated manner while he listened intently. No trace of the fatigue she had just feigned. Surely she had felt the urge to inform her son straight away of the outcome of their conversation.

Ramses. What was he supposed to do with him? According to the official version he was his, Seti's, offspring. The king's bodily son. But while Seti was looking at him, he wondered how anyone could believe that.

Ramses' looks resembled neither his mother's nor his alleged father's. He was unusually tall for his age, and in contrast to Tuya his lean body didn't show any traces of excessive flesh. It was a blessing that thanks to his intensive physical training he had started to develop the muscles of a grown man, so that his long limbs didn't look quite as lanky anymore as they used to. His most striking feature, however, was his large beaky nose which jutted out in a rather alarming manner and, together with his strong chin, gave his young face a hardened and imperious appearance. Not to forget the unusual hue of his flaming red hair which virtually lit up in the glare of the sun. No, Ramses' features could not in the least be compared to Seti's delicate, only slightly curved nose and his well-shaped jaw, however hard Tuya might try to convince him of the contrary.

It had been almost exactly eight months after Seti's return from a major expedition he had conducted in King Horemheb's service that Ramses had been born. Tuya had kept telling him that she must have fallen pregnant straight after his arrival, and that by all accounts little Ramses must have been born somewhat prematurely. Seti had had his doubts from the beginning, for the new-born Ramses had been an unusually big and strong child.

For the sake of peace and quiet and in order to save the family's reputation he had decided not to voice his doubts. Seti would have been prepared to regard the boy as his own, had it not been for that tall, skinny and big-nosed overseer of his estate whose bright red mop of hair used to show up in the most unexpected places. The older Ramses had grown, the more obvious it had become. Finally, when Seti hadn't been able to cope with all the malicious gossip anymore, he had dismissed the man. Of course, the problem had remained the same. But what else could he possibly have done about it? All that was left for him now was to keep quiet and bear his shame. He had no other son.

Remembering what Tuya had said, a daring thought fleeted into his mind. What if he really ignored Ramses and appointed Mehy heir apparent instead? But no sooner had he pondered this thought than he dismissed it. The consequences this move might have were too dire to contemplate. There wasn't much that Seti would have put safely past Ramses and his mother.

"Father?"

Startled, Seti shot round. He hadn't noticed Tia's coming. Here at his summer palace things weren't quite as formal as they were in the main residence.

He was glad to see her. "Tia," he said gently as he approached his daughter, extending his hands to embrace her.

"Is everything all right, father? You look distressed."
Seti sighed. "Your mother has just seen me," he said, feeling no need to elaborate. He knew that his daughter would understand.
"I do hope she hasn't spoken about me and Ramses again?" The despaired tone of her voice hit him hard, but he was relieved that he didn't have to lie to her. "No, dear, she hasn't. Don't worry; I assure you that in this respect nothing will happen against your will."
The young girl's pretty features brightened. "Thank you, father. I was unable to sleep, so I came to see what you were doing. What about a game of Senet?"
Seti smiled. "That would be just right," he said cheerfully. While he was watching his daughter setting up the game he tried hard to ignore the sharp pain in his chest which kept ailing him whenever he experienced great strain, or had exerted himself. He only wished that he was truly as unconcerned as he had just pretended.

Chapter Two

Meresankh couldn't believe that her younger sister had really done that. She knew only too well how inconsiderate, and at times unscrupulous Satet could be. But she would never have thought her capable of doing such an outrageous thing.
Satet had not joined them for breakfast. When Meresankh had gone to check on her, she had found her sister's room empty. Her bed had clearly not been slept in, and a few of her garments were missing. The conclusion that Satet had left the house in the dead of night was inescapable.
Poor Meritamun had been so upset that she had been on the verge of rushing off to look for her foster-daughter on her own. Meresankh had had a hard time to prevent her from doing so and make her see reason. Ever since Meritamun just sat there, crying and raging in turn and heaping reproaches on herself. Meresankh was immensely relieved when Taneferet arrived who was horrified at hearing the news of Satet's latest escapade.
"I don't believe it," she hissed furiously. "Whatever did she think? If she doesn't care about us, at least she should think of mother! It is completely unheard of that a young woman runs off in the dead of night without even so much as leaving a message behind! Why, anything might happen to a beautiful-"
Taneferet bit her lip when Meresankh shot a warning look at her and jerked her head in Meritamun's direction. There was no need to point out all the dangers to her that were lurking

out there.

When Taneferet's little daughters started to become fretful, Meresankh instructed the servant to lead them out into the garden along with her own boys. The two women followed them, seizing the opportunity to talk without Meritamun overhearing them while seemingly watching the children play.

"What do you think has really happened?" Taneferet asked.

Meresankh shrugged helplessly. "All we know is that Satet made off at some point during the night, and that she was careful not to wake anyone. Nobody has seen or heard anything. The servants have searched the whole area, but there isn't a single trace of her. A few of her garments are missing, as is most of her jewellery. I assume she just walked down to the riverbank and waited until dawn. Then she probably got on one of the first ships, and off she went."

Taneferet looked at her doubtfully. "But how did she pay for the passage?"

"Have you forgotten how much her jewellery must be worth? For a precious ring or two most sailors would be most happy to bring her to wherever she wanted to go."

Taneferet nodded thoughtfully. "That's quite true. But where would she want to go anyway, and why?"

Meresankh let out a sharp breath. "I assume that she has gone to Mennefer in order to meet Siamun."

Her friend's eyes widened in surprise. "Whatever gives you that idea? And why now, of all times?"

Noticing the curious look of the servant girl, Meresankh turned to move and motioned Taneferet to follow her. "Yesterday we received Siamun's first letter, and…"

"What does he say?" Taneferet interrupted. "Is he alright?"

Meresankh smiled for the first time that day. "Yes, fortunately everything went well so far, better than expected even. He writes that he is going to set out on a tour of all the main royal monuments soon. I believe that Satet made off to get hold of him prior to his departure. Before he left us, Siamun told me that Satet wanted to go with him right from the start."

"But what for?" Taneferet's voice sounded indignant. "Her place is here with her family!"

"You should know her better than that by now," hissed Meresankh between clenched teeth. "Satet has always been bored with us. All that she's after is some excitement. She wants to roam the streets of the great cities and have fun, and she doesn't care one bit for either her reputation or mother crying her eyes out. Satet behaves like a stupid child when she is a grown woman at twenty-one years of age. She could have had two or three children by now, had she cared to marry in time!"

Taneferet lifted her brows and smiled wryly. Clearly she hadn't forgotten the disaster they had gone through with Satet's various suitors either. Each time Satet, who simply hadn't wanted to get married, had misbehaved so badly that the family had eventually stopped any further advances in their tracks for fear of damaging the family's reputation.

While they walked on in silence, Meresankh looked at the young woman beside her with great affection. The two of them didn't share the same parents, but they had grown up together from birth onwards. They had always felt like sisters, and even now that they both were married they were still as close as ever. Right now Meresankh cherished her company more than anything else. She knew that she and Taneferet shared the same thoughts about Satet who had always appeared to be somewhat removed from the rest of the family. She wasn't really a bad sort, but her vanity and arrogance made it difficult at times to get along with her, and as long as there were men around who melted away like fat in the sun at the sight of a coquettish bat of her eyelid she wasn't likely to change her ways. In contrast to her, Meresankh had never thought much of her own exquisite beauty which she owed to her Nubian mother. The shade of her skin, though, revealed almost nothing of her foreign heritage, for her father had been one of the people of Kemet, and their king at that –one of the kings whose names were not spoken anymore.

"This time Satet really must have taken leave of her senses," Taneferet muttered at last. "She doesn't even know if she will be able to get to Siamun in time. And what if he has left the city already? Do you think she'll just give up and come back home, full of remorse?"

Meresankh shook her head wearily. "I believe we both know the answer to this question. I only hope that we will see her ever again."

****

Siamun and Nebnefer, his new friend and colleague, were hurrying along the busy road, trying desperately not to let their superior Wenamun get out of their sight. This was admittedly no easy task because the streets of Waset were overflowing with people, and the scores of merchants who were lining both sides with their goods spread out in front of them certainly didn't make things easier.

Ever since the day that Siamun had passed his test his heart was filled with joy. He had solved difficult mathematical problems and correctly calculated the areas and volumes of all kinds of shapes. He had determined the most suitable angle of inclination of a ramp employed for the erection of an obelisk of a given length and worked out the number of mud-bricks required to build said ramp. Thus he had now been admitted into the ranks of the royal architects, albeit the lowest one. In order to gain the sorely needed practical experience, he had been allowed to accompany Wenamun on his inspection tour along with Nebnefer and Hatiai –both of them apprentices like him.

They had just finished the inspection of the works on His Majesty's mortuary temple which was situated on the west bank. Siamun had been rather disappointed. The appearance of that temple didn't quite agree with his aesthetic sense. The columns were too clumsy for his liking, and the crude execution of the reliefs made the lack of craftsmanship all too apparent, but of course he hadn't voiced his thoughts. Now, they were on the east bank, headed for the temple of Ipet-Reset.

The two young men had just entered a particularly narrow street and were now weaving their way through the throng of people as well as they could when they became aware of the sound of approaching horses behind them.

Just what we needed, thought Siamun in disgust. *How can anyone try to get their chariot through this mess?*

He turned to look back and saw people jumping aside in fright, some of them stumbling and falling over in their hurry to get out of the way. Not one but three chariots forced their way through, hardly slowing down to avoid an accident. One of the big wheels very nearly caught the leg of an old man who had been sent sprawling in his bid to escape. In a flash Siamun had gotten hold of Nebnefer's sleeve and dragged him to safety. They hardly had time to catch their breath when indignant shouts and curses filled the air. The merchants whose goods had been upset and trampled underfoot by fleeing people had good reason to be furious. The chariots just carried on, their

riders seemingly oblivious to the frenzy they had created.
"Have these fellows lost their minds, dashing along a busy road like that?" Siamun scolded as he helped to gather the spilled contents of a large jar he had accidentally knocked over. "Look what they've done! It's simply outrageous!"

Nebnefer had remained remarkably calm. "This was one of the greatest men in the entire land and his entourage," he explained with a shrug. "He can do as he pleases."

"That doesn't mean that he has the right to be that reckless, though," Siamun insisted. "And who was that anyway?"

"The vizier of the north and excellent overseer of all royal building projects, Nebamun," Nebnefer droned out with a meaningful lift of his brow. "Among much else, he decides the fates of us architects, so you'd better be on your guard."

Siamun felt his eyebrows knitting together even more. "Well, being a vizier he should take better care of his people than that."

"Come on, we must go," Nebnefer urged. "Can you see Wenamun anywhere?"

"No, he's probably long gone. Forget Wenamun. We can find our way to the temple without him."

It didn't take them long to reach the first court of the temple complex which was enclosed by a tall wall. Wenamun and Hatiai were waiting next to the tri-parted chapel which served as a repository station for the divine barges during the Festival of Opet.

"I am sorry we're late," Nebnefer panted. "We were caught up in-"

"I know," interrupted Wenamun, nodding in sympathy. "Just keep your voices down, will you? It's been a while since the great man has proceeded into the temple, and he might emerge from it at any moment because, as always, he has precious little time."

The small group passed through the gate of the only pylon and found themselves standing under the high roof of a pillared hall which was supported by fourteen elegant papyrus columns, featuring open capitals. There were no priests to be seen, but the heavy scents of incense and myrrh wafting over from the direction of the cult rooms nevertheless reminded them of their presence.

The overall impression this structure made on Siamun was one of elegance and perfect harmony. His gaze travelled admiringly up the slender columns and fastened on the gap between the roof and the enclosing walls which admitted just enough light to see by. His heart started to beat faster when he looked at the brightly coloured reliefs which adorned the faces of both walls. He already knew what they represented, but seeing them with his own eyes for the first time was an overwhelming experience. The depictions were a detailed account of the various stages of the Beautiful Feast of Opet. Here the king offered incense and flowers to Amun, there he could be seen on his barge leading the procession on the river. The royal cartouches designated him as Horemheb Djoserkheperure, but that was wrong. It was a blatant lie, yet nobody except him seemed to take offence. The king's true name was Tutankhamun Nebkheperure. Siamun's father. Horemheb had simply usurped most of the beautiful representations in this colonnade like he had done with many other depictions and statues commissioned by the young king.

Siamun had already encountered many instances of usurpation. Not only Horemheb, but also the current ruler King Seti Menmaatre had not been slow to appropriate numerous monuments belonging to earlier kings, foremost those of Tutankhamun, erasing their names and replacing them with his own. In order to justify his actions Seti made extensive use of the formula *shemawi menu*, the renewal of monuments. He didn't seem to mind the fact that many if not most of these reliefs and statues had already been restored following their destruction during king Akhenaten's reign, who was nowadays only referred to as the rebel of Akhetaten.

This was certainly an easy way to acquire a great number of monuments in the shortest of times, but to Siamun it just didn't seem right. It was an outrageous thing to do. In fact, in his eyes, it was an offence against Maat, the concept of truth, justice and perfect order in the Two Lands and the entire universe, which every king was supposed to maintain.

Meanwhile they had been slowly moving on. Eventually they reached the far end of the hall, where works on the reliefs were still in progress. Fascinated, Siamun looked on as the sculptors' chisels chipped away flakes of limestone, accurately following the black outlines that had been drawn on the surface and gradually making signs and figures appear, virtually bringing them to life. His experienced eye spotted at once the difference between these and the representations on the greater part of the walls. In contrast to the only slightly raised relief employed by Tutankhamun and Horemheb, the style favoured by Seti had the figures stand out higher from the background, the way they used to do during the reign of King Amunhotep Nebmaatre. This resemblance was perhaps no coincidence, for Seti did all he could to associate himself with that king, as if he wanted to draw a veil over all that had come in between their respective reigns.

A sharp pain in his side jolted Siamun out of his reverie. Nebnefer had given him a forceful nudge, a habit that Siamun had come to dread. He opened his mouth to protest, but his friend cut him short, tilting his head in the direction of the open court which lay beyond the pillared hall.

"Watch out, here he comes," he hissed.

Siamun turned his head to see three men approach them, two of whom were engaged in animated conversation. The third was, strictly speaking, still a boy; he could hardly be more than fifteen years of age.

Although Siamun had never come face to face with Nebamun, he could easily identify him to be the man in the middle. The official garb he was wearing was unique and reserved only for the vizier: an ankle-length wide garment which reached just below the arm pits, held in place by two thin shoulder straps. In his right hand Nebamun carried a long gilded staff which he pounded vigorously on the ground with each step he took. Two servants followed in his wake carrying a fan and a tall sceptre, the insignia of his office.

Nebamun appeared to be in his forties. He was of medium height and extremely slim. His bare shoulders looked bony, and his clavicles showed unattractively below his scrawny neck. His gaunt face was dominated by a sharp hooked nose which was somewhat at odds with his receding chin. The small close-set eyes darted about while he spoke, and a deep furrow had engraved itself between his brows, giving a clear indication of how often they must have been drawn together.

While Siamun watched the vizier coming closer, he couldn't prevent his mind from conjuring up the image of a vulture. He didn't know why, but he took an instant dislike to this man who was clearly someone not to be trifled with.

Siamun leaned over to his friend. "Who is the one Nebamun is speaking to?" he asked as inconspicuously as he could.

"This is Ptahnakht, Wenamun's superior," Nebnefer returned just as carefully.

"And that youngster to his left?"

Nebnefer grinned. "Nebamun's son, Penre."

Meanwhile Wenamun had stepped forward to address the vizier. Apparently they were talking about his new apprentices, for Nebamun's gaze swept over the small group of young men without lingering on a particular face. With a final satisfied nod he started to move, heading for the opposite end of the hall. Siamun and his young colleagues waited with bowed heads until the great man and his entourage had passed by them before they followed several steps behind. From the few shreds of their conversation he could overhear Siamun gleaned that the men were discussing the enlargement of the first court. They had to walk slowly, because for some unfathomable reason the vizier didn't seem to be in a hurry anymore. In fact, Siamun felt as if they were hardly moving at all.

All of a sudden, a weird feeling began to creep all over him. The sensation of eyes staring hard at him. Siamun glanced around furtively. None of the men in front of him or those by his side payed him any heed. His uneasiness didn't subside, though. Quite on the contrary, it grew worse with every breath he took. Profoundly confused, Siamun cast a tentative glance at the wall to his right. There, now he could see who it was. It were the dark eyes of the king that looked at him. Wherever Siamun directed his gaze, his father's intense stare followed him. And not just his. All the deities that were depicted on the walls stared accusingly at him.

Hastily Siamun averted his gaze and fastened it on the ground by his feet, but to no avail. He could still *feel* their eyes boring into his back, piercing his skin and flesh right through to the bone. But that wasn't all.

Softly and barely discernibly at first, like the gentle whisper of the north wind, he heard their voices speak. But it was only when they grew louder and more urgent that Siamun was able to understand what they said.

Prince Siamun, they went, *what are you doing here? You are the bodily son of a king and the rightful heir to the throne of the Two Lands! Follow Maat and seize what is yours! What are you waiting for?*

The voices began to combine and interfere with each other, growing steadily in volume until Siamun could hardly resist the urge to slap his hands over his ears in order to block them out. Not that it would have helped, anyway. The voices had already penetrated his heart, and his whole innermost being reverberated with their sounds.

Siamun could feel a cold sweat breaking out on his skin. He needed to get out of here, away from staring eyes and demanding voices. Why in all the gods' names didn't the men in front of him hurry up a bit?

Just when he was sure he couldn't stand it any longer they emerged from the pillared hall. Siamun was struggling for breath, panting hard like someone who has just run a race. Nebnefer turned to him at once. "Whatever is the matter with you?" he asked, concern ringing in his voice.

"Why, Siamun, you are all covered in sweat!" Hatiai pointed out, quite unnecessarily.

"Quiet," Nebnefer demanded. "There's no need to let everybody know."

After a few deep breaths Siamun managed to calm himself down. Angry with himself, he pulled his sleeve across his sweaty forehead.

"I'm all right now," he said. "Come on, let's go! The others have already left."

"Are you sure?" asked Nebnefer, anxiously searching his friend's face.

Siamun nodded emphatically.

"Now, aren't you going to tell us what was wrong with you?" Hatiai urged. "Was it the vizier who has upset you so much?"

Siamun was about to reply when Nebnefer came to his aid.
"Do you really have to be so nosy?" he scolded. "How would you like it if someone was pestering you like that?"
Hatiai didn't ask any more questions. In silence the three young men hurried down to the riverbank where a boat was waiting for them to carry them a short distance downstream to the huge temple of Ipet-Sut, the most excellent of places.

****

After a short walk up the avenue leading to the temple Siamun stood in front of the great pylon erected by King Horemheb. Amazed, he let his gaze travel up the eight flag staffs and fasten on the colourful pennants which were dancing in the breeze at a dizzy height. The surfaces of the pylon were covered with representations of the ever victorious pharaoh, their vibrant colours lighting up in the sunshine. And deep inside its two mighty towers, hidden from view, lay scores of just as brightly painted stone blocks that used to belong to a beautiful memorial temple King Tutankhamun had commissioned on the west bank, in remembrance of his military successes in Nubia and Kadesh. Later, Horemheb had seen to it that the whole temple was dismantled and their stone blocks used as filling material for his new pylons.
Siamun's jaw tightened when he thought of the pitiful remains of his father's temple which were by now almost entirely covered with sand. Not a word had been said about it when they had passed by it earlier that day, and Siamun had hardly been able to contain his fury, knowing full well that he could do

nothing to undo this abominable desecration.

He was glad when his companions moved on before he could start to hear more ominous voices. Beyond the pylon a most impressive sight lay in wait for them. A huge construction site extended from the pylon they had just passed through to the next, divided into two halves by a double row of twelve massive roofed papyrus columns. The pylon at the far side was an even more splendid sight than the first one, embellished with gold leaf and precious stones as it was. This didn't take Siamun by wonder; after all, this magnificent structure had been built by Siamun's grandfather, King Amunhotep Nebmaatre, who was well known for his lavish building style. Behind it the gleaming tips of four tall obelisks rose proudly into the deep blue sky.

Reluctantly Siamun tore his gaze from this overwhelming sight to let it roam across the large expanse of bustling activity in front of him. Apart from the roofed columns in the middle, the whole area was surrounded by a low mud-brick wall and covered with sand up to the height of roughly two cubits. The stumps of countless columns protruded from the sand, reminding Siamun of the broken tusks belonging to some gigantic beast. In between them, scores of workmen clad only in loincloths were milling about, hurriedly preparing the stumps for the reception of an additional layer. Here the stony surface would be rubbed down with the help of granite pebbles, there mortar would be spread and smoothed before huge sandstone discs would be heaved into place. By adding more and more discs the columns would rise until they eventually reached their final height. All the while more sand would be brought in to raise the level of the ground that was being worked on. Once the capitals would have been attached to the columns, the sand would gradually be removed in order to facilitate the decoration of the columns. This long-standing procedure had proved successful from time immemorial as it rendered the use of scaffolding superfluous and thus reduced the number of work-related accidents to a minimum.

"Never in my life have I seen so many columns in one place," Nebnefer remarked, with admiration in his voice.

Wenamun, who had joined his apprentices once again, nodded. "I fully agree with you. It is indeed a unique project, and after its completion it will undoubtedly be the most impressive part of the whole temple complex."

"Who has designed the plans for it?" Siamun asked, feeling far more comfortable now that Nebamun and his followers were out of sight.

"The then supreme overseer of all royal building works Merimose, who served under His Majesty Osiris Ramses Menpehtire. Unfortunately he went to the West shortly after he had completed the building plan which decrees that one hundred and twenty-two columns are to be added to the twelve that already exist. The intention is to make this place appear like a huge thicket of papyrus stems."

"Will the new columns all have the same height as the ones in the middle?" asked Siamun.

"Yes," Wenamun replied. "They are supposed to form a harmonious unity together."

As he stroked his chin, Siamun's mind started to wander. Wenamun, who had come to know this gesture well, laughed. "May I ask if the aspiring architect has any objections?"

Siamun had come to realize that Wenamun already had a very high opinion of him. In fact, he treated him more like a colleague than a mere apprentice. However, Wenamun had never uttered anything in the way of an apology for his brusque behaviour when they had first met. Perhaps this was just the way he dealt with new arrivals. Nebnefer had been right, though, that on the whole their superior was affable enough a man.

"It is plain to see that the circumference of the additional columns is much smaller than that of the existing ones," Siamun pointed out. "This means that compared to them the new columns will look a great deal more slender and elegant, making the twelve columns in the middle appear too massive and clumsy."

Wenamun just shrugged. "There is obviously not enough space to accommodate so many columns with the same circumference as the old ones have. Apparently the number of columns matters more than anything else. I think we're finished here. Let's go!"

He got moving, followed by Nebnefer and Hatiai. Siamun stayed behind, feeling that there was something not quite right about the intended building plan. He was convinced that it was in need of some improvement. And he already had a vague idea of what was to be changed. But first, he needed to have a clear picture of what the completed pillared hall was going to look like. Siamun's mind set to work immediately, causing the columns in front of him to grow until they reached their final height. Then they were fitted with capitals and decorated, and finally they were covered with a single large roof. The work was done, but Siamun didn't like what he saw. As he had anticipated, the double rows in the middle appeared unattractively clumsy compared to the ones surrounding them, and the interior of the imaginary hall was far too dark. What had to be done to improve things? If the additional columns weren't quite as high as the twelve existing ones...

"Is there something wrong with my columns, young man?" a sonorous voice rang out right behind him.

Siamun's trail of thoughts came to a sudden halt when the words penetrated his mind. *My columns?* Who was that to speak in such a presumptuous manner?

He spun round and came face to face with a man dressed in a magnificent robe who looked at him expectantly. He wore the Red Crown of the north, and a rearing uraeus serpent adorned his forehead.

Hastily Siamun stepped back and bent over into a deep bow. "I beg your pardon for not having noticed Your Majesty's approach," he muttered.

"You are pardoned," King Seti said in a friendly voice. "You may straighten up. It doesn't happen often that I manage to surprise someone with my coming. But tell me, young man, why you have been staring so hard at this construction site."

"I would be honoured to do so, Your Majesty," Siamun said, gradually recovering from the shock the king's sudden appearance had given him. "I have the pleasure of accompanying the royal architect Wenamun on his inspection tour, and I have just been trying to imagine what this magnificent pillared hall will look like upon completion. No doubt it will be a most impressive structure, but there are a few aspects which in my opinion could be improved."

"Really?" asked Seti in a curious voice. "And what exactly would that be?"

Siamun sucked in a sharp breath. What had he done? Did he really dare criticise the building plans that had already met with the king's approval? Well, it was too late now to think of that.

"In my opinion the columns shouldn't all be of the same height," he explained, "because this will make the twelve pillars in the middle appear overly broad and clumsy. Besides, there will be no point of attraction, nothing the spectator's eye can focus on. However, if the new columns would be lower in height, they would be in an interesting contrast with the existing ones, thus emphasizing their majestic appearance. The difference in height would have another great advantage, because the gap between the different roof levels could easily be fitted with gutter windows. The play of light and shadow would render the interior of the hall more mysterious compared to the plain near darkness a single roof would create."

With a slight inclination of his head Siamun fell silent. While he waited anxiously and with bated breath for Seti's reply, the tension within him rose. Had he been too bold for his own good?

"I think your ideas are well worth a second thought," the king said slowly. "In fact, what you say sounds quite appealing to me. But before I can make my mind up, I'd have to see the draft in front of me. Would you be able to design a clear drawing by, say, tomorrow night and bring it to me?"

With his mouth gone dry all of a sudden, Siamun could only nod. His heart began to beat faster. Could it really be true that the king wanted to take the suggestions of a mere apprentice earnestly into consideration?

"Don't worry about how to find me," Seti added. "I'll send someone to pick you up. That's all for now."

Siamun bowed deeply while Seti turned to go. When Siamun straightened again he caught sight of a group of spectators standing just a few paces off and thus well within earshot. He felt deeply embarrassed when he realized that they must have heard every single word he had spoken. To his utter dismay he recognized not only Ptahhotep, Wenamun and his two young colleagues among them, but also Nebamun with his entourage and a man who, judging by the garb he wore, could only be the vizier of the south. Whatever were they going to think of him? Quite by accident Siamun's gaze met Nebamun's. The vizier's eyes narrowed to slits as he shot him a long appraising look before he turned to follow the king into the temple. This time there was no doubt that Nebamun had indeed taken notice of him, but Siamun suddenly wished that he rather hadn't.

In an instance Nebnefer and Hatiai were by his side.
"In all the gods' names," Nebnefer hissed excitedly, "I thought you were digging your own grave when you started to rip into those building plans in front of His Majesty!"
"Honestly, Siamun," Hatiai butted in, "you can deem yourself lucky that pharaoh took no offence at all. Quite on the contrary, he seemed to be rather intrigued with your ideas."
The note of envy in his voice was not lost on Siamun.
"Nothing has been decided yet," he said airily. "Anyway, it is highly unlikely that His Majesty is really going to change the original plans just because some lousy apprentice proposed a few suggestions."
"Don't be so shy," Nebnefer said eagerly. "If pharaoh hadn't been impressed already, he wouldn't have asked you to make the drawings in the first place."
Talking with excitement, the three friends made their way back to their quarters which were not far off the temple complex. They were grateful for the refreshments that were waiting there for them.
"Just tell me," Nebnefer began when Hatiai was out of earshot, "what really bothered you back in the hall of Ipet-Reset. Of course, you don't have to, if you don't want to," he added quickly.
Having anticipated that this question was about to come, Siamun had already thought of an explanation which didn't reveal the true reason behind his great distress, but which contained a grain of truth nevertheless. He shrugged casually.
"Actually, it was nothing worth mentioning. It's only that at times I don't feel comfortable in enclosed spaces. Then I get a

feeling that the walls are closing in on me, trying to crush me, which causes my breathing to become erratic. That's probably the reason why, unlike my father, I'm never going to design any plans for tombs, if I can help it."

Nebnefer chuckled. "Really? Who would have thought? Well, at any rate you'd better be off to design the plans His Majesty has asked for, or you won't get them ready in time."

****

Siamun was sprawled out on his bed, trying hard to get to sleep. But it was no avail; far too much was going on in his mind. If he wanted to get at least some rest, he would have to come to terms with all that had happened that day.

First there had been the unpleasant experience in the pillared hall of Ipet-Reset. Or had it really been only that? At first, Siamun had felt some strange, intimate connection with his deceased father. After all, King Tutankhamun's depictions were all that was left for him, all that he had to cling to. Of course, there were his memories, too. Memories that were not his own, but felt as familiar to him as if they were. Siamun's half-sister Meresankh, who had been almost five years old at the time of Tutankhamun's untimely demise, had treated her little brother to many tales about her loving father and the royal wife Sitiah, daughter of the King's Son of Kush Huy. The two of them had been blessed with an unusually deep love, and Siamun had kept pestering his sister and his foster-mother Meritamun, who had been Sitiah's close friend, with questions for more and more details. He had never given up, until there had nothing been left to tell him. And all the things that he had found out about his parents had deeply engraved themselves on his heart. So deeply that at some point he had truly started to take them for his very own memories.

Siamun also knew that King Tutankhamun had not pronounced his new-born son heir to the throne. He had wanted to avoid Siamun being forced upon the throne at an early age in case of his own premature death. Instead, Tutankhamun had appointed his elderly uncle Ay as heir apparent, who had in his turn designated the little prince as his successor during his own short tenure in order to continue the royal blood-line through him.

But then things had turned out quite differently. Following Ay's death, his daughter Mutnodjemet and General Horemheb had seized the opportunity to finally ascend the throne of the Two Lands. At that time, Siamun had barely been five years old and was living with Meritamun, her children Panakht and Taneferet and his own sisters on her estate near Iunu.

Of course... his sisters. As if the load on his mind hadn't been enough already, his thoughts wandered inevitably to Satet. Where Meresankh had always been easy-going and jovial, his younger sister had been defiant and self-centred for as long as he remembered. Ever since she had come of age, she had also started to display a downright unbearable arrogance which made it often difficult to get along with her. Siamun sometimes thought that perhaps it had been these characteristics that had helped her to be born alive when her twin had remained stuck in Sitiah's womb and died along with her mother. Be that as it may, he fervently hoped that Satet had calmed down and wouldn't be up to any nonsense.

Determined not to dwell on these gloomy thoughts, Siamun pushed them away in order to focus on the here and now. Quite unexpectedly, a great opportunity had presented itself to him.

Certainly it didn't happen every day that pharaoh himself instructed a low-ranking, inexperienced architect –an apprentice at that- with the designing of the plans for such an important structure. Siamun didn't know yet if his ideas were going to meet with the king's approval, but if they were it could lead to his entering into His Majesty's services in the shortest of times. He, the prince of royal blood and legitimate heir to the throne, was going to serve a king whose father had been a mere commoner who in his turn had been made king by the commoner Horemheb. It was downright grotesque.

But Siamun didn't allow himself to be bothered by these things. He had never intended to assert his right on the throne, anyway. All he had always wanted was to design grand structures and to build them. He was longing to prove himself, to show what he was able to do, and now that he had got the chance, he wasn't going to waste it.

****

Seti had enjoyed a light meal and was now resting in his bedchamber. He had come alone to Waset. Tuya and Ramses had both preferred to stay in Mennefer. This hadn't been an option for him, though. An inspection of his numerous building projects had been overdue, and the Beautiful Feast of Opet was going to be celebrated in about three weeks' time. On his way back to Mennefer Seti would have to stop in Abedju in order to carry out the annual rites in honour of Osiris on that god's very own sacred ground. Then it would be high time already to prepare for another campaign to the northern territories.

Seti sighed. He was indeed a very busy man.

He wondered if that young architect was really going to show up. The remarkable young man whose name he had learned to be Siamun had deeply impressed him in a way. Siamun hadn't in the slightest appeared to be shaken by his unexpected encounter with his king. He had seemed calm, self-confident, yet at the same time modest. The way in which he had described his vision of the great pillared hall had shown him to be both enthusiastic and imaginative, and if his drawings could live up to his promise, the hall may well be built according to Siamun's plans.

It was to be expected that not everybody was going to appreciate Seti's decision, least of all Nebamun, who had already tried hard to dissuade him from paying any attention to Siamun and his mediocre ideas. And Seti knew the reason behind his reservations all too well. The vizier hoped that his own moderately talented son would soon be given the golden opportunity that would smooth his way to a splendid career. But Seti wasn't going to settle for less than he could get. He had other, even more ambitious projects on his mind, for which he needed someone with truly great abilities. Someone, perhaps, like Siamun.

Seti sat up and reached for his cup. He had only had a few sips of his favourite wine when his chamberlain Ptahmai appeared to announce the arrival of a certain Siamun.

"Let him enter," Seti told him.

He rose and made for his small reception room where he settled himself on a cushioned chair. A few moments later the young man stood in front of him, carrying a large scroll under his arm. Having performed a deep bow, Siamun waited with lowered eyes to be addressed.

Seti took the opportunity to watch him closely. He marvelled at the regularity of Siamun's pleasant features which were so unlike those of his alleged son. Besides, there was something about them that struck him as familiar. It was just as if he had seen him before, but Seti couldn't for the life of him imagine where this might have been.

"I am pleased to see that you have followed my summons," Seti began. "Did you succeed in designing a plan according to your ideas?"

"Yes, Your Majesty," Siamun replied. "I believe I did succeed in doing so. I have to admit, though, that the drawings are currently not exactly true to scale because the original plan wasn't available to me."

Seti nodded. "Don't worry about that. Once your plans will have found my approval, you will be given all you need. But first let me see what you have got there."

"Of course, Your Majesty."

Siamun walked up to the table which Seti had indicated to him. He unrolled the papyrus and waited until Seti had weighted both ends down with two fist-sized scarabs.

Seti looked eagerly at the drawings. There were two of them, one showing the pillared hall in front view with the lateral view shown underneath.

Siamun cleared his throat discreetly. "With Your Majesty's permission, I would like to elaborate on the details of these drawings."

"Go ahead!"

"Here in this drawing which represents the frontal view the proposed difference in height becomes most apparent," Siamun explained while his index finger pointed to the corresponding parts of the immaculate black lines. "The difference must not be too slight, because this would give the impression that the new columns have accidentally turned out too short. I have settled on a height of two thirds of the already existing ones which means that the two sets of columns are in clear contrast with each other. Apart from that, this difference in height corresponds closely with the one in circumference which also amounts to about two thirds. This means that although the new columns will be shorter in height, their relative proportions will match those of their taller counterparts in the middle, thus eliminating the danger of the latter looking clumsy and out of proportion. Another additional advantage would be that the bases of the new columns that have already been built won't have to be abolished. They can simply be raised to their new established height. Regarding their capitals I believe that they should be fitted with closed bud ones so that they contrast nicely with the open capitals of the twelve columns in the middle. When it comes to the roof," Siamun's finger slid down to the drawing below, "the lateral view shows clearly how the difference in height can be used to its best advantage. The gap between the middle roof and the lower roofs to each side can either be left open, or they can preferably be fitted with gutter windows which will admit enough light to illuminate parts of the interior without the use of lamps or torches. On the whole," Siamun concluded, "the differing heights of the columns will not spoil the appearance of this building, nor will they compete with each other. Quite on the contrary, they will complement each other, thus enhancing the overall impression of harmony, and at the same time the gaze of the spectator will be drawn to the main part in the middle which he is about to enter."

A short silence followed Siamun's impressive words. Seti took his time to let them sink in. Even prior to this meeting he had been inclined to entrust this young architect with his currently dearest project, but hearing his enthusiastic explanations had strengthened his resolve even more. Rarely had he seen someone speak and act with such deep conviction. Siamun's words hadn't been said lightly or in a deceptive manner, the like of which Seti got to hear all too often. No, they had come from the very depths of his heart.

"I don't believe that the suggestions you propose can be improved in any way," Seti eventually said. "Nor can I find any fault with them. Therefore I decree that the plans be changed according to your wishes. The original drawings will be sent to you first thing in the morning in order to enable you to design the final draft. Until then, building works at the temple of Ipet-Sut will be put on hold. Once I have approved of the final plan, they will be resumed under your supervision. This is all for now."

Siamun bowed before he gathered the papyrus from the table. Seti watched on as he carefully rolled it up and secured it with a string. Then a sudden thought hit him. There was one more thing he needed to know.

"I have only one last question, Siamun."

"Yes, Your Majesty?"

"I have been told that you spent the last three years in the House of Life of the great temple in Iunu," Seti said.

"This is correct, my king."

"Did you by any chance attend the ceremony which was held in honour of my coronation in that temple?" Seti asked, raptly watching the young man in front of him.

"Indeed, Your Majesty," came the reply he had hoped for. "Back then I was an assistant to one of the lecture priests who took part in the rites."

"Good," Seti said with a satisfied nod. "I thought I might have seen you before."

Having dismissed his visitor, Seti pondered the question of why on earth he should have memorized the face of a single priest among scores of others.

Well, he told himself, *apparently this is exactly what happened. There is no other plausible explanation.*

Or at least, he couldn't think of one.

****

Once again, building works were in full swing. But even so Siamun estimated that it would take several years to complete this gigantic structure. In the northern part of the future hall which was already enclosed by walls adorned with numerous depictions of Seti's first campaigns, works were progressing faster than on its far end. Here, some of the columns had already reached about half of their final height. But altogether there were one hundred and twenty-two of them, all of which had to be raised, decorated and covered with a roof.
Siamun attended the construction site every single day, ignoring the noise and the dust that hung in the air and rendered breathing difficult. In his mind he kept double-checking his calculations in order to make sure that nothing would go wrong. Every now and then pharaoh would visit and exchange a few friendly words with him. And of course Nebnefer would often turn up and provide him with the latest news. Thus, Siamun came to know quite soon that pharaoh's decision to entrust him with the supervision of this important project had not met with everyone's approval. As he might have expected, Nebamun had accepted it with rather bad grace.
"It is said that he is quite beside himself with fury," Nebnefer reported one day. "Nebamun clearly fears that this might not have been the only opportunity that you have snatched from his son."
"Why?" Siamun asked, surprised. "Are there other royal projects coming up?"
"His Majesty plans the construction of a temple on the sacred ground of Abedju," his friend replied in a mysteriously lowered voice. "Didn't you know?"

"To be honest, I didn't. How comes that he has chosen Abedju of all places?"

Nebnefer shrugged. "Apparently His Majesty's father had already planned the construction of a temple there, but works had barely begun when he went to the West. Now, King Seti wishes to complete this structure, but he is not at all happy with the existing design. He has set his mind on something really special. The new temple will be dedicated to various deities, so by all accounts it will be a grand project. And now pharaoh is looking for the right man to carry out his ambitious plans."

Siamun had been listening with rapt attention. Abedju. The most sacred of all places in the entire land, and the site where Osiris was allegedly buried. The most recent kings had somewhat neglected it, focusing all their attention on great cities like Mennefer, Iunu and Waset. Suddenly the columns became blurred in front of his eyes, and his mind started to wander. Siamun tried to imagine how such a temple might look, but he didn't get far. His contemplations were cut short by a forceful slap on his shoulder.

"Honestly, Nebnefer!" he protested while tenderly rubbing the sore spot. "What did you do that for?"

He turned and found himself staring into a pair of roguishly twinkling eyes.

"Panakht, what are you doing here?"

"Is that any way of greeting an old friend?" Panakht complained in a good-humoured tone of voice, broadly grinning.

"It's just that you took me completely by surprise," Siamun explained after a warm embrace.

Panakht eyed him warily. "A pleasant one at that, I trust."

"Of course, how could it not be? Just tell me, how did you manage to get down here?"

"Well, all of His Majesty's brave soldiers have been granted leave on the occasion of the upcoming celebrations, so that they can thoroughly indulge in all the feasting. And that's exactly what I'm going to do."

"Sounds good," Siamun said.

Panakht nodded slowly. "It certainly does, but things will turn quite serious soon after."

Siamun lifted his eyebrows. "You're going on campaign, I take it?"

"Yes, and a quite ambitious one it is too. First we will have to subdue all the important sea ports on the northern coast. As you might guess, this is mainly to ensure our troops' provision with further supplies on our campaigns against all those petty princes. The long-term goal, however, will be the recapture of the city of Kadesh."

"These are truly grand plans," Siamun said. "I hope you are well prepared."

"Of course I am," came the sure reply. "I've been working really hard during the past month, you know. *You* on the other hand," he added pointedly, sweeping his arm around the site expansively, "let others do the work for you. I told you that you'd make it to the top in no time at all."

Siamun pulled a face. "It was just a stroke of luck that the king came across me and heard of my ideas."

"And, more importantly, approved of them," Panakht pointed out.

"By the way, where are you going to stay while you're here?" Siamun asked, not wanting to dwell on this topic.

Panakht rolled his eyes. "In the barracks close to the docks. It's a soldier's life after all."

He tilted his head in Nebnefer's direction, who was talking to one of the foremen a few paces off. "Have you befriended him?"

Siamun nodded. "Yes, he's an amiable fellow. His name is

Nebnefer. Everyone else I have met so far are quite all right, too. Except for the vizier Nebamun, that is. When I first saw him, I was instantly reminded of a vulture circling above his prey."

Panakht laughed. "Not everyone can be to your liking." Then, growing serious, he lowered his voice almost to a whisper. "Are you sure your secret is safe as yet?"

He didn't have to elaborate.

"Yes, fortunately I am," Siamun replied just as softly.

Panakht nodded, looking relieved.

"Do you happen to have any news from home?" Siamun asked.

"I do. On my way down here I got off the boat at Iunu. I spent only a few hours with them, though. Thankfully, everyone is alright. Taneferet has arrived with her children, but Kenamun still hasn't returned yet."

Siamun grinned. "As usual. Will they come here for the celebrations, then?"

"No, I'm afraid they won't," Panakht said, shaking his head slightly. "Mother is not feeling well."

Siamun glanced at his friend enquiringly. "But you just said they were fine!"

Panakht's smile looked somewhat forced. "That's true. It's only that mother's notorious headaches keep her from coming here. She says the strain of the long journey would be too much for her."

"That explains it all, of course. May Sekhmet ease her pain and make her better," Siamun said compassionately.

"The celebrations only start in a few days," Panakht began after a short silence. "Why don't we meet up before then and do something more exciting than standing about in this horrible dusty place? You look as if you could do with some exercise. What about a spot of hunting?"

Siamun hesitated. "I would love to, but how are we going to get hold of a chariot?"

"No worries, I can take care of that," Panakht said, visibly swelling with pride. "What about tomorrow? If you can spare a few hours, come to the barracks first thing in the morning. Should you have trouble finding me, just ask for the commander of troops Urhiye. He's a good friend of mine."

****

It was a sensation of freedom that Siamun hadn't experienced for a long time. He let the smooth leather of the reins slide through his fingers and clicked his tongue. The two brown stallions fell into a fast trot, and Siamun enjoyed the ride even more.

Panakht had kept his word and organized a number of robust chariots along with their teams. One of his comrades called Pawer stood next to Siamun in the driver cabin, and they intended to take turns with holding the reins and shooting arrows.

It was a small hunting party; the vehicle in front was shared by Panakht and the troop commander Urhiye, two of their comrades rode in the middle, with Siamun's chariot following behind. It wasn't even certain if they would be able to track down any worthwhile bag so close to the city, but they had armed themselves with bows and arrows nevertheless. To Siamun it hardly mattered anyway.

He had taken an instant liking to Panakht's new friend. Urhiye couldn't be much older than himself, and he appeared to be friendly and easy-going. He didn't seem to fancy himself at all for being in command of several hundred royal troops already. Quite on the contrary, the fuss Panakht was continually making over his rather elevated status seemed to embarrass him. Apart from his name, Urhiye's golden-brown hair and the light shade of his skin betrayed his foreign origins. His ancestors hailed from Mitanni, as he happily related, but his family had come to live in Kemet ever since the warlike Hittites had launched a devastating offensive against their homeland and raised their cities to the ground.

Unlike most foreign immigrants, his parents hadn't deemed it necessary to give their son a name common in Kemet. And apparently this hadn't been harmful to his career either. As Panakht had already proudly whispered into Siamun's ear, Urhiye's prospects of being raised into the rank of a general were excellent.

They had been riding along for more than an hour without spotting anything other than the omnipresent vultures, when Urhiye brought his chariot to a sudden halt and raised his hand. His companions understood that they were to do the same. He must have spotted something. When Siamun craned his neck in order to see, he caught sight of several brown bodies darting along. It might have been a family of hares trying desperately to find shelter behind a rock or one of the tough bushes that dotted the sandy ground.

Panakht turned around, grinning wryly and indicating with a shrug that this wasn't what he had hoped for, but it would have to do. Siamun smiled back and pointed at his quiver. Urhiye nodded and urged the horses on.

A short while ago Siamun's companion had taken over the reins, and Siamun stood there trying hard to keep steady while at the same time clutching his bow with one hand and clinging

to the top rail of the cabin with the other. He wasn't bold enough to think that he would be able to strike such small and quick animals. It had been far too long since he had practised his archery skills. During his time on their estate near Iunu, he and Panakht had been instructed in this art. They had also been taught how to handle horses and ride the chariot. Siamun had thoroughly enjoyed it, but when he had joined the House of Life his practical lessons had come to an end and he had gradually lost the skills he had acquired. Panakht on the other hand had continued to practice and brought his skills to perfection.
While they were racing along, Siamun kept a lookout for the hares or anything else worth shooting at. Finally he spotted several of the panic-stricken animals, and they followed in hot pursuit. When Siamun saw one of them darting sideways in its bid to escape, thus accidentally coming within his reach, he readied his first arrow and released the string. It hissed through the air but missed its target by several cubits. His ensuing attempts were hardly any more successful.
Pawer slowed the horses down so that they would gain a better overview. Siamun spotted several furry bodies lying scattered across the ground. The other chariots slowly came to a halt, too, and it seemed that the chase was over.
Siamun knew all too well that he hadn't exactly covered himself with glory.
"I should have been the one holding the reins and let you do the shooting," he told his companion with a wry smile.
Instead of answering, the young man raised his brows and jerked his head sideways. When Siamun glanced in the indicated direction, he caught sight of a movement. He had to strain his eyes to discover the sand-coloured creature with strikingly large ears which was slinking by, heading towards one of the cadavers. The desert fox had apparently set its mind on feasting on the dead hare. The small predator had to be

ravenous in order to take such a risk, or perhaps it had more hungry mouths to feed.

This was the last chance for Siamun to prove his worth. Making no sound at all, he retrieved an arrow from his quiver and took aim. For a moment, the fox stopped dead with one front paw suspended in mid-air, but instead of turning to flee it continued to steal towards the carcass, watching Siamun intently all the time. It was so close that it would have made an easy target for anyone, but Siamun suddenly wondered why on earth he should kill this poor creature at all when it wasn't even edible. Was he really that desperate to prove himself?

Slowly, he lowered his bow and looked on unmoved as the fox seized the hare in its mouth and dragged it behind the nearest rock.

Just then the remaining hunters joined them.

"Look what I've got!" Panakht cried excitedly, grabbing one of the cadavers by its hind legs and waving it around like a flag. "We killed seven of them between us! There's going to be lots of nice roast meat tonight. What about you, Siamun?"

His face fell when he peered into the cabin and saw that it was devoid of any bag. "Seems that this wasn't one of your best days."

"No, you can say that again. Things can only get better," Siamun replied, trying to sound cheerful.

"They sure will," Panakht said, nodding encouragingly. "All you have to do is come with us as often as you can, as long as we're still around. Just turn up at the barracks whenever you have some spare time."

Siamun smiled. "All right. The columns can sure do without me from time to time."

****

The throngs of people that filled the streets of Waset and lined the riverbanks stretched out almost endlessly. An expectant silence had descended on the masses after news had spread that the royal family had already emerged from the vast temple complex of Ipet-Sut, accompanied by the sacred barges carrying the golden images of the Holy Triad. Now they would embark on their magnificent gilded boats and travel a short way upstream to visit the southern sanctuary of Ipet-Reset. It was here that the sacred mysteries of the Beautiful Feast of Opet were going to unfold, during which the king was going to be equipped with a new Ka and confirmed in his right to rule. Actually, Siamun would have preferred to stand near the embankment in order to have a good view of the approaching ships, but Panakht had insisted that they position themselves as closely to the temple as possible. Now the two friends and Nebnefer were standing crammed between countless bodies, waiting for things to happen.

"By the way, where is your friend Urhiye?" Siamun asked in a low voice.

Panakht hesitated slightly before he answered just as softly. "He told me that he wasn't going to watch the procession because he simply can't stand crowded places."

Siamun sighed. "It's quite the same with me," he admitted truthfully. "Why did you have to choose this spot of all places? It's absolutely packed."

"I know, and there is a reason why this is so," Panakht replied happily. "See how close we are to the temple portal? Once the gate opens, we will be among the first to enter the forecourt, and we'll be able to secure ourselves the best places in the front row when the oracle will be consulted. This is incredibly entertaining, as you will see."

Siamun wondered what could possibly be entertaining about a consultation of the divine oracle. In the past, he used to avoid such gatherings whenever he could. The candid manner in which people revealed their most intimate problems which were then usually discussed at length by onlookers had always appalled him.

Meanwhile, the tension had almost reached breaking-point. It couldn't be long now that the royal family appeared in all their glory. The delicious smells of freshly baked bread and roast meat filled the air and made Siamun's mouth water. It was a relief that they also helped to mask the far less pleasant odours which some of the bystanders exuded.

From the excited whispers around him Siamun could glean that the fleet was about to moor after being towed upstream. All of a sudden, the crowd began to fill with life. People were shoving and jostling hard from behind in order to get to the front, eliciting angry hisses from those standing in their way. Young children were lifted onto their parents' shoulders, while the older ones simply stood on their toes and craned their necks. At long last, overwhelming cheers rose from the throats of those closest to the river and spread rapidly along the lines of spectators.

The first thing that caught Siamun's eye was the glint of gold. High-up on the shoulders of his litter bearers, King Seti sat on his gilded throne, clutching his royal insignia to his chest, his composure one of perfect regal dignity. With the tall double-crown on his head and the robe which was adorned with countless golden discs he was indeed a magnificent sight. The barge of the great god Amun followed on the heels of the royal fan-bearers, its prow and stern displaying rams' heads and being carried on sixteen poles and twice as many shoulders. A single priest in an immaculate white robe preceded it with a most solemn expression on his face. It wasn't hard to tell that this was Wenennefer, Amun's long-standing high priest since King Horemheb's time. The lavishly decorated divine barge was carried solely by priests with clean-shaven heads who were accompanied by more priests holding incense burners and chanting songs of praise as they went. The somewhat smaller barges of Amun's wife Mut and their son Khensu followed closely behind.

Then the Great Royal Wife Mut-Tuya, as she called herself officially, came into view. A golden vulture cap which resembled that worn by the goddess Mut encased her proudly raised head. The heavy wig she wore underneath framed a small but chubby face. Staring unwaveringly ahead, she looked like a statue clad in a glamorous gown.

Next came Prince Ramses. A lock of his longish red hair had been made into a braid which protruded from an opening in the tight-fitting skull cap that covered the rest of his hair. A thin golden diadem encircled his head, adorning his brow with a small rearing serpent. While his guise obviously associated him with the divine son Khensu, his posture betrayed the spoilt youth in him just as clearly: Slumping in his elaborate chair, Ramses rested his elbows casually on its arms, and the look on his face could best be described as bored.

Siamun was about to turn his attention to the musicians and dancers whom he expected to follow in the wake of the royal procession when he caught sight of yet another litter which was occupied by a young girl. He was surprised, for he had almost forgotten that King Seti also had a daughter. Soon enough, he found himself staring intently at her while she floated slowly past him. The princess wore no wig, and her luscious brown tresses cascaded freely down her back. The small head of a gazelle was attached to the front of her golden circlet, thus designating her as a female member of the royal house. But how different were her features from those of her brother! Where the contours of his profile were sharp and disagreeable, her delicate chin and the slight curve of her small nose were a pleasant sight to look at. Her cheeks were full and soft, and the subtle auburn tinge of her hair reminded Siamun of the mild glow of the setting sun. But what fascinated him most of all was the air of sadness that surrounded her, as if there was some secret sorrow hidden in the depths of her heart. He kept staring as the princess moved along, mesmerized, until her litter had long vanished from his sight.

"Come on, what are you waiting for?"

Nebnefer's words hardly penetrated his mind. Siamun didn't even feel the nudge that undoubtedly accompanied them.

"Why, what is the matter?" he asked absent-mindedly.

"You're asking me what the matter is?" Nebnefer returned indignantly. "I'd rather like to know what is wrong with you all of a sudden! They have opened the temple gates, and Panakht has since long gone to get us the best places. Come on, he's waiting for us!"

When Siamun still didn't react, Nebnefer grabbed him by the sleeve without any further ado and dragged him along. With the help of some serious prodding and jostling they managed to shove past the scores of people who were pouring through the open gates and eventually found Panakht.

"Finally!" he exclaimed, impatience ringing in his voice. "What took you so long? Weren't you able to tear your eyes off the pretty dancers? Well, there will still be plenty of opportunity to catch up on that, but the consultation of the oracle only happens once, and it is about to begin."

Siamun decided to ignore his friend's rude remark and focused on what was about to happen instead. As Panakht had promised, they had an excellent view of the vast court, for they were standing in the front of the crowd that took up a good part of it. Two of the bases in the repository shrines were occupied by the barges of Mut and Khensu, but the third one in the middle was empty. Amun's sacred barge still rested on the shoulders of his priests who had positioned themselves right in the centre of the remaining space. The double doors of the wooden shrine that housed the god's golden image stood wide open, for today everyone should be allowed to catch a glimpse of the Hidden One who usually resided in the mysterious darkness of his sanctuary.

Next to the barge stood the High Priest, whereas the litters of the royal family were lined up behind it.

The rows of the spectators stretched across the entire width of the court. Heavily armed security guards soon put a stop to the shoving and pushing that was still going on in places.

Eventually, all went quiet. The booming voice of the high priest rent the ensuing silence.

"Whoever wishes to consult the divine oracle of the great god Amun may step forth!"

Heads turned, and curious glances were cast all around. Then a woman standing in the front row took a big step forward.

"Divine oracle, will my husband Huy recover from his illness?"

Everyone was staring intently at the sacred barge. Would it move forward to say yes, or would it destroy this poor woman's hopes by moving backwards? The barge jerked, seemingly forcing the priests to take a large step backwards. Disappointed muttering rose among the spectators. Only those who had seen the contented smile on the woman's face made either outraged or amused remarks.

"I bet that woman can't wait until her husband breathes his last," Panakht whispered into Siamun's ear.

Another woman stepped forward. Two young children were clutching her hands while a third one clung to her dress. In addition to them a tiny baby was strapped to her back.

"Divine oracle," she began in a rather timid voice, "will my sister Isisnofret finally fall pregnant this year?"

She watched the barge closely until, to her obvious relief, it moved in her direction.

"Well, it's plain to see that she doesn't share her sister's problems," a man standing close to Siamun murmured to someone beside him.

Once again, Siamun was at a loss. He couldn't understand how people could bring themselves to exposing their most personal worries in front of everyone. For him, this would be the last thing he'd ever do. Not only did he not believe that it was really the god who acted. He knew for certain that it were merely the priests who answered the questions of the innocently trusting people quite arbitrarily, which in itself was an offence against Maat. What was even worse was the fact that the whole system was open to corruption. Siamun was convinced that at least some of those posing questions might well have paid the priests beforehand in order to get the desired answers. And he knew that he wasn't the only one who doubted the divine origin of the oracle. As it were, it was all nothing but a big hoax, but as long as it was entertaining nobody seemed to mind.

Distinctive murmurs went through the crowd, and further down the lines someone seemed to fight his way to the front. Soon a big burly man with coarse features emerged and advanced briskly towards the barge until a warning shout stopped him.

"Divine oracle," his hoarse voice boomed, trembling with barely contained fury, "has my wife been cheating me with that wretched scoundrel Hunefer?"

Startled, Siamun caught his breath. He stared hard at the

priests on whom depended the weal and woe of a woman who might well be innocent. The barge jerked, and the priests took a large stride forward.

With a blood-curdling howl the man turned and stamped off, uttering the worst curses Siamun had ever heard while he forced his way through the throng of people.

Despite the warm sunshine a cold shiver ran down Siamun's spine as he tried to stop himself from imagining what this bad-tempered fellow would be doing to his allegedly unfaithful wife. To a woman who had just been found guilty by a handful of ignorant priests.

Pushing these unpleasant thoughts aside, he let his gaze roam until it fastened all by itself on a particular royal litter. Even across the distance he was still touched by the princess's allure. He was unable to make out her features, but his mind started to stray nevertheless. Siamun wondered what she was thinking, whether she believed in the divine origin of the oracle and that it was truly the god who judged people's affairs. And he asked himself how she felt, sitting in her litter, high above the heads of everyone else, and whether she loved the life she led.

Stop that nonsense, he scolded himself at once. *What is it to do with me? It's none of my concern what the princess thinks or feels. I'm never going to learn, anyway.*

He tapped Panakht on the shoulder. "I believe we have seen enough. Let's go!"

Both Panakht and Nebnefer shook their heads. Apparently they enjoyed themselves too thoroughly to leave just yet.

Groaning silently, Siamun resigned himself to his fate. He was determined not to pay any more heed to the ongoing consultations. But this proved impossible when he caught sight of the next petitioner. Apart from the fact that he was rather tall and thus most probably male, not much could be said about him, for he was completely covered with a baggy garment that had clearly seen better days. Siamun was surprised to see that he had even veiled his head and face so that only his eyes were visible. He couldn't believe that someone who obviously didn't want to be recognized was allowed to approach the sacred barge at all. And he was not the only one to be taken aback, as he could glean from the many surprised glances around him. After a couple of bold strides, the man planted his sandaled feet firmly on the ground.

"Divine oracle of the great god Amun," he boomed in a loud and clearly altered voice, "is King Seti Menmaatre the legitimate ruler of the Two Lands?"

There were a few startled gasps, followed by an almost tangible silence. Everybody seemed to hold their breath. All those present glued their eyes on the sacred barge, waiting for the answer that didn't come.

Siamun assumed that the priests were simply too surprised to react, and he could hardly blame them. What an outrageous question to ask! Siamun was shaken by the sheer audacity of challenging the king's right to rule in his very presence. He directed his gaze at Seti who was leaning forward in his chair, craning his neck and staring hard at the barge as if willing it to move.

The air was thick with tension, but it wasn't until the man had repeated his insolent words that the priests came to their senses and took a large step forward. Throwing his head back, he broke into a chilling laughter before he turned and disappeared into the crowd.

Nobody seemed to even try and hold him back. The security guards just stood there, dumbfounded. It was only when a few cutting commands split the air that they started to move, forcing their way through the throng of people to go after him. Naturally, that put an end to the consultation of the divine oracle. Royal litters and sacred barges alike were hurriedly carried inside the temple and the crowd dispersed, chattering excitedly.

****

The beer was lukewarm and tasted horrible, and the wine, a rarity even in a beer house of some status like this one, made Siamun screw his face up with every sip he took. But nobody seemed to be bothered by those little shortcomings. Quite on the contrary, the mood was exuberant. People were singing, or rather bawling, so loudly that the musicians had a hard time to make themselves heard.

Feeling quite subdued, Siamun looked around. Everyone was having fun. Everyone except him. He cursed himself for letting himself be talked into visiting this packed establishment when he had simply wanted to go home. The excited discussions of the recent happenings had long ceased, giving way to different, less distinguished talk.

But Siamun couldn't bring himself to doing the same. The preposterous incident back at the temple had shaken him to the core. The longer he thought of it, the less comfortable he felt about it. Was it mere coincidence that someone had dared challenge pharaoh's authority just now that he, Siamun, had appeared on the scene? Who could this insolent person be, anyway, and why had he taken the risk? What could he possibly gain from it?

Siamun tried in vain to fight the growing feeling that Panakht might have something to do with it. He knew all too well how boastful his old friend could be at times, and Siamun wouldn't put it past him to reveal his secret in a bid to impress some of his new friends. Or, perhaps, it might have been just a slip of his tongue. He would have to ask Panakht as soon as possible. Then Siamun's gaze lingered as he watched Urhiye who was engaged in a lively conversation with the woman next to him. It suddenly struck him as odd that the troop commander seemed oblivious to the crammed space and the terrible stale air. Hadn't he told Panakht that he abhorred crowded places? Somehow, this didn't make sense, but Siamun was too exhausted to care. Having thoroughly tired of all the racket and the clumsy advances of the heavily made up lady beside him who had come too close for comfort, he decided to leave. When he rose and bade his farewell to his friends, they hardly seemed to notice. Siamun weaved his way carefully through the throng of sitting and standing guests. He had almost reached the door when someone close by went off into a peal of laughter that somehow struck him as familiar. Startled, he turned his head, searching for a face he could associate with that sound. Siamun's gaze fastened on the unusually pretty features of a young woman. His heart skipped a beat as he took in this startling sight. Wasn't that…?

No, this couldn't possibly be his sister. Satet was safely back at home, not here in Waset, and most certainly not in a place like this.

Just to make sure, Siamun rubbed his eyes and looked again. But where he had just caught sight of his sister –if it had indeed been her- was now a middle-aged woman with a brightly painted face.

Utterly relieved, he realized that he had been wrong after all. Perhaps it was not surprising that he was imagining things, since encouraged by his friends, he had forced a considerable amount of wine down his throat, too. Hurriedly, he took himself off and reached his quarters soon after.

Not bothering to undress, Siamun flung himself on his bed. But before he could drift off, the picture of a beautiful face with melancholic eyes flitted into his mind.

Don't be stupid, he berated himself at once. There were hundreds of pretty girls around. One day, he was going to marry one of them and lead a decent life with her. The princess was not for him. She was a king's daughter, and he was… a different king's son. This was never going to work. He had to forget her, and quickly at that.

But the harder he tried to banish her image from his thoughts, the more it persisted. And to make matters worse, it even haunted him in his dreams.

Chapter Three

"How can it be that there is still no trace of the perpetrator?" Seti's black expression betrayed his growing annoyance, as did the menacing tone of his voice. He knew it, and he didn't care. Clutching the royal crook in his right, he allowed the fingers of his other hand to drum impatiently on the armrest of his throne.

"Your Majesty, I fear that we may soon have to give up any hope of getting a useful hint as to the whereabouts of the culprit," Paser said as cautiously as possible. "Ten days have passed since that unfortunate event, and it becomes increasingly unlikely that we will ever be able to get hold of him."

"This scoundrel cannot possibly have vanished into thin air," Seti growled, drumming his fingers even harder.

"But in the meantime he has probably left the city behind," the vizier of the south pointed out. "In fact, he may have done so straight after his despicable performance."

"Which should not have been possible for him."

Nebamun's cutting remark almost elicited an angry hiss from Seti. The northern vizier was getting thoroughly on his nerves with his constant butting in.

"The whole city should have been sealed off immediately in order to cut off any possible route of escape," Nebamun went on unwaveringly. "This would have been the only sensible thing to do when the time was right. It is most unfortunate that this opportunity was missed."

"It is always easier to judge things with the benefit of hindsight," Paser explained, irritation ringing in his voice. "The incident came as a complete surprise, as everyone present will recall. As was my duty, I had directed all my attention at the sacred ceremonies in order to ensure their smooth progress. "

"In your capacity of mayor of this city, however, your foremost duty was to make sure that the security forces stayed on high alert throughout the ceremony," Nebamun snapped. "Had you cared to do so, they would have been able to react much faster than they actually did."

Seti just managed to stifle a groan. He deeply regretted to have summoned the northern vizier to attend this audience, but then there was barely any way of getting around this man. Nebamun's attempts at throwing an unfavourable light on his southern colleague thoroughly annoyed him. Seti didn't believe for a single moment that he would have done any better, had he been in Paser's place.

"Gentlemen, all this bickering gets us nowhere," Seti said sharply. "It is true that all the streets should have been sealed off straight away, at least the main ones. But it is equally true that nobody could possibly have anticipated an incident of this sort. The security guards had become just a bit too relaxed once they had sorted the throng of spectators out, a fact that the perpetrator was undoubtedly well aware of. We were all taken by surprise. Even the answer of the divine oracle came unusually late," he concluded, shooting a withering glance at Wenennefer who instantly lowered his eyes with a guilty look on his face. Seti didn't fail to notice Nebamun's gleeful smile.

"But rather than dwelling on past mistakes we should focus on the present," he continued, furrowing his brow. "What worries me most is the fact that apparently nobody in the crowd tried to stop that scoundrel. There should have been at least a few who were quick-witted enough to do so. It rather looks like they wanted the man to get away with it unscathed. This in turn leads me to suspect that a good part of the population may secretly share his view."

The ensuing uncomfortable silence was broken by a man in his early thirties who had hardly spoken so far.

"Your Majesty," General Mehy said in a calm voice, "perhaps it is still too early to speak of a particular view. Presently we don't know his motive, if he had one at all. For all we know, this could simply have been a madman, or an imposter who just wanted to cause a great stir."

Seti cast a grateful glance at his trusted friend. "You may be right, Mehy. It is never advisable to jump to conclusions. For now, we should rather concentrate on the two last remaining days of the celebrations, and on the final consultation of the divine oracle in particular. Paser will undoubtedly take appropriate measures to avoid any more disturbances. This is all for now."

It was with a great sense of relief when Seti dismissed the two viziers along with the high priest. He longed for a private talk with Mehy. Leaning back in his chair, he took a few deep breaths. Once he felt more relaxed, he placed the crook across his knees and searched the gaze of his friend who was leaning his shoulder against one of the pillars supporting the royal canopy.

"Do you really believe in a harmless explanation, or did you just want to appease me?"

"At any rate I think this is far more likely than the assumption that the perpetrator wanted to undermine your royal authority," Mehy replied quietly. "Supposed this was indeed his motive, what would have been the good of publicly exposing it? There is nobody who can lay even the remotest claim to the throne beside you and Ramses, thus challenging your right to

rule would be completely pointless."
Seti still wasn't convinced. "Who knows?" he said thoughtfully. "Sometimes I wonder if there is a possibility that someone with links to the former royal house is still out there, gathering support in parts of the population."
"If this were indeed true, we would know it," Mehy said firmly. "Trust me."
Seti nodded absent-mindedly, trying hard to muster as much confidence as his old friend seemed to have. He pushed himself up and took to pacing to and fro in front of the dais, clasping his hands behind his back.
"What if my own family were behind all that?"
Mehy looked puzzled. "What do you mean?"
Seti stopped short and trained his gaze on his friend.
"Unfortunately I have reason to believe that this might well be the case."
"What kind of reason would that be?"
Seti resumed his pacing before he spoke. "Yesterday, the Great Royal Wife has made the suggestion to have Ramses officially designated as heir apparent by the divine oracle. She pointed out to me that this was the most suitable way of silencing any malicious gossip regarding my alleged lack of legitimacy which might have started following that tiresome incident. Her reasoning is quite comprehensible, because if the god is happy to appoint Ramses legitimate heir to the throne it can be implied that he also acknowledges my own legitimacy. Pretty clever, isn't it?"
Mehy furrowed his brow while he pondered this new information. "And, are you going to comply with her wish?"
Seti exhaled sharply. "There is hardly any way of getting around it. I must remove the taint that clings to my authority ever since in some way or other. And the most effective way of doing so seems to be the one proposed by Tuya. Appointing

Ramses crown prince is by far more credible and inconspicuous than any attempt to have my own legitimacy directly confirmed by the oracle. Even the most simple-minded peasant would see through such a plot."

Seti paused to draw a laboured breath. All at once, he felt so incredibly old and powerless. And there it was, as he might have expected, the treacherous pain in his chest he had been waiting for all the time. He pressed his hand hard on the aching spot.

"Tuya thinks she has outwitted me," he muttered, as he gazed at the deep-blue section of sky that showed in the high-set guttered window, "but we'll see about that. I will find out whether or not she has really gone to such great lengths in order to achieve her aim. She might have beaten me this time, but she is never going to have her way with Tia. My daughter won't ever be married to Ramses. She is far too good for him."

Again, he fell silent and breathed heavily.

"Had I not better send for the physician?" Mehy asked with a worried look on his handsome face.

Seti chose to ignore this question. When he spoke again, his voice was tinged with menace.

"If I ever find out that Tuya has indeed arranged that despicable performance back at the temple to serve her own and Ramses' ends, her days as Great Royal Wife will be over."

****

"What a charade!" Siamun scoffed disdainfully. "I believe I would never let myself get involved in something like this."

"Well, Prince Ramses clearly doesn't share your view," Panakht pointed out. "And who can blame him? Someone who fancies himself as future king cannot afford to be squeamish about those things. Now he has finally got what he always wanted. Have you seen how his mother was swelling with pride when the voice of the divine oracle pronounced him the future ruler of the Two Lands? Though how they pulled that one off really beats me."

Siamun smiled wryly. The two friends went with the tide of the masses that were pouring through the temple gates into the city.

"Shall we go down to the riverbank to watch the procession returning to Ipet-Sut?" Siamun asked casually.

As he had anticipated, Panakht shook his head. "No, I think I've had enough of this."

"Same with me. Let's be on the lookout for something to eat, then. I could do with some of the scrumptious roast meat they are handing out everywhere."

Even after eleven days people hadn't tired of celebrating in the streets and alleyways of their city. Today was the last day of free handouts of beer, bread and roast meat, and everyone seemed determined to make the most of it. From tomorrow on, things would inevitably return to normal.

Siamun had been queuing up at one of the stalls for a while when his gaze fell on two women who were strolling past, chattering animatedly. Coincidentally, one of them looked in his direction, then turned her head abruptly and hurried on. For a moment, Siamun was struck dumb. He was convinced that this had been Satet. But how was this possible? How had she come here?

He left the queue and made to follow the women. Someone grabbed his sleeve and pulled hard at it.

"Where are you going?" Panakht complained indignantly. "It

was nearly your turn to be served. My stomach is growling like mad!"

"Forget your stomach and tell me instead why I have just seen Satet passing by," Siamun hissed. "Isn't there something you may have forgotten to tell me?"

Panakht bit his lip and fastened his gaze on his sandals, a guilty look flitting across his face.

"All I know is that some time ago she ran away from home. It is quite possible that she roams about here somewhere."

It took Siamun some considerable effort to swallow the caustic remark he had been about to hurl at his friend. With a violent jerk he freed himself from Panakht's grip and stormed off.

He heard curses of the worst kind as he forced his way through the crowds, pushing people aside in his bid to catch up with his sister. He didn't care. Siamun was boiling with rage. How could Satet have done that to him? And why hadn't Panakht told him of her disappearance?

He followed the direction Satet and her companion had taken, glancing into every alleyway he passed, but to no avail. He was about to give up hope when he caught sight of the two women, standing in front of a merchant who offered cheap jewellery.

"Satet!" he panted, struggling for breath.

Satet tore her gaze from the bangle she had just been appraising and directed it at her brother.

"Siamun, what are you doing here?" she asked, eyes wide with mock surprise.

The innocent tone of her voice made him finally lose his self-control.

"What *I am* doing here?" he lashed out. "You'd better tell me what *you* are doing here! What ailed you to run away from home and come this far all on your own? Did you spend a single moment thinking of mother and how dead-worried she must be?"

Satet put a soothing hand on his arm, exchanging meaningful glances with her friend.

"Siamun, please, do calm down. Whatever are all the people supposed to think?"

"The people?" he spat. "As if you had ever cared for other people's opinions! And your own family doesn't bother you one bit anyway. You are coming with me, now, and I'll take you straight back home."

Grabbing Satet's wrist, he made to pull her along.

"Just one moment, young man!" a booming voice called out just then.

Reluctantly Siamun turned round and came face to face with a burly Nubian. Judging from the leather throngs that crossed his torso and the truncheon in his hand he had to be one of the security guards patrolling the streets.

Just what I needed, Siamun groaned.

"You'd better leave this young lady alone and take yourself off at once," the man growled.

"Listen and let me explain," Siamun said, trying to stay calm. "This is my sister, and I'm only taking her back home with me."

"So, back home," the Nubian repeated, raising his eyebrows. "And where exactly is your home?"

"We live in Iunu," Siamun replied.

The guard's eyes widened. "Iunu? Quite some way off, isn't it?" he muttered, tapping his truncheon menacingly on the open palm of his hand. It was clear that the man didn't believe a single word Siamun had said, and he made no effort to conceal his distrust.

As if this were not enough, a second security guard appeared on the scene, offering his full support to his colleague.

Exasperated, Siamun glared at his sister. With a few simple words she could clear up the situation. Why didn't she do it then?

Seeing her gleeful half-smile, he suddenly understood. This unexpected interlude was just to Satet's liking. She clearly enjoyed playing with that dim-witted Nubian while leaving her brother in the lurch.

Just as he was about to throw all caution to the winds and yell at her, Satet opened her mouth to speak.

"Good man, this here is really my brother," she said in a patronizing manner. "Even though he is very strict with me, I am willing to go with him. After all, there isn't always any choice when it comes to one's own relatives, don't you agree?"

The Nubian nodded vigorously while his thick lips stretched into the most stupid grin Siamun had ever seen. He was itching to slap it off his smirking face, but then perhaps – do to him justice- it wasn't entirely his fault. Satet seemed to have that kind of dulling effect on most of the men she encountered, and she certainly knew how to make the most of it.

Once again he grabbed her wrist and pulled her along, this time unmolested by anyone.

"Really, Satet, I am lost for words," Siamun ranted as he weaved his way through the crowd with Satet trailing behind. "You are simply impossible. Aren't you ever going to change your ways? Where have you been all the time, and who was your companion?"

"I have been enjoying the celebrations just as you did," Satet replied with unnerving calm. "And as to my whereabouts, I have been living with my new friend whom I got to know a while ago. I have been looking for you everywhere, but as I was unable to track you down I had no other choice."

So it had been Satet whom he had seen the other day in that beer house after all. But it was no use reproaching her for it. She'd only have brushed his concerns away with a shrug.

Siamun let out a deep sigh. He was about to give up all hope of Satet ever bringing honour to her family and becoming a respectable lady of the house. If only she didn't run towards her ruin one of these days.

Having arrived at the stall where he had first spotted his sister, Siamun kept a sharp lookout for Panakht as he went along, but to no avail. His friend seemed to have vanished into thin air, and he wasn't going to search for him any longer.

Curse him, Siamun thought, still angry with him. Panakht must have come to know of Satet's disappearance when he visited at home. Why had he kept the truth from him? Perhaps Panakht hadn't thought much of it, just as he never thought much of anything and never seemed to worry.

"Do you really have to run like that?" Satet complained, panting hard. "And where are you taking me, if I may ask?"

"We are on our way to my living quarters in the heart of the city, which you were unable to find," Siamun snapped, glancing at her over his shoulder. "And that's where we're going to stay until our departure in two days' time."

"Oh, do we really have to leave so soon?"

Siamun ignored the obvious disappointment ringing in her voice.

"Yes," he said sternly. "As soon as possible."

Later that day Panakht turned up to say his good-byes. His ship was due to leave for Mennefer early next morning. There he would stay until the returning troops were fully assembled and ready to head subsequently for Avaris.

Although he was still mad with Panakht, Siamun decided that now was not the time to heap reproaches on him and explained his own plans in a calm voice.

"I'm not certain if I will reach Mennefer in time to meet you," he said, "because pharaoh has decreed that he wants to have his architects around when he stops in Abedju to carry out the annual rites in honour of Osiris. I don't know for sure yet why this is so, but I assume that it has something to do with the new temple he intends to build there. Whether I see you or not, I wish you all the best for your first campaign. Take good care of yourself and make sure you come back safe and sound."

****

They arrived in Abedju in the early afternoon of the third day following their departure. Siamun had been sharing a boat with his superiors Ptahnakht and Wenamun as well as Nebnefer and Satet. The royal family and their entourage had arrived one day earlier in order to witness the first part of the sacred mysteries. Their ship moored in a broad canal that led from the Great River to a small harbour situated close to the main cult centre, the temple of Osiris. Except for a few trees, no greenery could be seen, for the waters of the river had flooded all fertile ground, bordering the desert and encroaching perilously close on a few peripheral mudbrick houses. They were not really in danger of being flooded, though, because the water had risen its highest and would gradually subside, leaving the soil thoroughly soaked and covered with the nutritious black mud that had given this land the name Kemet, the Black One.
It was a short walk from their mooring place to the temple. Ptahnakht and Wenamun were hurrying on ahead, leaving the young people to follow them in their wake. Satet had insisted on accompanying them, and Siamun had known better than to reason with her. He was glad that nobody had asked any awkward questions. If Nebnefer was confused by Satet's

sudden appearance, he chose not to show it.

It wasn't long until they saw the vast site opening up in front of them. It was shaped like a drawn-out valley, bordered on the near side by the moderately high cliffs they had just passed through, while the impressive rocky plateau of the high desert formed a natural boundary on the far side. The rocky wall receded considerably opposite the great temple, but advanced steadily the further Siamun looked to his left, thus narrowing the valley noticeably. From where he stood Siamun could already make out two royal monuments that had been built by earlier kings: one was an impressive enclosure wall diagonally opposite him, and the other was an ancient temple nestling against the high cliff.

The most important structure of all, however, was situated within the huge cliff-lined bay which opened up before him as he turned right. The brilliant white temple that lay in its very centre was one of the most breath-taking sights Siamun had ever seen. And it was filled with life, too. A crowd of pious people had gathered to both sides of the entrance gate in order to witness the performance of Osiris' sacred mysteries. Judging by the rather small number of moored ships, most of them had to live locally, a fact that distinguished this event clearly from the celebration of the Beautiful Feast of Opet, as did the rather solemn and despondent mood. On coming closer, Siamun was able to glimpse the sadness on people's faces, and he sensed their grief at the death of Osiris which had been re-enacted just the day before. Osiris had been murdered by his evil brother Seth, and during the night his body had rested in a tent-like pavilion backing the temple where it had been mummified and wrapped up with bandages. Now was the time to carry his body in a long procession to the sacred site of Poker where he was going to be buried.

Meanwhile, Siamun had joined the silent crowd along with Satet and Nebnefer, waiting eagerly for things to happen. They had arrived just in time to see the sem-priest emerging from the temple at the head of the procession. His right hand was clutching a long staff, and the imitation of a leopard skin was slung around his bare torso, its gilded head dangling just above the broad sash of his white kilt. The gaunt face of the man who appeared to have lived through at least six decades and his extremely slim frame reminded Siamun immediately of the vizier Nebamun. Nebnefer, with whom he shared his observation, nodded. The sem-priest was Ramose, Nebamun's father.

Hard on his heels followed another priest whose high status was apparent from the standard he carried, on top of which a sinister, jackal-like figure was crouching. This was Wepwawet, the Opener of the Ways, whose duty it was to ensure the smooth progress of the procession and its safe arrival at Osiris' tomb by eliminating any dangers lurking in its path. In doing so, Wepwawet avenged Osiris' murder as he enabled him to be properly buried and resurrected to new life.

The next face was a well-known one, although Siamun had never before seen King Seti in his guise of Horus, Osiris' son. His features were set in a mask of solemn grief which made him appear older than he was. Seti was clad in the traditional garb which was lavishly adorned with stylized feathers, thus associating him with the falcon Horus. This time, he wasn't sitting in a litter but walked on foot like everyone else, for in this procession the honour of being carried was solely Osiris' due. The god's bandaged body lay on the sacred neshmet-barge which rested on the shoulders of twelve priests. A gilded canopy draped with garlands spanned its entire length. The heavy scents of burning incense and myrrh mingled with the sweet fragrance of the flowers as the barge floated past.

Trailing behind were more priests, headed by Prince Ramses who didn't seem happy at all to find himself relegated to this rather inconspicuous position, and scores of wailing and shrieking women with dusty and tearstained faces, bemoaning Osiris' violent death. Just like professional mourners were an integral part of any burial -at least if the deceased had been someone of some status- they played an essential role in this funeral procession. When Siamun spotted the Great Royal Wife and the princess among them, he quickly averted his eyes and hurried after the pious who accompanied the procession on its way into the sacred valley.

First they had to climb a gentle slope which rose immediately in front of the entrance gates. Covering the top of the hill were countless memorial chapels belonging to people who had lived and died centuries ago, and who had wanted to share in the blessings of this most sacred of sites while being buried elsewhere. The size of the shrines varied greatly, but almost all of them had a vaulted roof and were covered in thick layers of sand. There was no trace left of the trees that must have adorned their tiny yards other than the occasional deep pit. Siamun was deeply touched by the sight of those forlorn testimonials of past times, and he hoped that whatever these pious people had wished for would come true. Glancing sideways, he saw with surprise how Satet's lips moved as if in silent prayer. Could it be that she was actually praying for the Kas of the deceased? If so, there must be a side to her he had never known. For the first time in his life, Siamun felt that he shared something really valuable with his sister.

However, he didn't have time to dwell on this thought. The procession continued on its way, leaving the rows of shrines behind to trail down the hillside and enter the so-called sacred valley, which was in fact not much more than a drawn-out hollow extending to the rocky cliffs of the desert plateau beyond. Progress was slow, and the shrill shrieks of the mourning women were increasingly straining on Siamun's nerves. He longed for it all to be over.

To his utter relief, the procession came to a halt fairly soon. They had reached the far end of the hollow which was now so shallow that it could hardly be distinguished from the surrounding desert. The neshmet-barge was carefully lowered onto a large wooden sledge. Six of the priests who had been carrying the barge stepped forward and took up the ropes that were attached to the front. Straining on them, they towed the sledge and its precious load along, turning first to the left and then heading towards a distinct rise in the distance. Only the sem-priest and Seti followed. From time immemorial, nobody else was entitled to visit the sacred tomb of Osiris and to witness the mysteries that unfolded there, and nobody was ever allowed to speak of what he had seen, not even pharaoh.

A soothing silence descended as the shrieking and wailing ceased. Mourners and spectators alike turned to make their way back to the temple. Furtively, Siamun glanced around, eager to catch a glimpse of the princess.

"What are you craning your neck for? Are you looking out for someone in particular?"

The teasing tone of Satet's voice made Siamun's cheeks burn. "Of course not," he snapped, angry with himself. "I was only surveying the landscape."

Having said that, he looked hard in the direction of the magnificent white pyramid he could make out in the distance. Satet laughed brightly. "You can't fool me that easily, but I'll leave it at that. What are we going to do now?"

"I would like to have a good look around while I have the chance," Siamun replied, feeling his embarrassment gradually subside. "After all, we're not going to stay in this place for long."

"I reckon that you're going to spend more time here than you might think," Satet said, raising her eyebrows meaningfully.

"What do you mean by that?"

"I'm speaking of the time when you will have to supervise the construction of pharaoh's new temple, of course."

"There's no way that's ever going to happen," Siamun retorted. "There are other, more experienced architects than me."

"But there is no-one as competent as you," she said casually, as if this were a matter of fact. "Hasn't His Majesty already entrusted you with another important project?"

Siamun waved dismissively. "True, but that was only a columned hall. This is different. The design of an entire temple involves a lot more planning, even more so, since the king appears to make great demands on this one. Are you coming with me?"

Satet shook her head. "No, I'd rather like to wait here for you and enjoy the silence."

For the second time this day, Siamun was baffled. "You want to enjoy the silence?" he echoed, his voice full of incredulity. "At home you always keep complaining about how silent and boring everything is!"

"This is different," Satet replied slowly, as if trying to find the right words. "This is not the kind of silence that makes you feel bored, but rather a soothing, comforting silence. I have never felt so close to death as I do now, being in this place where everything around me reminds me of death and the transience of life. But despite this fact –or should I say, owing to it- I'm not frightened of death anymore. If it ever becomes clear that death is only a way station in the transition to eternal life, it is here."

Never before had Siamun heard similar words from his boisterous sister who had always been eager to live life to the full. His stupefaction must have been mirrored in his face, for

Satet threw her head back and laughed out loud.

"You would never have expected me to say things like that, would you?" she said in a good-natured tone of voice.

"No, but all the nicer it was to hear them," he replied softly. He felt that there was something going on. Perhaps Satet was really about to change her ways after all, who could tell?

"I'm going to sit there by these rocks and wait for you to come back," she said, pointing to the left.

"All right," Siamun nodded, beckoning to Nebnefer at the same time. The young man had been standing a few paces off, apparently not wishing to intrude on their private conversation.

As Siamun had anticipated, Nebnefer was of the same mind as he. Having been here before, he couldn't wait to show his friend around. It was a short walk to the pyramid Queen Ahmose had erected on the far edge of the plain, the one that Siamun had already admired from the distance. However, its impressive height only now became apparent that they were nearing it, as did its deplorable state of decay.

"It must be about as high as King Menkaure's pyramid, don't you think?" Nebnefer said with an appraising look.

Siamun nodded slowly. "Yes, that may be about right. It's a pity, though, that the top isn't intact anymore. And the limestone casing seems to have suffered a great deal, too."

"Sure it has. In some places it has vanished entirely, as you can see. But you can't help these things. Time will leave its marks on everything, no matter what. You mustn't forget that more than two centuries have passed since this pyramid was built."

"Time enough that someone might have thought of removing that ramp over there," Siamun said dryly while he glanced disapprovingly at the mudbrick structure which had once been used to drag the great stone blocks up.

Nebnefer only shrugged, seemingly undisturbed by such

laxness.

"At least this temple here is in a much better condition," he said, pointing at a small but very well maintained complex next to the pyramid. Meanwhile, Siamun had spotted a cluster of small houses in its vicinity which appeared to be occupied.

"And here live the priests who maintain the queen's mortuary temple and its cult, I suppose," he said, tilting his head in their direction.

"Quite right," Nebnefer replied merrily, clearly enjoying this private tour just as much as Siamun did. "But now let's go, there is still much more to be seen!"

They had to go round a great rock that jutted out considerably before they encountered the remains of a settlement which must have been far bigger than the one they had just seen. Judging by its dilapidated state it had to be much more ancient, too.

"Must have been a magnificent temple back in the day," Siamun muttered in dismay as he let his gaze roam across the pitiful ruins. "This is what will happen to everything we are constructing, too. We believe the monuments we build from hard rock to be solid and durable for all times, but the truth is that their splendour will fade very quickly. As soon as there is nobody left to look after them, they inevitably start to crumble away. Give it a few centuries, and all our efforts come down to nothing."

With a last regretful glance, they turned to go. The two friends had to surround yet another cliff that projected far into the plain.

"Sad as it is, I couldn't agree more," Nebnefer said. "And this is especially true for the royal monuments, because naturally every king gives preference to his own building projects over those of his predecessors. Fortunately, this is somewhat different when it comes to structures that are of more general interest, like the temple of Osiris which, as you will have noted, is not only in excellent condition, but is also being continually extended and embellished. But why should we care? The task of us architects is to serve the current ruler and to set his wishes in stone, nothing more and nothing less. Here we are, by the way," he concluded somewhat abruptly.

"Where?" Siamun asked, startled. He could see nothing of any particular interest.

"This is the spot where pharaoh wishes to have his new temple erected," Nebnefer explained in a low voice.

The projecting rock they had just surrounded was receding to form another deep natural bay. With about a hundred paces of width, it wasn't quite as large as the one housing the temple of Osiris, but its size was considerable nevertheless. What was more important, however, was the fact that the rocks lining it formed a backdrop that would be just perfect. They were high enough to embrace the future temple without overwhelming it.

"His Majesty has made an excellent choice," Siamun said admiringly while he let his gaze stray.

"Actually, this praise is His Majesty's father's due, remember?" Nebnefer pointed out. "Or, to be precise, his chief architect's Merimose, the same who had designed the original plans for the great columned hall. But as you can see, things haven't progressed far at all."

Siamun stared thoughtfully at the foundations outlining the shape of a good-sized building. He didn't know Seti's wishes yet, but he felt rather certain that the existing foundations would have to be abolished before building works could start.

"Are you already designing the plans for your next grand project, Siamun?" a cutting voice rang out behind him.

Siamun instantly recognized it although he had heard it only once before. He slowly turned to the speaker who eyed him intently.

"I have just taken the opportunity to commend His Majesty's excellent choice," Siamun said as calmly as possible.

"Indeed," Nebamun snarled. With his son and two servants in his wake, he slowly advanced on the two young men until he stopped a couple of paces off.

"Indeed there couldn't have been a better place," the vizier continued. "It is a pity, though, that Merimose's excellent plans aren't good enough anymore."

He surveyed the area with an air of importance while he seemed to consider, leaving young Penre to stand awkwardly beside him and throw occasional curious glances at his two colleagues.

"As rumour has it, this temple will be dedicated to seven deities," Nebamun went on in a mysteriously lowered voice, "each of whom is to have their very own sanctuary. Naturally, all the other elements essential to a proper temple are to be included, too. And in addition to that, His Majesty desires that a subterranean structure be built next to the monument, serving as a mock tomb for Osiris. All of this will have to fit into this not overly grand space. That's no easy task at all, come to think of it." Nebamun paused to cast a sly look at Siamun. "I do wonder whom His Majesty is going to entrust with this unique project. Don't you, Siamun?"

Without waiting for an answer, Nebnefer turned on his heel and strode off, pounding his staff forcefully on the ground as he went. Penre hesitated, as if he would rather stay behind than leave. For the fraction of a moment, his eyes met Siamun's, then he quickly averted his gaze and hurried after his father.

"It looks like Nebamun is going to do all he can to secure this opportunity for his son," Siamun remarked once the men were out of earshot.

"You can bet your life on it," Nebnefer replied. "Like he said, this project is going to be very special indeed, and it seems to be very dear to pharaoh. The name of whoever is going to design and build this temple to pharaoh's complete satisfaction is sure to last forever."

"I assume His Majesty will soon inform us of his wishes in more detail," Siamun said after a short silence.

Nebnefer nodded slowly. "Yes, most probably tomorrow. Given how important this project is to His Majesty, it should be on the top of his agenda once the sacred rites are over."

"I can't help feeling sorry for Nebamun's son," Siamun said thoughtfully, casting a glance in the direction of the quickly disappearing figures. "I believe he isn't happy at all having to live up to his father's high demands."

"Indeed he isn't," his friend agreed. "As far as I have come to know him, Penre doesn't take one bit after his ambitious father."

"Actually, things shouldn't be like that in the first place," Siamun mused. "What's the point of all this rivalry going on between fellow architects, anyway? I mean, rather than envying one another, we should work together and combine our various ideas and suggestions to get the best results possible."

Nebnefer sighed. "That's quite true, but unfortunately it's never going to be this way. All cooperation usually ends as soon as there are great wealth and glory at stake."

Siamun nodded in resignation, knowing full well that his friend was right.

"Let's go back then," he suggested, spotting the purple tinge of the western sky. "Once we have picked up my sister we can make for the ship."

But Satet wasn't where she had promised to wait. She wasn't sitting by the rocks she had indicated nor anywhere near them, for that matter. Satet seemed to have vanished without a trace. Siamun tried hard not to panic. He wasn't really concerned for her safety. It was very unlikely that anything bad might have happened to her just here. And hadn't she looked after herself for the past few weeks? Though what exactly she had been doing, only the gods knew; Siamun most certainly preferred not to.

The most likely explanation was that Satet had eventually tired from waiting for them and returned to the ship. The other, far more sinister possibility that she might have slipped away again didn't bear thinking. Just in case she was still anywhere around, Siamun called her name several times. He was surprised when he heard bright voices ringing out from somewhere high above his head. Looking up, he caught sight of a small group of young women who came slowly clambering down the great rock. Could Satet be one of them?

When the women had come close enough for him to distinguish their features, his breath caught in his chest. Satet wasn't among them. To his utter dismay, it was the princess instead who was nearing him, along with two of her companions!

A few moments later they had reached the bottom. All Siamun could do was stand and stare helplessly, not in the least knowing what to do or say. It was the princess who addressed him with a friendly greeting.

"I am glad that it's you I met and not the vizier," she added.

Siamun felt immediately lulled by the tone of her melodic voice.

"He is such an unpleasant person," the princess went on. "I'd rather encounter a snake than him. When we saw Nebamun and that little entourage of his coming this way, we quickly climbed this rock to get away from him."

On hearing this charming revelation, all tension left Siamun and he managed a smile.

"Unfortunately we weren't quite as lucky," he said. "By the time we noticed him it was too late."

The princess giggled. "Nebamun is notorious for his unexpected appearances. I assume he spoke to you about father's new temple."

Siamun nodded. "That's exactly what he did. Apparently he wanted to make a statement that none other than him, or rather his son, is going to be entrusted with this project."

"Poor fellow," she said, shaking her head in sympathy. "As a matter of fact, Penre is far more interested in the construction of ships than that of temples, but his father won't hear of it. Presumably there isn't enough glory to be had in designing ships. At any rate, I do hope that the new temple will be built according to your plans, Siamun. I know for certain that father pins high hopes on you," she concluded with a meaningful look.

It was rather strange. Only the princess and Siamun engaged in conversation, just as if there was nobody else around. They were complete strangers, but they talked as freely as if they were old friends when he didn't even know her name. Nebnefer and the princess's two young companions, on the other hand, were confined to the role of mere bystanders, exchanging shy glances every now and then while listening to the ongoing conversation.

"I heard you call out for your wife before," the princess said suddenly. "What happened to her?"

Siamun looked at her, baffled. His wife? What wife? Then, finally, the truth dawned on him.

"I have been looking for my sister Satet," he explained. "That's why I called out her name. We had agreed to meet here before returning to the ship. But I couldn't find her; maybe she has already gone back by herself. Anyway, I am not yet married," he added.

No sooner had the words left his mouth than he wanted to kick himself. What had he said that for? What was the princess now supposed to think of him? Surely she must take him for some kind of babbling fool. And yet, he thought he could see a look of relief flitting across her beautiful face when she nodded her understanding.

"By the way, my name is Tia," she said with an enticing smile. Siamun found himself staring helplessly at the gleaming row of her immaculate white teeth.

"Unfortunately, I have to return to the temple now," she continued, sincere regret ringing in her voice. "My parents surely expect me to have recovered by now. Earlier on, I feigned indisposition in order to get away from it all and stretch my legs a bit. I hope that we meet again soon, Siamun." Flashing one last smile at him she turned away -rather reluctantly, to Siamun's mind- and beckoned her companions to follow her.

Siamun stood motionlessly, his gaze following their fluttering garments until they disappeared behind another rock.

Nebnefer cleared his throat noisily. "We had better return to the ship now to make sure that your sister really is there."

Siamun nodded absent-mindedly and set off. He was immensely grateful that his friend didn't mention the encounter with the princess while they were on their way.

Back on their ship, Satet was awaiting them impatiently.

"As much as I enjoyed myself at first, I got finally bored, sitting there and waiting for you endlessly, so I decided to take myself off," she explained. "Though what took you so long, I can't imagine!"

Siamun preferred not to tell her. Quite unnecessarily, the litters of the royal family appeared just then to be carried onto their boats. The princess caught sight of Siamun standing at the rail and waved to him.

As Siamun had feared, this move hadn't been lost on Satet. "Now I know whom you were looking for so hard earlier on,"

she said pointedly. Then she shook her head in dismay.
"Siamun, if you'd care to listen to the advice of your unworthy sister just this once, don't do it. Keep well away from her. This can't turn out well."
But Siamun wasn't in a position to heed her advice anymore, even if he had wanted to. He had gone far beyond the point where there was no return.

****

His mouth set in a tight line, Prince Ramses stared sullenly at the water which was glittering with the rays of the afternoon sun. The euphoric mood he had been in ever since he had been pronounced official heir to the throne had apparently left him. And Seti thought he knew the reason why this was so.
Somewhat reluctantly he approached the young man and stood himself beside him. Ramses, who had been leaning himself casually on the rail, straightened up and bowed his head slightly.
At least he still displays some sort of respect to me, but that's probably all there is, Seti couldn't help thinking.
Of course it wasn't entirely Ramses' fault if he grew more and more impatient and found it increasingly hard to accept his alleged father's decisions. Seti knew full well who was stirring him up.
"You do not appear overly happy," Seti began cautiously. "Tell me why."
"Because I won't have anything to do but sit around idly while you lead the army north, father."

Every time Ramses used this word it felt like yet another stab into Seti's already wounded heart. Seti himself tried hard to avoid addressing him as his son. Once again he wondered if Ramses truly was as ignorant as Tuya would have him believe. Seti had never dared to find out, feeling that this matter was far too delicate to be pried into.

"Well, that's not quite true," Seti replied eventually. "Actually, knowing you as I do I believe you will have your hands full exercising and hunting. And for a change you can always throw a glance over Nebamun's shoulder and concern yourself with the affairs of administration."

Even before seeing the dismal look on Ramses' face Seti knew that none of this was what he really wanted.

"Father, I hoped to accompany you on this campaign as a commander of troops," the prince said with barely concealed reproach in his voice. The glimmer of hope that lit up in his greenish eyes while he spoke wasn't lost on Seti. Hope that wasn't going to be granted. Not yet, anyway.

"As a matter of fact, it is going to be more of a visit to the various sea ports north of Tjaru than a real campaign," Seti said lightly. "I presume that all of them will be prepared to cooperate with us. In the unlikely case that any of them are reluctant to comply, we will make them see reason in a quick and unspectacular fashion. So you see that this is no good opportunity at all to prove yourself."

As he might have anticipated, his words had done little to dissuade Ramses.

"This may well be true, but what about your ensuing advance on the territories that are controlled by the Hittites?" the young prince spluttered. "I simply have to be there when we give them a thorough smack!"

His childish eagerness nearly caused Seti to smile, but it also strengthened his resolve even more. It was quite obvious that

Ramses had yet to realize the seriousness of going to war. For him it was more of a thrilling game than anything else, and this attitude was fraught with danger.

"I promise you," Seti replied, "that you will join the army as commander of troops on next year's campaign. Until then you may want to prepare yourself by perfecting your various skills."

He had spoken in a voice stern enough to make it clear that this was his last word in this matter. Ramses hastily made a stiff bow and retreated to the spacious cabin in the middle of the deck from which his mother emerged soon after. Tuya headed straight for her husband who watched her with a sense of foreboding.

"Dear husband," she piped, "with your permission I would like to inform you of a rather unpleasant matter."

"Speak!"

"It has come to my attention that our daughter has recently been seen talking to this young architect towards whom you seem to be so well disposed."

Surprised, Seti drew a sharp breath. He had assumed that Tuya would be working on him for Ramses' sake.

"You are speaking of the architect Siamun, I presume?" he inquired.

His wife shot him an irritated glance. "Of course, that's the one. I have already spoken to Tia, and she admitted to it without wavering. She doesn't even believe this to be unseemly, but in my opinion it is very improper for a royal princess to engage in conversation with commoners, particularly if they are male."

A few years ago we were all commoners, Seti thought wearily. But now was not the time to point this fact out to his upset wife.

"If there is a cause for speaking to common people, be they male or female, every member of our family may do so," he replied calmly.

"There sure was no cause for Tia to talk to him," Tuya objected. "And just look what happened! Haven't you noticed how her demeanour has changed since our departure from Abedju? I am afraid that she might have taken an unduly interest in that young man."

Seti glanced furtively at his daughter who was sitting together with her friend Baket a good way off, playing with her golden brown tomcat. He had to admit to himself that he hadn't noticed anything out of the ordinary, but then perhaps men weren't just sensitive enough in these matters.

"Are you trying to say that Tia has fallen in love with him?" Seti thoroughly enjoyed the look of horror on Tuya's face.

"Indeed this is what I was implying, although I can only marvel at the ease with which these words come to your lips. As such a relationship is entirely inacceptable as a matter of course, I would like you to speak with your daughter. She never listens to me, but hopefully you can make her see reason. If she still isn't prepared to marry Ramses, another suitable husband has to be found for her, and the sooner the better."

"I can tell you straight that Tia won't hear of marrying Ramses," Seti said in a tired voice. How often had he tried to make Tuya understand, apparently without success?

"And because she has only one brother," he continued, "any other suitor will inevitably be a commoner like Siamun."

"I beg your pardon," she exclaimed in an aggrieved voice. "Surely you don't want to equate this young upstart that nobody has ever heard of with members of venerable families like Tija, Userhat or Iuny?"

"I will talk to Tia," Seti promised, hoping to end this rather unpleasant discussion. But Tuya wasn't finished yet.

"I trust you wouldn't support an alliance between her and that Siamun, would you?" she asked, scrutinizing his face suspiciously.

"I have no doubt that we are going to find a solution to the problem," was his noncommittal answer. "But now you'll have to excuse me, for I am in sore need of some rest."

Tuya inclined her head, her discontent obvious from the sour look on her face.

Safely back in his cabin, Seti poured himself a cup of wine and took a long swig. Then he positioned himself beside the small guttered window from which he could see Tia and her friend quite clearly.

Tuya's observations may well be correct, he thought. Now that he came to think of it, he realized that his daughter didn't appear to focus on what she was doing. He saw how Baket had to address her several times until she finally reacted. What if she had really fallen in love with Siamun? Was he going to approve of this alliance?

Admittedly, Tuya was right in so far as nothing much was known about the young man's background. But then, was this really necessary? Seti had always prided himself on being an excellent judge of character, and he had felt right from the start that the young architect was someone with a decent personality. Apart from his unusual talents he appeared to be serious and honest, and reading through the high priest's commendations he had requested from Wenamun had only confirmed Seti's opinion. The judgement of someone who had known him for three years could surely be trusted.

But Seti wasn't going to make any rash decisions. First, he was going to watch Siamun some more, and he was going to see what kind of ideas for the new temple he would come up with. Although, if truth be admitted, Seti was already strongly inclined towards entrusting him with his dearest project from the day he had gathered his best architects around him to show them the location, and to inform them of his wishes. He had sensed how Siamun had literally sucked up all his words, and he had seen from the look on his face how his mind had immediately set to work. Seti felt sure that if anyone could make this temple special, it was Siamun. Under his direction it wasn't going to become a lifeless monument built from dead rock, but rather the most excellent example of architecture that had ever been built throughout the Two Lands. It was going to be animated by the spirit of a man whom he would entrust his other treasure, his own daughter, without hesitation, once the time had come.

****

She had gone. Disappeared, again. Siamun knew this for sure when he returned to the spot where he had told Satet to wait while he was going to organize a porter. Yet he still clung to the last ray of hope of finding her somewhere in the milling crowd of Perunefer.

Muttering various curses under his breath, Siamun forced his way through the throng of sweaty bodies, furious with himself for being so trusting when deep down he should have known better. Instead of stopping in Mennefer to see Panakht he should have taken Satet straight to Iunu. Now she had run away again, and how on earth was he going to track her down in this sprawling city?

Every time he glimpsed the fluttering garment of a woman his heart leapt with joy, only to be seized with bitter disappointment.

Resignedly, he finally gave up the chase. When he returned to his luggage he found Nebnefer already waiting for him. Siamun tried hard to appear calm in order to prevent his friend from asking awkward questions. Whatever would he think if he knew that Siamun's grown-up sister had just run off for the second time!

Their attempt to meet Panakht in the barracks proved fruitless; the troops had already moved on to embark on their imminent campaign. Then there was nothing left but to head straight to their living-quarters next to Nebamun's estate. They didn't talk much. Siamun was boiling with rage. What an idiot he had been to think that Satet might have mended her ways! What was he supposed to tell Meritamun? He had already sent a letter to them in which he had proudly announced that he would soon bring his sister home. Now he had to think of a good excuse for the delay, and then he could only hope that Satet would turn up some time or another.

The next day, Siamun threw himself into his work. He was full of ideas, at least as far as the seven sanctuaries and the two pillared courts of the new temple were concerned. Things proved to be more difficult when it came to the numerous cult rooms, vestibules and galleries the king was envisioning, not to forget all the other indispensable elements like storage rooms, slaughter houses and living quarters for the priests. He tried various different layouts only to discard them and start anew. Siamun was extremely grateful for the many suggestions Nebnefer made, but even so their work wasn't making much progress. Siamun soon found himself to be far too distracted to focus properly. He frequently thought of Satet, what she might be doing and why she was the way she was. And he wondered what her parents would have done with her, had they lived to see their daughter's escapades.

But far more often his thoughts strayed to the lovely princess who had stolen his heart. Although they had only met once, he clearly felt that an invisible bond of affection had formed between them. He didn't believe it had been a mere coincident that Tia had been waiting by that rock. Surely she had anticipated that he was bound to pass by on his inspection tour. And she had only been talking to him, as if she had been unaware of Nebnefer's presence. He felt slightly uneasy, though, when he thought of the possibility that her parents might have learned of their private conversation. After all, he hadn't been alone with Tia.

Tia... Every time he recalled her name, he could hear her melodic voice. He had to see her again. But what would be the good of it? What exactly did he hope for? Siamun knew he could not, *must* not marry the princess. She didn't know who he was, was oblivious of his dark secret. How could he possibly spend his whole life with her without ever confiding in her? And even if he managed to keep quiet, what if she found out herself? What would she do if she ever learned that she had married her father's rival, a contender with a claim to the throne strong enough to snatch it from him?

The bitter taste of unfulfilled love began to form in Siamun's mouth. That was what his parents must have felt like, living separate lives for years, devoured by yearning yet unattainable for each other. At long last the gods must have taken pity on them, and the two desperate lovers were finally united. For a short time they had been happy, King Tutankhamun and his royal wife Sitiah. But what did the immortals have got in store for their son?

In utter disbelief Siamun stared at the man who had just asked him to pack all his belongings together, so that they could be moved to his new dwelling in the north of the city. He was undoubtedly a royal herald and claimed that His Majesty had granted the royal architect Siamun a sizeable house to call his own with immediate effect. Having made sure that there could be no mistake, Siamun did as he was told, wondering whatever could have prompted this unexpected gift. Had the king become suspicious already and wanted to put him under close surveillance in a place of his choice? Or did it have anything to do with his recent encounter with the princess? A hot flush came over Siamun when he thought of how much closer to the palace he would be living from now on.

Preparations didn't take long, and Siamun was ready to go. He said a quick good-bye to Nebnefer and promised to see him soon. Outside, a litter was waiting for him which he mounted with some hesitation. At first, Siamun wasn't comfortable at all in his swaying seat high above people's heads. He felt exposed, as if everyone was staring in curiosity at him. But when he realized that he was only imagining this, he began to enjoy the ride, watching the bustle around him from a new perspective. Having crossed the canal that separated the south city from the centre they arrived at the vast court surrounding the great temple of Ptah. On they went in the direction of the royal palace before turning right. Soon after the litter bearers stopped in front of a town house that was surrounded by a gleaming white wall.

Amazed, Siamun alighted from his litter and had a quick look around. His new home was situated in one of Mennefer's best neighbourhoods that stretched from the great royal palace to the so-called *Fine District of Pharaoh,* a cluster of smaller royal palaces and grand estates lining the riverbank.

"This is the property that His Majesty has assigned to you," the herald's voice rang out. "To your convenience a cook, a house-servant and a gardener will be at your service."

"When will I have the opportunity to thank pharaoh for his generosity?" Siamun asked, trying hard not to sound all too baffled.

"His Majesty is expecting you in the afternoon," the man replied. "I will be back to accompany you to the palace. You may want to use the remaining time to get settled in your new home."

****

"He will soon be here," Seti said, glancing at the waterclock. "Have a good look at him."

Mehy nodded. "I will," he promised. "Although I doubt that my opinion will be of much value to you. You have always been better at assessing people's characters than me, Seti."

Lost in thought, Seti peered deeply into his half-full cup. "This time I'm not so sure of myself," he said eventually. "I keep wondering if it is right to rush Tia into a marriage. But then, I have hardly another choice. If anything is certain it is my growing distrust of my wife. Before we embark on our campaign, I would like to be sure that Tia is in good hands. Unfortunately, there is precious little time left. First I have to leave for Avaris for the final inspection of our troops, then I would dearly love to carry out the foundation ceremony for my new temple, and quite on the side I want to marry my daughter to someone I have only recently come to know. Yet my heart keeps telling me that he is the right one for her, presuming that there is something in Tuya's talk, that is."

"Wouldn't it have been better to speak to the princess first?"

Mehy asked slowly, pouring himself some wine.

Seti shook his head. "She might be too ashamed to tell me the truth. That's why I have arranged this meeting. I want to see how they react when they come face to face with each other. Then it will become clear whether they indeed have any feelings for one another or not."

For a short while, neither of the two men spoke. The silence was broken by the chamberlain's announcement that the royal architect Siamun had arrived.

Seti rose from his chair. "Thank you, Ptahmai. Show him into the antechamber."

When he and Mehy entered the room that served for the informal reception of guests, Siamun already awaited them with a large scroll tucked under his arm. Having bowed deeply, he waited to be addressed.

"Welcome, Siamun," Seti greeted him. "I have summoned you to discuss the progress of your work with you. I can see that you have already brought your drawings with you. This is indeed praiseworthy, all the more so since I forgot to instruct my herald accordingly."

A smile flitted across the young man's face. "I deemed it appropriate to show Your Majesty my drawings in order to elaborate on a few unclear points. But first and foremost I would like to express my gratitude at being presented with this wonderful estate, an honour I hardly deserve."

"Being one of my best architects this is only your due," Seti replied warmly. "Besides, this gift doesn't come from entirely selfless motives. I hoped you might be able to work even better in more comfortable surroundings. But now let me see what you have got there."

Siamun walked up to the table he had indicated. Only now did he seem to notice the presence of another guest and inclined his head towards Mehy.

"This is the chief commander of the royal chariot troops, Mehy," Seti explained. "He knows even less about architecture than I do, but sometimes an untrained eye sees what the expert has overlooked."

Meanwhile Siamun had unrolled the scroll and weighted the ends down. Seti and Mehy stood on either side of the table, peering down on the neat drawings. With a slight nod, Seti prompted the young man to begin.

"One fundamental problem with this design is to find enough space to accommodate all the essential elements of the new temple," Siamun began. "Your Majesty's wish to have seven sanctuaries all side by side with an adjoining cult room for Osiris makes it in my opinion inevitable that all other rooms be built at the side. Only then will we be able to place Osiris' subterranean tomb right behind his cult room, which is Your Majesty's express wish. Here" – he pointed at the lower part of the drawing- "we can see the pylon with both forecourts and the two pillared halls. The partition wall between the second forecourt and the adjoining hall will have seven openings in accordance with the seven sanctuaries in the heart of the temple. In this part over there" –his finger slid across the sanctuaries to a large rectangle on their left- "additional cult rooms, storage magazines and the slaughterhouse can be allocated. I haven't designed the final layout of these rooms yet because I wanted to await Your Majesty's decision. After all, the overall design implies a considerable modification of the traditional layout, but in my view the obvious advantages offset this drawback."

Seti had been listening with rapt attention. To his great satisfaction, he realized that everything was the way he had envisioned his new temple to be.

"I believe this slight deviation from the norm is well worth the while," he said thoughtfully. "What do you think, Mehy?"

"I am deeply impressed," his friend replied. "I think this design could hardly be improved in any way. It is far better than anything we have seen so far."

Seti nodded slowly. "I am of the same opinion. Siamun, will you be able to work out the missing details and draw the final draft up in, say, two weeks? I intend to carry out the foundation rites before I leave the country."

He looked at the young man expectantly.

"This shouldn't be difficult," Siamun said after a short pause. "I give you my word that the plans will be ready by then."

Seti smiled, relieved. That was one problem solved. Now to tackle the next.

"Good, that settles the matter," he said cheerfully. "Why don't we go and sit in the garden to talk some more?"

He didn't fail to notice Siamun's bewildered expression as he took up his scroll and tucked it under his arm. Of course, he couldn't have anticipated this invitation for an informal chat. As they had agreed beforehand, Mehy led the young architect into the garden while Seti stayed behind to give his trusted chamberlain one more instruction before following them. He was glad to see that the two men were already engaged in a lively conversation. On coming closer, he could hear them talking about Siamun's brother Panakht who appeared to serve in the chariotry.

"Of course he has grand plans like every young soldier," Siamun told Mehy who listened with great interest. "Panakht has always dreamed of becoming a commander of the chariotry. Without giving him any undue praise, someday his dream may well come true. He is a natural for handling horses and all kinds of weapons, and an excellent archer at that."

"This surely sounds promising," Mehy smiled. "I'll sure keep an eye on him."

"And what about you?" Seti asked as he joined them at the table which was laden with refreshments. "Do you enjoy physical activity as much as your brother apparently does?"

Siamun hesitated slightly before he answered. "I am certainly not adverse to things like archery or a good hunt," he said cautiously, "but rather as a pastime than a real occupation. I'm afraid to say that unlike Panakht I would probably never make a decent soldier. My preferences have always been mathematics, writing and drawing."

Seti acknowledged his words with a nod. He liked the young man's sincerity. As Seti had anticipated, Siamun wasn't one of those braggers and flatterers who usually surrounded him.

"Even so, you may want to accompany us on our next hunting trip nonetheless," Seti suggested.

Siamun bowed his head in recognition of this extraordinary favour. Then he reached for his wine cup and raised it to his lips, but instead of taking a sip he suddenly froze. A startled look appeared on his face, and his eyes widened considerably. Seti followed his gaze to see Tia entering the garden from the opposite side and coming towards them with her pet cat hard on her heels. From the corner of his eye he saw Siamun lowering his cup, seemingly having forgotten all about his wine.

"Tia, you are coming just at the right moment," Seti called out cheerfully. "I would like to take the opportunity to introduce you to Siamun, the talented young architect I told you so much about."

By way of a greeting he took her hands into his. Tia cast a shy look at Siamun who hastily rose from his chair, accidentally spilling a little wine from the cup he was still holding.

"I am honoured by the presence of Your Highness," he muttered bashfully.

With a nod that was almost imperceptible, the young girl lowered herself into an empty chair next to her father's and lifted her beloved tomcat on to her lap. While gently stroking the purring animal, she seemed to be listening to Seti's description of the new temple and his praise of Siamun's talents. But Seti wasn't fooled; he sensed that she was paying no more attention to his words than Siamun, whose sudden self-consciousness was most apparent, no matter how hard he tried to conceal it.

To Seti, it was as clear as anything that the two young people were not indifferent towards one another, although they were too ashamed to even admit to the fact that they had met before. Just once or twice did they exchange furtive glances, only to avert their eyes again hastily.

When Siamun asked for permission to leave, Seti was happy to give it. He had seen enough, and he had made his mind up. All that was now left was a serious talk with Tia.

Chapter Four

Siamun was tearing his hair in despair. He just didn't get on. Time was running out, he was under pressure, yet he was unable to focus on his work no matter how hard he tried. His thoughts travelled constantly back to the day he had met Tia in pharaoh's garden. There had been something strange about it, now that he came to think of it. Right from the start the king had treated him like an old friend, almost as if he belonged to the family even. The mood had been casual and relaxed, at least until Tia had appeared on the scene. He knew that they both must have behaved in a most suspicious way. What if they had given themselves away? It was well possible that pharaoh had got wind of their secret. In fact, Siamun even suspected him of having arranged this meeting to find out. But if his assumption was right, what was the king going to do now?

He glanced sullenly at the drawing in front of him and lowered his reed brush. But what was he supposed to do with it? The marvellous idea that had just occurred to him a few moments ago had entirely vanished. His mind had gone blank again. Groaning with frustration, he tried once more to concentrate while tapping the tip of his brush impatiently against his teeth. Again, he didn't get far. Wensu, his man-servant, interrupted his developing trail of thoughts with the announcement that a lady had come to see him. In a trice Siamun leapt off his seat and hurried to his reception room, wondering all the while who this unexpected visitor could be. Surely, surely this wasn't...

"Satet!" he exclaimed, full of surprise. "What are you doing here?"

"I have come to visit you," she explained, smiling innocently. "Why, is that so unusual?"

"Indeed it is," he growled. Siamun wasn't prepared to let her get away with it that easily. "First, you just run off for the second time, leaving your trusting brother to worry about you for days and weeks, then you suddenly turn up out of nowhere pretending nothing bad has ever happened. But don't let us discuss this matter here. Follow me!"

He led the way into his study where Satet slid gracefully into a chair opposite his desk without being asked. While she started to arrange the rich folds of her pale yellow dress with dainty movements, Siamun caught sight of her golden bangles and her lavish necklace.

"Where did you get this expensive outfit from?" he asked suspiciously. "And how did you find out where I live?"

"I have made a few enquiries," she replied airily. "It wasn't hard to find out the whereabouts of pharaoh's new favourite."

"So you call me his *favourite*?" Siamun snapped, feeling his anger rise.

"To come back to your first question," Satet went on, quite undeterred, "it is some time that I move within the best circles of society."

"Really? And what exactly are you doing in those best circles, if I may ask?"

"If you do have to know," she replied pertly, "I entertain the gentlemen and their guests with my dance."

Siamun felt his jaw slacken as her words sank in.

"You do *what?*" he eventually uttered with considerable effort. "Do you really mean to say that you have turned into one of those cheap dancers?"

"No, I haven't!" Satet exclaimed, shaking her head vigorously. "I told you that I only move in the best-"

"Oh, just stop it!" Siamun was beside himself with rage. "As if there was any difference between the vile rabble in the beer houses and the high and mighty devouring you with their greedy eyes! And surely there is still more to it than meets the eye, isn't it?"

Satet shrank visibly back from his fury. Lips firmly clamped together, she began to fiddle about with one of her rings. Siamun recognized it instantly. Made of silver and set with little gems of turquoise and lapis lazuli, it had once belonged to her mother, who had died giving birth to her twin babies. Meritamun had kept it and then given it to Satet as a memento.

"I simply can't believe that you got involved into something like that," Siamun hissed. "Have you entirely forgotten who you are?"

Satet rose slowly from her chair, her expression darkening as she glanced at the drawing on the desk.

"And you?" she asked coldly. "What about you with your tireless drawing and building for pharaoh? Haven't *you* forgotten who you really are?"

At that point, something inside Siamun broke. This was more than he could bear. How *could* she compare his honourable occupation with her detestable doings?

His eyes narrowed to slits as he glared at her.

"Satet, I really do believe that it would have been better if you had died along with mother instead of your twin," he blurted with barely suppressed rage. "We would all have been spared a lot."

For the duration of a few heartbeats, Satet just sat there, mouth agape, and stared at him with a look of utter incredulity on her face. Then she jumped up from her seat and stormed out of the room without another word.

Siamun made no attempt to hold her back.

****

The hunting party in the western desert consisted of a good fifteen chariots, all manned exclusively with young people. This didn't surprise Siamun, since the hunt had been organised by the crown prince who had invited Siamun and Nebnefer to take part in it along with his peers. Pharaoh was not present, since he had gone north to inspect his troops and wasn't expected to return for another week.

For Siamun this invitation had come at a most inopportune moment, but he hadn't deemed it advisable to turn it down. Ever since Satet had come to see him three days ago he had fallen even more behind with his work. Once his anger had subsided somewhat, Siamun had tried his hardest to figure out who might have sponsored Satet's costly outfit. He must be a rich man indeed, or else he wouldn't have been so generous towards an ordinary dancer. But then, perhaps there wasn't only one man involved but several, each of whom had done his bit. The mere thought of it made Siamun's stomach lurch.

But there was something else that kept nagging his mind. How could Satet have found him so easily? After all, he had moved into his new home just recently. Perhaps, he mused, she had first gone to his former living quarter where someone might have informed her of his current whereabouts. But, having never before been there either, how had Satet come across it in the first place?

Siamun groaned silently. Try as he might, he couldn't make head or tail of it. At any rate, he was utterly relieved that he had moved home and thus didn't have to live in the vicinity of that spiteful vizier anymore. Every time he thought of Nebamun, a cold shiver crept up his spine.

Nebamun...

All of a sudden, that name left an even more unpleasant taste in Siamun's mouth than usual. Apart from pharaoh, Nebamun was one of the two highest and mightiest men in the entire Two Lands, and as rumour had it, he had little sense of morals. Being a vizier, he was naturally also well-informed of all the things that were going on, and Siamun felt certain that neither pharaoh's generous present nor Siamun's subsequent move would have escaped Nebamun's attention. Given the fact that his precious son hadn't yet been granted any kind of royal favour, this wouldn't have gone down all too well with him. However, Siamun couldn't think of anything that connected the vizier with Satet. Perhaps, if he made a few enquiries…

The thought struck him so suddenly that it almost hurt. Could it possibly be that Nebamun had coincidentally hired Satet as a dancer and now intended to use her to bring him into disrepute by showing everyone what a wretched sister he had? This would necessarily imply, though, that the vizier knew of Satet's connection to him. Maybe she had told him, or he could have found out himself. For a man with a true network of informants at hand like him, this was surely not overly difficult. Siamun cast a furtive glance at Penre who was standing in a chariot not far from his. The young fellow certainly looked innocent enough, but as far as his father was concerned Siamun felt sure that he might stick at nothing to attain his own ends.

"Whatever are you thinking about all the time?"
Nebnefer's question put a sudden end to Siamun's trail of thoughts.
"I am thinking of a way to get out of this without making a complete fool of myself," Siamun said with a light shrug. "After all, we are in the company of some of the finest archers around,

and unfortunately neither you nor I can count ourselves among them."

A look of deep concern appeared on Nebnefer's face. "Rather than that I'm worrying about my own skin. Couldn't the prince have thought of something else than hunting wild bulls? Those beasts can turn pretty nasty, you know!"

Siamun laughed. "Never mind the bulls. I'm sure that measures have been taken so that they can't turn nasty on us, as you call it. As far as the crown prince is concerned, nobody is prepared to take any chances. His person is much too precious for that. Besides, haven't you noticed how young all the participants in this hunt are? Most of them are hardly older than Ramses himself. Compared to them, I feel like an old man already."

"If you're saying that at only nineteen years of age, what about me? I'm nearly twenty-five!"

Siamun opened his mouth to reply, but hurriedly closed it again, catching himself just in time. Dismayed, he thought of how easy it was to make a mistake. He had nearly blurted his true age out to his friend.

"Be that as it may," he said eventually, "I think we should try and get the best out of it. I'm glad for the few times I went hunting with Panakht while we were in Waset. This might come in useful now."

He let his gaze stray across the chariots until it lingered on Ramses who was leading the party. Like his companions he was well prepared for the hunt. Broad strips of cloth had been wrapped tightly around his torso for support during the chase, his hands were encased in gloves made from the finest red leather, and his head was protected by the tassageled bronze helmet usually worn by charioteers. The well-defined muscles of his arms and shoulders made the prince appear older than he was, even if his longish legs still looked somewhat lanky. As if he had sensed Siamun's gaze on him, Ramses let his chariot fall back until it was level with his. Grinning broadly, the prince cast him a challenging glance.

"Fancy a few wild bulls, architect?"

"Of course, Your Highness," Siamun replied calmly. "Why not? Have any of them been spotted yet?"

"Indeed," Ramses sneered. "They are already waiting for us. I hope you are as skilful with bow and arrow as you are with your reed brush."

Siamun ignored the mocking tone of his voice. "I will try my best, Highness."

"We'll see if your best is good enough, architect."

With that, Ramses motioned his driver to urge the horses on, and his chariot picked up speed.

"What a braggart," Nebnefer snorted in contempt once the prince was safely out of earshot. "Pretty conceited fellow, isn't he?"

Siamun sighed. "Sure he is, and being a prince he can afford it. You know what, Nebnefer," he went on after a short pause, "I keep wondering all the time why they haven't taken a single hunting dog with them."

"Perhaps that's because the dogs wouldn't get on well with his tamed lion," his friend suggested, warily eyeing the young predator that was trotting along beside Ramses' chariot.

Siamun shook his head. "I rather believe that there are no dogs because we won't need them."

For a while, the chariots kept rolling on with moderate speed. Then a number of huge brown bodies could be discerned in the distance. These had to be the wild bulls Ramses had been talking about. What struck Siamun as odd was that the animals stood rather still, herded close together, without there being a fence apparent. On coming closer, the reason soon became clear: The bulls were penned in on a large rectangular surface which was surrounded by a broad ditch. Being at least five cubits wide and perhaps three cubits deep, it proved to be an insurmountable obstacle for the animals.

Siamun was filled with growing uneasiness. He felt sorry for the magnificent animals that were standing there crammed together, unable to escape the volleys of arrows that would soon be raining on them and equally unable to turn on their attackers.

On Ramses' command the chariots began to spread out evenly around the whole enclosure, positioning themselves as close to the ditch as possible. The bulls, about thirty in number and all of them most impressive animals, were sensing danger and started to move about aimlessly, bumping into each other due to the confined space and kicking up heaps of dust with their hooves.

Then all eyes were on Ramses whilst he readied his first arrow and pulled the string. The lethal missile hissed through the air, and the bulls scattered, or rather tried to, but to no avail. Not surprisingly, Ramses' arrow was right on target, as were all the others that followed suit, raining down on the miserable animals from all sides. In fact, it would almost have been impossible to miss them. Soon blood was gushing forth from countless wounds, streaming down the furry bodies and tinting the sandy ground a deep red, but it took some time until the first bull broke down.

By then, neither Siamun nor Nebnefer had fired a single arrow. Siamun was watching in horror as a magnificent bull close to him staggered, swaying from side to side until its legs buckled under its weight. With a blood-curdling roar it finally fell over, its lifeless body being trampled underfoot by the remaining panic-stricken animals.

A little later only a few bulls were alive, albeit weakened by

continuous blood loss. Roaring and snorting furiously, they stomped towards their tormentors only to braze their front feet against the ground just before plunging into the ditch, as one of them inadvertently did. At once Ramses was on the spot and killed the bull with a well-aimed throw of his spear. Having done this deed, he glared expectantly at Siamun who slowly retrieved an arrow from his quiver and shot, hoping that it wasn't too obvious that he had taken such a bad aim on purpose. He didn't want to be involved in this kind of massacre. At long last, only one last bull remained still on his feet. Bleeding heavily from numerous
wounds, it ran around in a frenzy, stumbling over the bodies that littered the ground in its bid to get away from more lethal arrows.

A prod in his side made Siamun look in the direction Nebnefer indicated with a jerk of his head. Ramses had alighted from his chariot with a long rope in hands and positioned himself as close to the edge of the ditch as possible. He waited until the bull stood quite still and was staring at him with unblinking eyes, then threw the loop towards its mighty head. However, it slipped off the horns, and Ramses had to try again. This time, the loop fell neatly over the horns and remained there, tightened by a strong tug on the rope. At once a few of Ramses' comrades jumped to his aid. With joined forces they held on tight to the rope, while the panic-stricken animal pulled into the opposite direction for all it was worth. Once or twice it jerked its head so violently that its adversaries were nearly yanked off their feet and plunged into the ditch; but from then on, its strength diminished rapidly.

Now Ramses detached himself from the group and, grabbing another spear, swaggered over a broad wooden plank that had hurriedly been put across the ditch. Brandishing his dagger, Ramses then proceeded to separating the bull's tail from its root with a few quick cuts. Wondering at first what the meaning of this cruel mutilation was, the truth soon dawned on Siamun. Of course, being one of the most important symbols of pharaonic power, the bull's tail was an object much sought after by those holding this power and those craving it. Oblivious of the deafening roar that escaped the poor creature's throat, Ramses raised his bloody trophy high above his head, basking in the applause of his comrades. Then he took up his spear and rammed it between the bull's ribs. A moment later, there was silence, but Siamun's ears kept ringing with the agonized sounds of the tortured animal.

To the acclaim of his friends, the prince crossed the plank and sat down on the platform of his chariot, where he started to wipe his dagger clean before sheathing it.

"I can't tell you how glad I am that this dreadful spectacle is finally over," Siamun whispered into Nebnefer's ear.

"For me this was definitely the first and the last royal hunt I have taken part in," his friend returned equally softly. They had to be careful, for the prince was well within earshot.

"I don't think that pharaoh would have wanted anything to do with it," Siamun replied. "He surely would have organized a fair, decent hunt, and not such a disgusting carnage."

While he watched the prince, who was now crouching on the ground beside his chariot and expertly examining the arrows brought back to him by his followers, Siamun heard loud whinnying some way off. At first, he didn't think much of it; but then the sound grew more urgent, panic-stricken even, and he saw one of the horses shying from something, attempting to rear up as far as the yoke would allow and infecting the second horse of the team with its unrest. Soon the driver lost his struggle to regain control over them, and a young man who tried to grab the first horse by its halter strap was sent sprawling after being hit on the head by its hoof.

"Whatever is the matter over there?" Siamun wondered, knitting his brows.

Nebnefer shrugged. Before he could open his mouth to reply, both watched in horror as the chariot moved off, gaining speed ever so rapidly as the panicking horses tried to get away from whatever had scared them. Siamun gasped in surprise as he spotted a second chariot following close behind, but what was far worse was the fact that the horses were coming exactly in their direction, oblivious of anything in their path. Several of the young hunters had to jump out of their way, least they would be crushed underneath thundering hooves and huge wheels.

Siamun's gaze fell on Ramses who was still crouching on the ground, stunned, an arrow in one hand and gaping at the approaching horses. He seemed as rigid as a statue, unable to move, while the first chariot was almost on him, its driver clinging on for dear life!

Siamun leapt off the platform, and in one bound he was by the prince, clutching his arms and yanking him out of the path of peril just before the two chariots thundered past them. The force of their own momentum caused them both to roll over a few times before they came eventually to lie still on the ground. Siamun could tell by the gust of wind he had felt what a narrow escape it had been. While he waited for his pounding heart to slow down, he could hear muttered curses and spluttering as Ramses cleared his mouth from sand. Siamun was relieved to see him rise and stagger over to his chariot, supported by two or three of his friends and without so much as a backward glance at his saviour.

A moment later, Nebnefer was crouching at his side.

"Are you all right?" he asked, peering down at him with deep concern etched on his face.

Siamun nodded briefly. "Yes, I think we both got away with a fright and a few scratches."

Aided by his friend, Siamun scrambled to his feet. He was grateful for Nebnefer's support as he walked up to his chariot because his legs felt strangely weak. When he mounted the platform, his eyes met with the prince's who quickly averted his gaze.

"That fellow doesn't appear in the least grateful that you just saved his life," Nebnefer hissed through gritted teeth.

Siamun just shrugged. "Let him be. I believe that most of all he is ashamed to have gotten himself into this awkward situation in the first place. He is of an age when one hardly realizes the presence of danger, but all that counts is to look good under any circumstances."

It was in a very subdued mood indeed that they made their way back. Hardly a word was spoken, and Ramses just kept staring ahead of him, lips pressed tightly together. On the way they encountered both runaway horses along with their chariots. Having completely exhausted themselves, they had finally given up their flight. Drenched in sweat and with quivering flanks they were a truly deplorable sight.

At last it became clear what had caused the whole frenzy: According to the driver, a cobra had reared itself up nearby, probably afraid of being crushed under the hooves of those giant creatures.

When they eventually arrived at the royal stables and Siamun was about to hand his chariot over to one of the stable-boys, Ramses told him curtly that it was his to keep.

Nodding his thanks, Siamun accepted the gift without another word.

****

He was lying spread-eagled on the ground, somewhere in the middle of the desert. He didn't know what had happened to him, or why he was unable to move. It was as if he was pinned down by invisible restraints. Then, the ground shook, and he could hear the thundering sounds of approaching horses. They were getting louder and coming closer.
They are heading straight for me, he thought in despair. I must get away from here.
But try as he might, he couldn't move so much as a single finger. Then he saw them, a team of two stout brown stallions, kicking up the sand as they tore along like mad while flocks of foam flew from their mouths. They were harnessed to a chariot, but he couldn't see who was riding it, or whether there was anyone standing in it at all, for that matter.
Now they were almost on him. He could clearly see the white in the stallions' wild eyes. Just one more moment, and their lethal hooves were going to tear the flesh off his bones. He wanted to scream, but the sound got stuck in his throat. The only thing that was left for him was to close his eyes before...

Siamun woke with a start. He was drenched in sweat and his heart was hammering furiously in his chest. It took him some time to realize that he hadn't really been lying out there in the desert, but when he did, he was overwhelmed by relief. What a bit of luck it had been that he had been spared that horrible fate.

Panting, he sat on the edge of the bed and rested his forehead on the heels of his hand as the memories washed over him. Indeed, they hadn't been gentle with him. He hadn't wanted them to be, either. Even as a little boy, Siamun had been keen to know all about his father's horrible death. Whereas

Meritamun had always tried to get around the gruesome details, Meresankh –never one to mince her words- had told him bluntly all that she had been able to find out. His father's tragic demise had always affected him so deeply that he sometimes felt as if he was suffering the same fate. Just like he had in this terrible nightmare.

Perhaps it had been his knowledge of that disastrous event that had allowed him to act swiftly when all of Ramses' companions had been too stunned to come to his aid. Siamun had felt the impulse deep inside him. His heart had commanded him to save the prince, and it had also enabled his body to do so.

There was something else, too, that his heart was telling him. Next time he saw Satet, he wanted to apologize for his harsh words. He had been carried away by his fury, and he had regretted to have spoken them as soon as his anger had been spent. He could never want her dead, not even in the face of all the trouble she had caused.

But in order to hear his apology, she would have to come and see him again. And only the gods knew when this would be the case.

****

Siamun came to see his sister sooner than he would have thought. However, she was unable to accept his apology. Satet was dead.

A few days on, the gardener found her body early in the morning when he was about to tend to the vegetables. Someone had wrapped it tightly into a large sheet and then simply thrown the bundle over the rear part of the enclosure wall.

The man had been terribly upset by his find, and it was with great difficulty that Siamun persuaded him to help him carry the body inside. However, he didn't think it advisable to reveal its true identity just yet. This could wait. First he would have to come to terms with the gruesome fact of Satet's unexpected death.

There was no doubt that it had been a violent one. Her blood-smeared throat was slit from ear to ear. The blank stare of her wide eyes was horrible to look at. What made it all even worse, however, were the countless marks on her face that marred its beauty, left by the blade of some very sharp knife. They also covered her neck and, as Siamun saw to his horror when he moved the sheet a little, her shoulders. Presumably her whole body had been mistreated this way, but Siamun wasn't going to find out.

He fervently hoped that these terrible cuts had been inflicted on her only after her death. But what for?

It looked as if Satet's murderer had intended to rob her of her beauty. The cuts were not deep. They hadn't been meant to kill her, but to mar and disfigure her. And, of course, to give him, Siamun, an even greater shock. Siamun had no doubt that whoever had killed Satet had wanted to make sure that he was going to find her body. There was no way that of all places the garden of his own house had been chosen for its disposal quite by chance, as he would make his servants believe.

But who was behind this despicable act? And why did Satet have to die in the first place?

It seemed certain that she hadn't been murdered in the close vicinity of his property. A quick search of the surrounding area had yielded nothing to be suspicious of, especially no traces of blood.

What was Siamun supposed to do now? In any case, Satet's body would have to be brought quickly to the nearest house of life to have it mummified. But it was equally important to find and arrest her murderer. In order to achieve this aim, Siamun would have to report this heinous crime to the security forces immediately.

Having decided that for the time being Satet's body best remained where it was, Siamun left for the docks where to his knowledge one of the most important security bases complete with prison was situated. Instead of using his litter he walked, preferring not to be noticed by anyone. On his way he kept asking himself if it could really be his sister who was lying dead in his house. This was almost like one of those nightmares that occasionally haunted him.

Siamun's first notion upon entering the two-storey building was the distinct feeling that he was in the wrong place. He had expected a hive of activity; after all, in a great city like Mennefer the security forces had to be in high demand. Instead, the pillared hallway in front of him lay completely deserted. This seemed to be equally true for the smaller corridors that branched off it. It wasn't until Siamun had rounded a few corners that he encountered a living being, albeit a sleeping one. The man was slumped on a stool with his head and shoulders leaned against the wall, snoring softly. Siamun cleared his throat as noisily as he could. The man woke with a start and sat bolt upright, opening his eyes with obvious difficulty.

"What's the matter?" he mumbled sleepily.

"I have come to report a murder," Siamun told him.

"Really?" the other returned in an even voice. "You'll have to wait some more. All the officers have either gone out, or they are busy."

"But there must be someone here to take my report down," Siamun insisted.

"I told you there is nobody available," came the rather moody reply. "Go and come back in about two hours."

With that he leaned himself back against the wall and closed his eyes. Siamun stared at him incredulously, surprised to hear him snoring again only a few moments later. Shaking his head, he turned away. In spite of the man's discouraging announcement, he decided to keep searching for somebody – *anybody*- in this building who might be able to deal with his request. He tried the door next to the sleeping guard, or whatever he was. Seeing that it was left ajar, he pushed it open a bit.

His gaze fell upon a man whose most striking feature was his enormous belly. He, too, was slumped in his chair with his eyes closed and his head tilted against the back rest. He had his hands clasped above his protruding tummy while his feet were resting on the desk in front of him. All in all this man was the very definition of peace and quiet.

Exasperated, Siamun pulled the door shut. He was appalled by this unexpected laxness, but it didn't put him off. Quite on the contrary, his determination grew with every passing moment. He tried another door, not bothering to knock. In the room behind it he spotted a young man who quickly shoved a large bite of some sort of meal into his mouth. Relief was mirrored in his face when he realized that it was only a visitor. Siamun felt likewise at having finally encountered someone who wasn't asleep.

"Who are you, and what do you want?" the young man asked. Siamun chose to ignore the fact that the tone of his voice wasn't all too obliging, either.

"My name is Siamun, and I have come to report a murder."

"Who has been murdered?"

Siamun swallowed hard before he answered. "My sister."

Less than impressed, the other hardly raised an eyebrow. "You'll have to wait until the officer in charge becomes available," he declared with a vague indication towards the wall.

Siamun watched the young clean-shaven face intently. "Are you talking of the man who is having a nap next door?"

A nod confirmed his suspicion.

"What about you?" Siamun asked, not caring to conceal his growing irritation. "Can't you help me?"

"No, I can't," came the firm reply. "I'm merely an ordinary scribe. I only write down what my superior tells me to. I said you...wait, you can't go in there just like that!"

But Siamun had already left the room and stormed into the neighbouring one. He wasn't going to stand any more nonsense.

"Wake up!" he called out, giving the fat one a thorough start.

"What in Amun's name-"

"I told him he couldn't do that, but he didn't listen," the young scribe whined from behind Siamun's back.

"That's quite true," Siamun said, undeterred by the black expression on the other's face. "I have come to report an urgent matter that brooks no delay."

"And what would this urgent matter be, if I may ask?"

As he spoke, the man rose and drew himself up to his full unimpressive height with his fleshy arms akimbo.

"A murder."

"A murder?" the other echoed.

Siamun could hardly believe his eyes when the man's mouth stretched into a scornful grin. Then he broke into a laugh that made all the excessive flesh under his flabby garment shake.

"Murder, indeed," he panted when he had calmed down

somewhat. "My good man, did you really think you could just drop in and ask for help? You ought to know that the authorities only deal with matters that concern the crown or a great one. Therefore I suggest that you leave us alone and think of a way to solve your problem on your own."

Siamun felt that this was more than he could bear. He took a large step forward and glared at the chubby face in front of him.

"Then let me tell you," he hissed, "that I am a royal architect in charge of His Majesty's latest building project and personally acquainted with the king at that. I'm not entirely sure if that alone makes me one of your so-called great ones, but I do know that this murder affects me very deeply because the victim happens to be my own sister. Now you'd better do your damned duty and write down a proper report, launch your investigations and find the murderer before he strikes again. Or what else are you being paid for so generously out of pharaoh's coffers?"

His gaze settled meaningfully on the man's enormous mid-riff. With some satisfaction he saw that his scolding had not failed to produce the desired effect. The man shrank visibly and lowered himself back into his cushioned chair which creaked dangerously under the strain of his considerable weight.

"Very well," he said in a far more obliging tone of voice. "Sit over there and tell me what happened."

He indicated a stool that looked as if it was going to collapse at any moment. Siamun sat down gingerly and looked expectantly at the portly figure behind the desk.

But the man wasn't quite ready yet.

"Min, bring me some refreshments, and be quick about it!" he barked in the direction of the door. "And make sure you strain the beer properly this time, or you'll get a real good hiding one of these days!"

Then he glowered at the young scribe who was by now sitting cross-legged on the floor, a piece of papyrus on his lap and busily chewing the tip of his reed brush.

"Hurry up, Sobek!" his master demanded. "I don't have all day!" Sobek obediently dipped his brush into the shallow water bowl next to him before working the dry black cake on his scribal palette with it until the fibres had absorbed enough paint to write with.

"Get on with it," his superior urged, impatience ringing in his voice. "Date, location, witnessed by the chief of the security forces Bakenkhensu - you should know all that by now."

While Sobek's brush started to flit across the papyrus, a servant appeared –the man whom Siamun had met sleeping by the door- carrying a tray laden with a jug, a bowl and a plate with what looked like dried figs. Forgetting all about the report, Bakenkhensu grabbed first the jug and then the bowl from which he slurped noisily for some time. Placing the plate on his lap, he then leaned back with a contended sigh and started to fan himself vigorously.

Meanwhile, Siamun had had ample time to survey the room. Not that there would have been much to see, for the furniture was sparse and had clearly seen better days. Even the state of cleanness left much to be desired. A thick layer of dust covered most surfaces as well as the floor, and on close inspection the little black dots that littered the ground by the window turned out to be the remains of the last flies of the bygone summer.

Following Bakenkhensu's request, Siamun gave his details and explained the circumstances under which he had found Satet's body.

"Did your sister last live in Mennefer, and if so, where?" the chief of security then asked.

"Well, she spent her last time here in this city, although I am unable to tell where exactly."

Bakenkhensu rolled his eyes. "Where does your family hail from?"
"We hail from Iunu."
"Then this case is not within my responsibility," Bakenkhensu announced with obvious relief. "You must contact the authorities of your home town."
Waving a dismissive hand at Siamun he began to busy himself with his dried figs.
"Wait a moment," Siamun protested. "You can't tell me that you're not responsible for a murder that happened in this very city!"
A sly look crossed the plump face. "How do you know that?"
"Know what?" Siamun shot back, genuinely irritated.
"That the murder was committed here in Mennefer. You just told me yourself that no traces of blood have been found in the vicinity of your property, thus your sister can have been murdered anywhere."
Determined not to let his growing annoyance get the better of him, Siamun took a deep breath. "Maybe I forgot to mention that my search was only very superficial, therefore any deductions are preliminary at best. A more thorough investigation might yield entirely different results. But this is your duty, not mine. Besides, the last time I met my sister was shortly before her death, and she didn't speak of any intention to move from here. Quite on the contrary." Siamun paused briefly to prepare for what he had to say now. "She seems to have found a wealthy sponsor with whom she presumably lived."
"Really? And in which capacity did your sister serve this wealthy sponsor?" Bakenkhensu asked with rapt attention, a lecherous grin spreading all over his face. Even Sobek had stopped in mid-sentence, leaving his brush poised in the air.
Siamun swallowed hard. "Apparently she has gone into his

service as a dancer," he said in a strained voice.

Bakenkhensu's eyebrows climbed up until they nearly reached the line of his sparse hair.

"The sister of a respectable royal architect an ordinary dancer?" he jeered.

Presumably this was supposed to sound incredulous, but Siamun could tell that Bakenkhensu actually enjoyed this last bit of information immensely. Without another word he rose from his stool and was in one bound by the desk, bracing his arms against it and leaning forward as far as possible. The jug on it began to sway, but he paid it no heed.

"Listen, Bakenkhensu," he hissed right into the rotund face in front of him, which by now had lost all traces of amusement. "I've had enough of that. In every family there is someone who is different from all the rest. I admit that I was far from happy with my sister's ways, and I also admit that I severely reproached her because of her doings last time she came to see me, but she left my house alive and unharmed. Soon after, she came across her killer who badly mistreated her body and threw it into the garden of my house which I only recently moved into. Can all of this be a mere coincidence?"

Bakenkhensu shook his head faintly.

"That's just how I see it," Siamun continued, keeping up the menacing tone of his voice. "To be more precise, I believe that only those with close connections to the royal house can have been aware of the fact that His Majesty recently bestowed this property on me. In addition to that, it has to be someone who isn't at all well disposed towards me, who wanted to inflict pain and grief on me or intimidate me, possibly both. When I think of all that, the name of one particular man instantly comes to my mind, a man whose displeasure I seem to have incurred. Whether you like it or not, I'm speaking of the vizier Nebamun. How about investigating in this direction first of all?"

Siamun straightened himself up and retreated from the desk. Relieved, Bakenkhensu exhaled the breath he seemed to have held all the time. Then he threw his hands up in dismay.

"I must say, you are going too far with your accusations," he panted. "The venerable vizier is most certainly above all suspicion."

Again, Siamun stepped forward and brought his face close to Bakenkhensu's.

"I'm telling you that no-one is above anything," he growled. "Just do as I said. Follow the lead I have given you, and if it proves to be wrong, all the better for us. Then you can turn your attention to whoever you want."

Feeling that enough had been said, Siamun turned away and made for the door. In passing his gaze fell on Sobek who looked very confused indeed, apparently at a loss what to include into his protocol and what to leave out.

"What are you waiting for, go on and write!" Bakenkhensu shouted.

"By the way, I need someone to come and examine my poor sister's body before it is going to be brought to the house of life," Siamun said, glancing over his shoulder. "What about you, Bakenkhensu?"

"I am not available," the chief of security forces declared quickly. "You can have Sobek as soon as he's finished here and one of the other men. They will assist you with everything you need."

Siamun noticed with glee how obliging the fat one had become all of a sudden, only to get rid of his troublesome visitor as soon as possible. Surely he had realized that Siamun wasn't someone to be trifled with.

On his way out a rather young man crossed Siamun's path, casting him a curious glance. Perhaps he had become aware of the row Siamun had made. The man appeared to be a messenger, for Siamun saw him handing a few scrolls and other small items to Min who had by now reassumed his role as a doorkeeper. Then the messenger received a number of scrolls and packages in exchange and made off with them. Lost in gloomy thoughts, Siamun waited for his helpers to arrive.

After a while Sobek turned up, accompanied by a surly looking man whose looks reminded Siamun somewhat of Prince Ramses. Together they left the building and made their way to Siamun's house. It wasn't long until they stood at the front door which was opened by a confused and terrified Wensu. The two men were being led to Satet to do their duty. Siamun didn't follow them; he didn't feel the need to be present when they examined her body. Instead, he stayed in an adjoining room where he dropped into the nearest chair, propping his chin wearily on his cupped hands.

Then Wensu appeared and announced the arrival of a royal herald. Siamun nodded briefly and went to greet his visitor. He was the same man who had shown him here not long ago, but this time he had brought a message from the Great Royal Wife who summoned Siamun to meet her at the palace. Siamun's question for the reason behind this summons remained unanswered.

Whatever the purpose of this meeting, it seemed to be urgent, since the herald had been instructed to bring Siamun straight back with him. However, upon request, Siamun was granted a little time which he used to discuss the fate of Satet's body with Sobek. Both men announced that she was ready to be brought to the house of life. Siamun gratefully accepted their offer to take care of the transport. Later on he could visit there and arrange for a coffin and other burial goods.

The time had come to say his final good-byes to his sister.

Tenderly he cupped Satet's battered face in his hands and told her in a soft whisper that he deeply regretted his last words to her, that he hadn't meant to say them and could never have wished her dead. He then assured her that he was already looking forward to meet her again in the Fields of Reeds. Maybe he was just fooling himself, but in a strange way he felt certain that Satet understood his every word. Could it be possible that her Ka was still around, lingering somewhere nearby? Whether his notion was true or not, at least it provided some much-needed comfort.

Abruptly, Siamun turned away from her and hurried to the litter that was waiting outside.

The antechamber where Siamun had been ordered to wait was lavishly decorated. The tiled floor sported a stylized reproduction of a fishpond or lake, whereas the walls were painted with images of lush vegetation and water-fowl. The visitor could easily gain the impression of being in the midst of a watery landscape surrounded by papyrus-thickets. The furniture –two small tables and a few chairs- was made from shiny ebony with contrasting inlays of ivory.

Naturally, Siamun didn't sit down yet. Instead, he stood close to the entrance, waiting for the queens' arrival, pondering what on earth could have prompted her to summon him. The only reason that came to his mind was the rescue of the prince –or Tia. His palms started to sweat as he thought of the latter possibility.

Thankfully, he didn't have to wait long. The sound of sandals slapping against the tiled floor announced Mut-Tuya's arrival. A few moments later, the Great Royal Wife came rushing through the door, followed by two women of whom Siamun could only catch a glimpse before he performed a deep bow.

While he remained in his bent position, his heart began to race. Surely she hadn't brought Tia along with her? He longed to see the princess, but he also felt sure he wouldn't stand another close encounter with her without being allowed to reveal the feelings he had for her.

"I welcome you, architect," the queen piped. "You may rise."

Siamun straightened up and cast a furtive glance at the two women who framed the Great Royal Wife. It was with both relief and disappointment that he realized they were only heavily made up court ladies unknown to him.

"Let us take a seat," Tuya said with an inviting gesture towards the chairs.

Siamun lowered himself gingerly onto the seat she had indicated. The queen occupied the chair opposite him, while the two ladies sat around the neighbouring table, where both immediately started to employ their handy ostrich-feather fans, although to Siamun's mind the air was neither hot nor stuffy. He ignored their curious glances and decided to focus on the queen instead.

He had already noticed how surprisingly short and nondescript she appeared, viewed at close quarters and without her elaborate queenly headdress. But the determined trait around her pinched mouth and the piercing stare of her smallish eyes betrayed the fact that this woman was a force to be reckoned with.

"I appreciate that you have followed my summons, architect," Tuya began.

"I was honoured to do so," Siamun replied, keeping to himself that he had hardly had another choice.

"I know what a busy man you are," she went on in wheedling tones. "Therefore I won't keep you long. It has come to my attention how stout-heartedly you have acted when my son had gotten into serious danger on that unfortunate hunt. It would surely have broken my heart if something had happened to him. In order to demonstrate my gratitude, I would like to reward you for your bravery. Request whatever you want from me, and it is yours."

Give me your daughter, he would have loved to shout. Instead, he bowed his head bashfully.

"I hardly know what to say. I am deeply gratified by Your Majesty's generosity, but for me the crown prince's safety is reward enough. I couldn't possibly demand anything for a deed that everyone else could have done in my stead, nor would I ever accept any kind of reward."

He quickly pondered whether to mention the chariot that Ramses had given to him along with the team of horses, then he decided against it.

Tuya watched him intently. "Your modesty is indeed commendable, but I cannot rest until I have shown my appreciation. Is there really nothing your heart desires more than anything?"

She could hardly have said anything more provocative than this question. The subtle change of her tone left little doubt that this was indeed meant as an allusion to Tia. So she had gotten wind of this affair already. But what was she bargaining for?

"There is nothing, Your Majesty," Siamun replied firmly. "Your attention is already more than I deserve."

Tuya exchanged quick glances with her two friends before she fastened her gaze once more on Siamun's face.

"Then you must allow me to present you with something of my own choice," she said smoothly. "It is common knowledge that in every household there should be a woman. As I happen to know that you are still unmarried, I have thought of something very special for you." She smiled mildly as she saw Siamun's alarmed expression. "Don't worry, architect. I am not going to impose a wife on you. It is not for me to do this."

While she paused for effect, Tuya watched Siamun out of fixed eyes. His tension rose, as it had doubtlessly been intended to. The irritating sound of the two ladies' girlish giggles made it even worse.

"However, I thought it would be a good idea to help you out until you choose a wife yourself. Merit, fetch Benret and show her in!"

A moment later a maidservant appeared, followed by a young girl. On Tuya's motion the former retreated at once, leaving the girl to stand self-consciously in the middle of the room.

So this was Benret, meaning the sweet one. With her large eyes and delicate features she truly lived up to her name. Her heavy eyelids were modestly lowered unlike those of the other women whose piercing glances were almost unbearable.

"What do you think?" Tuya asked, leering at him.

"I am almost lost for words," Siamun replied truthfully, thinking hard of a way to get out of this mess. "She is very beautiful, but this present is far too precious for me to accept."

The queen shook a chubby finger at him in mock indignation.

"Now, don't you say that, architect. For the saviour of my son's life nothing can be too precious. Benret shall be yours!"

Suddenly, Siamun's mouth felt as dry as the sand of the desert.

"I am deeply grateful for Your Majesty's generous gift," he muttered, bowing rather stiffly.

"Not at all," Tuya said with a dismissive wave. "But now you should better leave. I assume that you will have more important things on your mind than sitting idly and talking to me."

Siamun rose, hoping fervently that none of those present would notice how his cheeks were burning with embarrassment and anger. There was no escape. He had to take this girl home. Rejecting the queen's present might prove disastrous. Without a further glance at any of the women he made a quick exit.

On the way home he was so furious that all his other concerns melted into the background. That beastly woman! How she had played with him, enjoying every moment of it! Had she really just intended to reward him, she could have sent Benret to his house. But no, Tuya had wanted to gauge his reaction when he saw the girl. Without any doubt she would now see to it that the princess came to hear of the great impression his new slave-girl had obviously made on the royal architect Siamun. Reluctantly, he glanced at the young girl who was mincing alongside his litter. Judging by her dainty figure and delicate limbs she was only suited to one thing, and that was to entertain her master.

Furring his brow, he averted his eyes. Clearly the queen did not approve of an alliance between him and Tia, as she had gone to such great lengths to put him off the trail. Now she apparently believed that she had gotten the better of him. But he would show her that he wasn't going to give up that easily. Not if he could help it. Someday, the Great Royal Wife might well be in for a surprise.

****

Three days had passed since Siamun had been to the palace, and despite all the things that nagged his mind he had managed to bring the building plans for pharaoh's new temple to near completion. Now he felt that it was about time to pay Bakenkhensu another visit and enquire for the progress of his investigations, if he had made any. Siamun needed to leave for Iunu as soon as possible to inform his family of Satet's tragic death. He had already sent them a letter in which he announced his imminent arrival, but he hadn't broken the terrible news yet. Perhaps he could ease their pain and grief somewhat if he provided them with at least a hint at the murderer.

Again the hallways of the security headquarters lay generally deserted, but this time Siamun headed straight for the door behind which he hoped to find Bakenkhensu, opening it after a very brief knock.

"What in all the-"

The words got stuck in his throat when Bakenkhensu recognized his visitor.

"What brings you here?" he asked quite unnecessarily.

Siamun wasted no time. "Have you found anything out?"

With a sigh the portly man pushed a half-full plate aside, wiped his fingers on a cloth and motioned Sobek to clear both away. Having thoroughly inspected his fingernails, he rested his elbows on his desk, laced his fingers and propped his chin on them in a supposedly superior manner. Then he looked at Siamun the way a mother might look at her fretful child.

"You can deem yourself lucky that I have indeed discovered something," Bakenkhensu began with an air of importance. "As was to be expected, the ghastly allegation you uttered against the venerable vizier has turned out to be plain wrong. The honourable Nebamun was travelling the country for the past few weeks and has only returned the day before yesterday."

"And where exactly has he been four days ago, at the supposed time of the murder?" Siamun asked, quite unimpressed.

"That's none of either your or mine concern," the chief of the security forces snapped. "The only important thing is that the vizier wasn't here and therefore can't have been involved in the murder."

But Siamun was not deterred. "He could easily have instructed someone else to do the deed for him."

"Nonsense," the fat one snorted in disgust as he wiped his sweaty brow with his oversized sleeve. Siamun couldn't help wondering what made this man sweat in the mild weather of the late inundation season.

"You'd better simply accept the fact that your accusations were false. It is as plain as anything that the vizier has had nothing whatsoever to do with your dubious sister. And if you don't stop suspecting him, I'll-"

"Who was it then?" Siamun cut in.

"How am I supposed to know?" Bakenkhensu shot back, shaking his head at Sobek who had meanwhile returned and readied himself to start writing another protocol.

"It could have been anyone, for all we know," he continued, turning to Siamun once again. "A madman, for example, or a-"

"A madman? Then you'd better go about finding and catching him!"

Bakenkhensu's already narrow eyes turned to slits as he watched Siamun with a mixture of pity and disgust. "Do you happen to know how many maniacs there are out and about in a city like Mennefer? At any rate many more than I could ever accommodate in my prison," he sneered, raising his eyes meaningfully to the ceiling. "Apart from that, there is of course still another possibility that should not be disregarded," he added, dropping his voice mysteriously.

"And that would be?" Siamun asked raptly.

Bakenkhensu leaned forward as far as his enormous belly would allow. "Demons," he said in a hoarse whisper.

"What demons?" demanded Siamun sharply, hoping against hope that he may have misunderstood.

"The demons of the night," Bakenkhensu declared with utter

conviction, leaning back to assume a more relaxed posture. "Have you forgotten all about them? The dwellers of the Duat who sometimes come to the surface to haunt the living, or the doomed Kas for whom nobody cares anymore, and who are out for revenge when it's dark." He paused to stare hard at Siamun. "You said that you found your dead sister in the early morning hours, what makes it all the more likely that whatever happened to her happened in the night before, don't you think so?"

"I only think that you are wasting my time," Siamun said coldly. "Who is your superior?"

"My superior," Bakenkhensu returned pompously, "is the great Neferhotep who oversees all the different branches of security forces that exist in this city. Unfortunately, as he is a very busy man indeed, you will understand that he has neither time nor patience to listen to your story. If you heed my advice, come to terms with the fact that your sister got only what she deserved for her disrespectable way of life, and stop bothering the authorities."

His self-righteous words infuriated Siamun so much that he could barely stop himself from punching his fist into Bakenkhensu's smug face. But it was no use. Not wasting another look at him, Siamun jumped up from his chair and stormed off.

Standing outside the building he hesitated, unsure of what to do next. Would it be worth the while to try and find that Neferhotep?

"If you ask me, my lord, you're only wasting your time with people like them," a voice rang out close to him.

Surprised, Siamun swivelled round. The man whom he had identified as a messenger at the end of his last visit watched him intently.

"I share your opinion, but I can't remember having asked for it," Siamun returned gruffly.

The messenger shrugged his shoulders. "I only wanted to find out if I can help you. You must know that I come around a lot, and I might see and hear much more than others do. But if you don't want my assistance, suit yourself."

Having said that, he pushed another scroll carefully into a cylinder-shaped leather container which was attached to his sash and turned to go.

"Wait!" Siamun called out. "What do you mean by that? Do you know anything about my sister?"

"Not so loud," the young man hissed. "And anyway, we can't discuss this right here."

"Come with me, I'll take you home," Siamun suggested.

"Too risky. We must meet someplace where we don't attract any attention."

"And where would that be?" Siamun asked warily.

If he had expected a meeting in some dark and deserted alleyway in the dead of night, he was in for a surprise.

"I'll meet you exactly one hour before nightfall at the barracks of Perunefer," the other announced.

"What? Perunefer?" Siamun blurted, thinking that this man must be quite mad.

"Keep it down, for god's sake," the messenger insisted, casting furtive glances all around.

"But that place is crawling with people," Siamun whispered.

The man grinned. "Exactly. That's why it is the ideal place for people who don't want to be overheard, like us. Make sure you bring something along that I can carry for you, so that it will look as if I were your porter. And don't be late. I hate to be delayed. By the way, my name is Pashedu."

****

Siamun had positioned himself a short distance away from the entrance of the main barrack with a large sack by his feet and waited for things to happen. He wondered if this Pashedu was really going to turn up. He sincerely hoped he would, although he wasn't quite sure what to expect. How was a mere messenger supposed to help him where the security forces had failed?

Who knows, Siamun thought. Perhaps that man had already come across some useful information. He had definitely sounded confident enough.

From where he was standing, Siamun had a good view on the better part of the main docks. While he was watching the bustle, it dawned on him why Pashedu had chosen this spot of all places, and at that particular hour, too. Shortly before sunset was one of the busiest times of the whole day, since everyone was eager to moor their boats and disembark before nightfall. Afterwards, nobody wanted to spend any time on the black waters over which Sobek and Seth held sway in their respective guises as crocodile and hippopotamus, lurking in the depths and ready to lunge at any unsuspecting creature within their reach.

Thus, Siamun could see sailors fighting fiercely over the last remaining mooring places and fishermen hauling their nets in. Ships were unloaded and their cargo stacked along the quay only to be carried off in a hurry, and travellers were urging their porters to make haste. Each one of them endeavoured to reach his or her destination before darkness fell, be it a generous estate, a small mud-brick hut or even a beer house. At night, nobody was entirely safe when he was out and about even on dry land, for according to popular belief the night was filled with eerie figures, demons, fiends and the restless Ka*s* of the doomed.

All of a sudden, Bakenkhensu's words forced their way into Siamun's mind, ascribing Satet's murder to one of those ghostly beings. Siamun nearly snorted in disgust. He didn't believe for a single moment that they were able to inflict any kind of physical harm on living people, nor had he ever come across one, for that matter. Still, he agreed that it was strongly advisable to spend the night indoors, because the danger of falling victim to the robbing and murdering low-lives haunting the streets in the dark was all too real.

He shot round when someone cleared his throat noisily. With a lopsided grin, Pashedu adjusted the shabby wig on his head, then he grabbed the sack and swung it over his shoulder. With his rather short, stout build and the worn papyrus sandals on his feet he looked exactly like one of the porters who were milling about.

"Looks heavier than it is," he muttered with obvious relief. "Let's go."

Pashedu made to join the throng of people, not bothering to wait for Siamun to follow him - just like a real porter - and soon almost disappeared from view. Siamun had a hard time forcing his way through the crowd and catching up with him. When he did, Siamun decided not to lose any time.

"How can you help me?" he asked.

"First of all let me tell you that neither the fat one nor his superior are willing to assist you," Pashedu replied casually, apparently oblivious to all the pushing and shoving around him. "They have already been bribed."

Siamun's brow furrowed. "Bribed? By whom?"

Pashedu cast him a pitiful glance. "By someone who has something to hide."

"How can you be sure?"

"As you are aware," Pashedu said with a sigh, "I earn my modest living as a messenger, which means that I deliver all kinds of documents from one house or office to the other. These deliveries are sometimes accompanied by things that by all accounts shouldn't exist at all. Small but nonetheless very precious presents, if you know what I mean."

"And how does this relate to the murder of my sister?" Siamun whispered, drawing closer to his companion.

"I couldn't help overhearing that you suspect Nebamun," Pashedu explained in a low voice. "And perhaps it is no coincidence that I had to deliver a parcel from him to Bakenkhensu on the very day you turned up there."

"What kind of parcel was that?"

Siamun's question was followed by a curse when a bull of a man barged into him especially forcefully.

"I must say this kind of conversation is rather tedious," he complained.

Pashedu chuckled. "You may be right there, but it's well worth the while. Nobody can possibly follow us in this milling crowd long enough to make out what we are talking about."

Siamun secretly agreed with him.

"The delivery," Pashedu went on, "was a smallish parcel consisting of many layers of tightly wrapped cloth secured with string. Inside it I could feel several round hard items. Rings, of course, made of solid gold judging by their weight. Trust me, I have done this often enough to know what I'm talking about. Presumably half of them were meant for Neferhotep, and the other half for Bakenkhensu."

"These mangy jackals," Siamun hissed. "But how can we be sure that Nebamun was involved in Satet's murder, let alone prove it? After all, according to Bakenkhensu he claims to have been far away at the time in question."

"In all likelihood that's a lie," Pashedu told him, readjusting the sack on his shoulder once again. The bag was far from heavy as it contained only a few garments. Either he put on a show, or he just wasn't used to carrying anything heavier than scrolls and tiny parcels. "I can find out for you, if you want me to. But then there's something else."

He paused to gape at a pretty young woman who passed by him, until Siamun dug his elbow in his ribs.

"Get on with it," Siamun snapped. "What else is there?"

Pashedu hesitated slightly before he spoke. "You may not like to hear it, but a short while ago I had to hand something over to Nebamun in person, and his doorkeeper told me with a meaningful grin that the great man was unavailable because he had to put his new dancers to the test."

Siamun felt how an uncontrollable fury rose in him. Suddenly his heart pounded so vigorously in his chest that he thought everybody around him must hear it. Grinding his teeth, he fought his anger back until it subsided, enabling him to speak calmly.

"When will you be able to provide me with news?"

"Give me two days, and I'll get back to you," Pashedu replied confidently.

Siamun nodded. "Good. Just tell me one more thing: Why are you so eager to help me at all?"

The other shrugged lightly. "Because I hope to get a small reward from you, and to get my own back on one of those devious great men."

"Don't forget that you assist them constantly in their doings by delivering their little gifts," Siamun reminded him.

Pashedu shot him a desperate glance. "Believe me, I loathe it myself, but what am I supposed to do? I have to support my wife and children, and I can't do that by carrying only a few scrolls around. These little jobs on the side are much better paid."

Of course, Siamun thought grimly. Whoever wanted to bribe someone else using Pashedu's services had to buy his silence as well. A silence that the messenger had just broken, hoping for a handsome reward from Siamun. Could this man be trusted at all? But then, could Siamun afford not to trust him if he wanted that justice be done to his sister?

"We'll meet again in two days' time," he said in a determined voice. "Same place, same time. You'll get your reward once I am satisfied with your work."

Pashedu nodded briefly. Then he made for the edge of the crowd where he put the sack down.

"See you in two days," he said before he disappeared from Siamun's view.

****

Siamun used the following day to acquire a coffin for Satet along with a few other necessary burial goods, pay for her mummification and to see Nebnefer. He didn't want his friend to gain the impression that he didn't care for him anymore, now that he had moved into his fancy new home. But it was with a great deal of uneasiness that Siamun entered his former dwelling, which was triggered by the close vicinity of Nebamun's estate.

He told Nebnefer of Satet's death, but kept his suspicion against the vizier to himself. His friend was visibly shaken at hearing the news and offered to assist Siamun in any way possible, despite being busy enough himself with drawing the plans for an extension of the great temple of Ptah.

Siamun also informed him of his imminent departure for Iunu in order to break the terrible news to his family, then he left and made his way back home.

Night came, and Siamun couldn't find any rest. Would he be any wiser at the end of the next day when he met Pashedu? And what would he do in case the messenger really did find out anything that proved Nebamun's guilt? Would he dare to take action against the vizier? Should he let pharaoh know?

A tentative knock on the door jolted him out of his reverie. Slightly confused, he prompted whoever it was to enter. The door opened and the pretty Benret stood in the doorway, asking him rather timidly if she could be of any service.

For the fraction of a moment he was tempted to say yes, but then he just sent her away. What good would it have been, anyway? He didn't fancy the girl. He wanted the one at whose sight the words died away on his lips and his heart rejoiced. And deep down he felt certain that he was going to get her, whether the Great Royal Wife liked it or not. Her devious plan of using the beautiful slave-girl to drive a wedge between the princess and him was doomed to failure. Tia was going to be his wife, even if he didn't have the faintest idea at the moment how he should go about it.

****

The hours of the following day wore on agonizingly slowly. Finally the sun approached the western horizon, and Siamun made his way to Perunefer. He stood near the barracks as he had done before and waited, but Pashedu didn't show up. As time passed by, Siamun debated what to do. Slightly annoyed, he decided to go in search for the messenger and headed for the drawn-out waterfront, not joining the milling crowd but keeping close enough to see people's faces. There was no trace of Pashedu. Where could he be? Had he been delayed by something? Or had he simply forgotten all about their meeting? Disappointed, Siamun returned to his starting point and resigned himself to more waiting. Then he remembered Pashedu saying how he hated being late when they first met, and suddenly he didn't believe in a simple explanation anymore. A distinct feeling of uneasiness began to creep all over him. What if something had happened to him?

Siamun felt he had to try again, had to look harder for the messenger. Again, he paced up and down the whole length of the quay, but to no avail. Little by little, the numbers of people bustling about were dwindling. The sun had nearly dipped beneath the horizon, and by now the river lay almost deserted. Only a few fishermen were still in their boats, making haste to haul in their catch.

Siamun was about to turn away when one of the boats caught his eye. It was not far off, and he could see two men in it who, judging by their wild gesticulation, seemed to be engaged in some sort of dispute. Upon looking closer Siamun realized that there was something else on board. That something was large and looked rather like another person. Then the two fishermen stopped arguing, seized the large item on both ends and lifted it up. The movement caused the boat to rock dangerously, foiling the apparent attempt to throw that something over board.

Following a sudden impulse of his heart, Siamun started to yell and wave his arms about, hoping to attract their attention. To his relief the two fishermen caught sight of him and paused in mid-action. Now he gestured again, trying to make them come in his direction. When nothing happened, he removed a golden ring from his finger and held it up.

Whether the men really saw the ring in the last remaining twilight, or whether it was the telling movement of pulling it off, Siamun couldn't tell. At any rate, they picked up their oars and started to row frantically. A few moments later they reached the quay, and Siamun peered eagerly into the boat. He had been prepared for an unpleasant sight, but what he saw now made the blood run cold in his veins. It was indeed a body, and one he knew at that. Pashedu. He hadn't simply drowned, as was clear from the gruesome fact that his throat was slit from ear to ear, just like Satet's had been. Pashedu had suffered the same violent death as she had, probably at the hands of the same killer.

The fishermen told him that the body had got caught up in their net, and after a hot debate they had decided to rid themselves of it by throwing it back into the water. Siamun offered them his ring as a compensation for their efforts if they helped him carry the body to the next house of life, an offer which they were quick to accept. Somewhere from the depths of their boat they produced a large piece of cloth, probably an old sail, and quickly wrapped it around the unfortunate messenger's body. Having moored their boat, they followed Siamun on his heels, carrying their macabre load between them.

As he strode along at a brisk pace, Siamun's mind set to work. This dreadful discovery strengthened his suspicion against Nebamun, for it had been him whom Pashedu had wanted to sound out, but even so it proved nothing. He would have to find another way of getting hold of irrefutable evidence.

Siamun gave a despondent sigh. Pashedu had mentioned his family, so he would have to try and find out their whereabouts in order to break the terrible news to them. And of course he owed the dead messenger a decent burial, since there was little doubt that he had died in Siamun's service.

****

Meresankh was looking forward to her brother's arrival with mixed feelings. She was filled with joy at the prospect of seeing him and sharing his success with him, but then she had a foreboding that something wasn't quite right. The relief she had felt at his written announcement that he and Satet would soon be in Iunu had given way to deep concern, because in his second letter he hadn't mentioned his sister anymore. If this wasn't a mere mistake on his part, what had become of Satet?
"Are you worrying about Satet again?"
A tall, good-looking man had approached her from behind and slung his arms around her waist.
"How do you know?" she asked as she snuggled up gratefully against his body.
"It doesn't happen often that you are so deeply lost in thoughts," he explained.
"Oh, Kenamun," Meresankh sighed. "I have a feeling that something might have happened to her. Why else should Siamun come to see us alone, given that he had already found her?"
"Perhaps he just didn't bother to mention her, and they both arrive safe and sound," her husband suggested.
"How I wish this was true," Meresankh muttered.
"Time will tell. Anyway, I think I should go and make for the harbour. They can't be long now."

"What if I come with you?" Meresankh asked eagerly.
"No, dear," came the firm reply. "I'd rather you stay here with Meritamun and the children."
With a last affectionate squeeze Kenamun detached himself from her body and walked off. There was nothing left for her but wait. She went inside to give the cook some last instructions for the evening meal. Meritamun crossed her path, and the worried look on her face made Meresankh almost cringe. Deep down she suspected that her foster mother secretly shared her concerns, even if she had never admitted it.

When Siamun finally stepped over the threshold, Meresankh knew for sure, for his grief was mirrored in his face. She felt as if her heart must burst as the pain washed over her. Even if there had been quite a few things she had disliked about Satet, she had still been her sister, and she was never going to come back home.
With a rather gloomy expression on their little faces, Ranefer and Amunmesse received a pair of wooden crocodiles from Siamun and disappeared with them into the garden. The family gathered in the living room. The air was filled with delicious smells that would normally have made everyone's mouth water, but as it were, nobody seemed to crave food.
Once they had settled down, Siamun began to tell how he had come across Satet quite by chance and how they had travelled from Waset to Abedju. He spoke about their short stay at the sacred site and of his tentative hope that Satet might have changed to the better. He went on with her sudden disappearance in Mennefer and the unpleasant end of their last and final encounter.
It was a sad reunion. Siamun had to repeat everything he said at least twice, and his narrative was constantly interrupted by loud shrieks and wails. But the mood changed dramatically

when he started to talk about his visit to the security forces, his suspicion against Nebamun and Pashedu's tragic end.

Kenamun had been listening in silence for the most part, but then he suddenly said something that made everyone sit up. "I am sure that Bakenkhensu told you a blatant lie when he claimed that the vizier had been away travelling. And I think I can prove it."

Everyone stared at him with rapt attention.

"How?" exclaimed Siamun.

"One of my most recent deliveries was meant for Nebamun," Kenamun explained. "The great man was present himself. He personally inspected the timber and even haggled with me over the price. And after all I've heard so far this must have been about the same time that Satet's death occurred."

"Do you have any definite proof for that?" Siamun asked, visibly excited.

Kenamun wrinkled his brow as he thought hard. "Well, the delivery must be recorded somewhere in my paperwork. It will become clear from the date on it whether my suspicion is right. The vizier's presence cannot be gleaned from it, of course, but I am ready to bear witness against him should he ever be tried."

"That's brilliant!" Siamun cried, full of enthusiasm. "This surely must suffice to file a case against that scoundrel."

"I'd rather you let this matter rest," Meritamun said, in a voice drained of all emotion.

Siamun looked at her in dismay. "But why? Don't you want that Satet's killer be brought to justice?"

"Of course I do," she replied, "but I also want you and Kenamun to live. I couldn't bear losing either of you. Have you forgotten how badly poor Pashedu fared? If you pursue this matter any further and present conclusive evidence on top of that, you're both as good as dead. Besides, not even the best evidence is of any use if the judges have been bribed. You must not forget that in his capacity as vizier Nebamun also presides over the Great Kenbet which deals with serious matters like murder. Nobody can get around him, I tell you."

Siamun cast her a defiant look. "Not even pharaoh? He can dismiss Nebamun and strip him of all his offices, or even exile him if need be."

Meritamun shook her head wearily. "It will hardly come to that. And even in the unlikely case that pharaoh should turn against his powerful vizier, he might not be able to prevent another disaster from happening."

"I' m afraid to say that I share mother's opinion," Meresankh said, feeling that it was high time to join the conversation. "Satet and Pashedu's deaths were meant as a warning to you, Siamun. Clearly, Nebamun wanted to drive the point home that he can do as he pleases. Please don't tempt your fate. It looks like there isn't much that can be put safely past that unscrupulous vizier."

Ignoring her pleading glance, Siamun leapt from his chair and began to pace briskly to and fro. His agitated movements betrayed his inner turmoil. Meresankh's heart went out to him. It was maddening to know that Satet's violent death might never be avenged. However, it was vital not to succumb to emotions, but to give way to reason instead.

Meresankh looked at her husband imploringly and shook her head ever so slightly, trying to make him understand that he shouldn't go on encouraging Siamun any further. Then she rose and walked up to her brother.

"Stop tormenting yourself," she said as she put her hand gently on his shoulder, causing him to stop short. "We are all full of grief and furious at our own impotence, just like you. But the pain will ease, as will our anger at those who caused it, you'll see. Let's not dwell on our gloomy thoughts for a while. We might all feel better after a good meal."

Not waiting for a response, she turned away and left for the kitchen to instruct the cook accordingly.

It was surprising how good the food tasted, all the more so, since Meresankh hadn't really believed herself capable of swallowing a single bite. The same seemed to apply to all the others, who tucked in just as heartily as she did.

I do hope he takes our advice to heart, she thought as she cast a furtive glance at her brother. *I could never bear losing him.* For as long as she could think, she had felt much closer to him than to Satet. All of a sudden, a distant memory leapt into her mind. It wasn't about some very important event at all, but for some unfathomable reason it had engraved itself on her memory nevertheless. Shortly after Siamun had been born, Meresankh had come to visit him in the birth pavilion. Naturally, her father and Sitiah had also been present. At nearly five years of age, Meresankh had already been a bright child with an inquisitive mind. Her father had asked her something she couldn't quite recall. What she did remember, however, was Sitiah's ringing laughter at her answer. Frightened by the startling sound, little Siamun had broken into a loud and indignant wail. Even now, Meresankh saw this touching interlude as clearly in her mind's eye as if it had only been yesterday.

Suddenly, a strong sense of yearning took hold of her. She badly longed to see her father and Sitiah, who would have been a good mother to her, had she been given the chance. Wistfully, she tried to imagine what her life would have been like if King Tutankhamun hadn't died prematurely. She felt certain that they would have led a happy life together, a life without the need to hide away and the constant fear of being discovered. But being a king's daughter, whom would she have married? It was never easy for a royal princess to find someone of sufficiently high status to be well suited to her. For this reason, they often married one of their brothers, or sometimes even their own fathers.

A sudden thought crossed her mind.

"Haven't you thought of marrying yet, Siamun?" she asked bluntly.

Baffled, Siamun looked at her blankly, then he smiled.

"No, sister dear, I think it's not the right time yet."

His reply had been airy enough, but Meresankh didn't fail to notice how awkward her brother appeared to be all of a sudden, just like someone who has been caught doing something forbidden. The strange lustre of his eyes wasn't lost on her either.

Who might she be, the lucky one whom he has apparently fallen in love with? Meresankh couldn't help wondering. If only it was someone who could be trusted.

Early next morning Siamun took his leave. Meresankh didn't like to see him go, but she didn't hold him back either, since he had already explained in his letter that he wouldn't be able to stay long. Pharaoh's return to Mennefer was imminent, and then the foundation of the new temple in Abedju was waiting to be dealt with.

"I am so sorry that we couldn't celebrate your success at all," Meritamun said sadly. "I do hope that you'll be entrusted with the supervision of pharaoh's latest project."

"I hope so, too," Siamun replied, letting out a deep sigh. "I expect to be much more at ease in Abedju than I am in Waset, where I constantly feel the demanding eyes of my ancestors and the gods upon me."

Meresankh nodded emphatically, feeling his subliminal distress as if it was hers.

"We can hardly tell you how proud we are of you," she said as she stepped forth to reciprocate his warm embrace. "Take good care of yourself. Whatever happens, remember to be always on your guard."

Chapter Five

With a solemn expression on his face, Seti paced along the rope that made up one side of a huge rectangle. Whenever he arrived at one of the knots which were ten royal cubits apart from each other, he let a handful of pulverised gypsum trickle on the ground, thus marking the outline of the new structure that was going to be built to honour Osiris, Isis, Horus, Amun-Re, Ptah, Re-Harakhti and Seti himself. According to the importance of the occasion, he was dressed in a magnificent robe and balanced the tall double-crown on his head. Everything had to be perfect, since not only the legitimacy of the new temple, but also its ritual functionality depended on the flawless performance of the foundation ceremony.

When he came back to his starting point, Seti was handed a hoe so that he could break up the ground at the four corners of the future building and deposit small votive figurines and other items inscribed with his name in the shallow holes.

Having done all this, he straightened his back and handed his tool back to the high priest of Osiris. His gaze strayed across the site where his dream was about to come true. In the past few weeks, the workers hadn't been sitting idly. The whole ground had been levelled and cleared from stones and other impurities in preparation for the building works. A canal had been dug that led from the already existing waterway directly to the new building site in order to facilitate the transport of the scores of limestone blocks and other building materials needed in the process. The ramp that connected the jetty with the causeway was later going to be replaced with a flight of steps.

Those privileged enough to attend the ceremony bowed deeply before the majesty of the king as he turned to face them. However, Seti didn't fail to notice the sour look on Nebamun's face. Together with his father Ramose and his son he stood a good way off, as if to express his great displeasure.

Seti couldn't care less. He had done the right thing to entrust Siamun with the construction of this temple, for his plans were the only ones to be in full accordance with his, Seti's, ideas. And after careful consideration he had given him his own daughter in marriage, because the two young people seemed to be destined for each other. If Nebamun had secretly been hoping to get Tia for his son, his disappointment must have become even greater than it had been already.

Seti's gaze flitted along the line of bystanders, across Ramses whose features were set in their usual haughty expression and settled on the young couple standing beside him. Ever since they had been married to each other during a simple ceremony in the great temple of Ptah, the two young people emanated a happiness that was almost tangible. It was with a heavy heart that Seti remembered his first years with Tuya. They, too, had been a happy couple at first, but then something must have gone badly wrong, even before she had started to cheat on him with that red-headed scoundrel of an overseer.

Seti sighed as he pushed these unpleasant thoughts aside. Anyway, he sincerely hoped that his daughter and Siamun would be granted ever-lasting love and happiness. And quite on the side he took a mischievous pleasure in the knowledge of having snatched Tia from the clutches of her brother and any other ambitious upstart, for that matter.

A little later, he was sitting in the reception room of his local palace, discussing future plans over a good meal with his most trusted friends. That was, if Ramses could be called that.

"I'm glad that everything went smoothly," Seti said, wiping his fingers on a damp cloth. "Once you arrive in Waset, make sure you withdraw as many workers as possible. This new project has priority over everything else."

Siamun, at whom Seti's words had been addressed, nodded. "I'll take care of that. I believe that I can easily double the size of the workforce we have currently on the spot, without slowing down the progress of the building works at Ipet-Sut too much."

"Don't bother about those columns," Seti replied, waving airily. "They can wait for once. I wish to put my new temple into operation as soon as possible."

Apart from Seti and Siamun, only Tia and Ramses were present. The latter hardly joined in the conversation, having his eyes glued on the golden shebiu-collar that hung prominently around Siamun's neck, as if willing it to disappear. Apparently, this constant reminder of his near-disastrous hunt distracted him from everything else.

"With Your Majesty's permission we would like to leave for Waset in a couple of hours' time," the young architect declared, seemingly undisturbed by Ramses' incessant stares. "In doing so, I will hopefully be able to arrange for the transfer of workers to Abedju the day after tomorrow. If Your Majesty would excuse us, we can start to prepare for the journey."

"Of course," Seti said, smiling benignly. "You are free to go whenever you please."

He acknowledged Siamun's bow with an approving nod and turned to his daughter.

"I will pray for your safe return every single day from now on," she announced in a choked voice as she slung her arms around her father's neck.

"Thank you, my dear. May the gods bless you both. And now you'd better leave, or else your journey will have to be delayed until tomorrow."

Seti released his daughter from his heartfelt hug and watched her going, accompanied by her young husband. His heart was at ease as far as Tia was concerned, but unfortunately the same could not be said with respect to Ramses. As to himself, he knew perfectly well that nobody could ever be certain to return alive from battle. Only time would tell what the gods had got in store for him.

****

The shady figure stole across the deserted hallway like a demon in hot pursuit of his next victim. And just like a demon of the night it seemed to shy away from light, because it gave the halo of the few torches that were fixed to the wall a wide berth. Eventually, the figure stopped in front of a closed door and knocked, three times in a row, pause, then three more times. This action betrayed the human nature of the figure more than anything else, since presumably a demon wouldn't keep to an obviously agreed signal.

The door opened a crack, not making the slightest sound, and a female hand appeared in the opening, holding a smallish bag out for the figure which instantly disappeared in the folds of its wide garment. The sinister shape made off in a trice, and the door was shut again ever so softly.

This time you have definitely gone too far, the woman on the other side of the door hissed between clenched teeth. I have let you do as you liked, but now you shall find out that I don't stand for any more nonsense! You will soon come to regret your cheek, that's for sure.

****

"I wonder how much longer it will take," Siamun said dreamily as he played with one of Tia's soft curls.
"How much longer *what* will take?" she asked.
"Until I finally realize that all this is true, and not just some kind of glorious dream," he explained.
Tia laughed softly. "Things were happening quite fast, weren't they?"
"You can say that again. If I told you that I was completely overwhelmed it would still be something of an understatement."
This was certainly no exaggeration, given how seemingly insurmountable difficulties had piled up in front of him at first, only to be replaced by the various favours pharaoh had heaped upon Siamun after his return to Mennefer: the Gold of Honour for the rescue of the crown prince, the sole supervision of works on the temple *Menmaatre is content in Abedju* and on top of that the lucrative office of an overseer of the royal granaries in Mennefer. Not to forget the hand of the princess, which meant more to him than all that taken together.
"Father had a notion that we were meant for each other," Tia said in a low voice. "He already suspected me to have fallen in love with you before I even told him. Father always quickly

senses what is inside people's hearts."
Inadvertently, Siamun had to swallow hard. If Seti had even the faintest clue whom he had entrusted his daughter...
Impossible. He must never know.

Having arrived in Waset, they disembarked and went to see the temple of Ipet-Sut straight away. Siamun was pleasantly surprised by the progress the building works on the great hypostyle hall had made so far, but he knew that from now on they would proceed at a far slower pace. He would have to withdraw two thirds of the total number of workers, which amounted to about two hundred men, in order to comply with pharaoh's express wish of having the core of his beloved new temple completed by the beginning of his fourth regnal year. The northern part of the hall was already nearing completion, and the proportions of the different sets of columns were clearly recognizable.
"Can you imagine how all this is going to look once it's ready?" Siamun asked in an excited voice.
"I think I can, and I'm sure it's going to be beautiful," his wife returned, eyes shining. "The columns will appear inviting and awe-inspiring at the same time. Without any doubt this will be the most stunning part of the whole temple complex."
With a satisfied nod Siamun tore his gaze from the impressive sight before him and went in search for Neferronpet, the foreman of the local workforce, in order to inform him of pharaoh's latest decision. As it turned out, the man wasn't particularly surprised to hear that he was going to lose a good many of his workers, for it had quickly got around how fond the king was of his new temple.
As Siamun turned away, his gaze fell on the magnificent pylon at the far end of the hall and lingered, as if attracted by some

powerful invisible force. Instantly, he felt the watchful eyes of his ancestors upon him. He gave his head a slight shake, determined not to fall under their spell again. This wasn't what he was after. Siamun wanted to make a fresh start, just like Seti did when he proclaimed his reign proudly as the beginning of a new era. And in order to do so, he had to be in Abedju, far away from everything that reminded him of his heritage.

With Tia by his side and two guards following in their wake, he crossed the courtyard and made for the entrance gate where their litters were waiting for them. But before they could mount them, Siamun caught sight of a small group of men standing a short way off and talking animatedly.

"I don't believe it," he hissed between clenched teeth.

"What's the matter?" his wife inquired, looking at him with surprise.

"Whatever is Nebamun doing here?" Siamun demanded indignantly. "Has he been following us?"

Tia gave a hearty laugh. "I don't think so. Being a vizier, he has to travel much and far. He will have some kind of business here, just like us."

Siamun turned away and made to ascend the litter. "Come on, let's get away from here before they see us!"

But it was too late. Nebamun had already spotted them and walked briskly up to them, followed by his two companions.

"What an honour to meet the great architect at a site the splendour of which is solely his due," he drawled. "Not to forget Your Highness, of course," he added with a stiff bow in Tia's direction. "May I take the opportunity to introduce the successful architect to my dear friends, my southern colleague Paser and the treasurer Hormin."

Hormin looked exactly the way Siamun had always imagined a

treasurer to be: short of stature, plump and with countless rings on his chubby fingers which were raised in a casual gesture of greeting. Paser, on the other hand, cut a far more elegant figure, slim and with pleasant looks. For someone holding such a high office he was extraordinarily young; Siamun thought he might perhaps be in his late twenties. Paser, too, had raised his hand by way of a greeting. "Your reputation precedes you, Siamun," he said. "All the greater is the pleasure to meet you in person. When may I invite you and Her Highness to be my guests?"

"The pleasure is all mine," Siamun replied, "and I thank you for your hospitality. Unfortunately I am not at all sure if I'll be able to accept your kind invitation, since I'm not going to spend much time here."

"Ah, of course not," Nebamun interrupted rather rudely. "You have other commitments to tend to, foremost of all your sister's burial, haven't you?"

For a moment or two Siamun was struck dumb by Nebamun's impertinence. How dared he to mention Satet's death and rub it in his face, he of all people? Siamun shot him a spiteful look. He had taken great care not to let this tragic incident become public. To this avail he had even broken with tradition and kept shaving his face clean when usually every close male relative of a deceased person was supposed to refrain from shaving during the period of mourning; but with his inappropriate remark the vizier had thoroughly destroyed all his efforts.

"I didn't have the opportunity to express my condolences yet," Nebamun went on unwaveringly, "but please allow me to make up for my negligence. May your sister be justified, and may her name live forever. Unfortunately, her tragic death just goes to show how dangerous the great cities can be for young women, particularly when they are on their own."

To Siamun these words sounded just grotesque. He clenched

his fists in an attempt to restrain his growing fury.
"Thank you, honourable vizier," he said in a strained voice. "Indeed, it is still unclear what caused my sister's untimely demise since the investigations launched into her death have yielded nothing. Therefore it is most likely that she fell victim to either a demon or someone whose heart is stricken by illness."
He had deliberately chosen the phrase that would often serve as a circumlocution for madness. The intended insult was not lost on Nebamun, as was evident from the angry flicker in his eyes. Indeed, to Siamun's mind the vizier's heart resembled that of a madman, devoured by ambition and beset with greed as it was.
Paser had been listening attentively.
"I am sincerely sorry to hear that," he said in a grave tone of voice. "All I can do is follow my colleague's example and express my sympathy. May your sister's Ka live forever. Under the given circumstances-"
"If we may excuse ourselves," Nebamun butted in once again, "I have to discuss a few urgent matters with the treasurer that brook no delay."
With a bow so curt that it rather resembled a nod he made off, beckoning Hormin to follow him.
Siamun couldn't prevent his gaze from boring into Nebamun's retreating back. When he managed to tear it off again he realized that Paser was eyeing him curiously.
"I meant to say that I am not quite sure if under these circumstances an invitation to my house would be appropriate," he concluded with an expectant look at Siamun, apparently wanting to leave the decision to him.
Siamun's interest had been awakened. He had taken an instant liking to the young vizier who seemed to be so different from his northern counterpart, and he was by no means averse to

making his acquaintance. After a short exchange with Tia, he accepted the invitation. That evening they were going to be Paser's guests.

****

Everyone was enjoying themselves thoroughly. Sitting on comfortable cushioned chairs, all one had to do was watch the servants bringing in ever more plates and platters laden with exquisite dishes and refilling cups with tasty red wine.
The spacious reception room occupied the better part of the ground floor of Paser's grand town house. As Tia had told Siamun earlier, only Paser himself, his mother and his sister lived here. His father Nebnetjeru, who had held the office of Amun's high priest prior to Wenennefer, had passed away several years ago. Paser's only other close relative, his brother Titia, who lived with his young family a few houses down the road, had come alone.
Once the lavish meal was over, the servants hurriedly cleared the small tables away, allowing the guests to move closer together. As was usual with such gatherings, men and women soon formed two separate groups. When Siamun exchanged glances with his wife, she flashed a happy smile at him. Tia seemed to enjoy the other women's company thoroughly.
At the far end of the room, a harp player and two young women with double flutes had settled down on thick cushions. Siamun liked the harmonious sounds that they coaxed out of their instruments. However, he did wonder whether the harp player was really as blind as he appeared to be, or whether it was just

pretence. For some unfathomable reason, blind harpists were held in particularly high esteem.

"Don't worry, he isn't truly blind," Paser's merry voice rang out close by, making Siamun believe that his host had been reading his mind. "I know for sure that when it's time for him to be paid, his eyes work marvellously. But there is certainly no harm in letting him believe he can cheat us."

Siamun chuckled. The young vizier's easy ways pleased him. They began to talk about Siamun's family and his work. Paser proved to be an attentive listener who asked appropriate questions without appearing overly curious. And he had the sense not to mention Satet's death again, for which Siamun was extremely grateful.

Paser's brother, however, turned out to be a rather taciturn person who hardly contributed to the conversation.

It's amazing how different brothers can be, Siamun couldn't help thinking. *Just like me and Panakht.*

Not for the first time Siamun had to remind himself of the fact that he and Panakht were not brothers, even if they had always been as close as if they were.

Suddenly a servant came along and whispered something into Paser's ear. The young man excused himself and hurried out of the room. Siamun wondered what might have prompted his hasty departure, but all he could do for now was direct a few polite questions at the silent Titia and listen to his monosyllabic answers. The rather difficult conversation ended when Paser appeared in the doorway, beaming all over his face.

"I am pleased to announce the arrival of two very distinguished guests," he called out.

Siamun caught Tia's eye. A worried look flitted across her face, and he knew that she shared his concern that one of those guests might be Nebamun.

"The venerable King's Son of Kush and one of his most trusted officials have come to honour us with their presence!"
When the new arrivals entered the room, everyone rose from their seats. Siamun did likewise, albeit with very mixed feelings. His gaze travelled to the young man who, as he noticed to his dismay, bore an uncanny resemblance to himself. This didn't come as a surprise, for Amunemopet, the King's Son of Kush, was his maternal cousin.
What if he recognized him and exposed him there and then?

In a hurry more refreshments were brought in and placed before the two men. Siamun cast wary glances at Amunemopet who had come to sit quite close to him. He hadn't been able to glean from his cousin's demeanour whether or not he had realized his, Siamun's, true identity. They had respectfully greeted each other, and then Paser had taken over his new guests. However, Siamun couldn't help overhearing much of their conversation.
"How long have you been staying in Waset already?" his host asked just now.
"It's been three days," Amunemopet replied.
Paser's eyes widened. "Three days? What took you so long then to come and see me?" he cried in a voice full of mock reproach.
The King's Son of Kush smiled amiably. "Well, you know what it's like. First I had to discuss a few things with Wenennefer, and then Nebamun caught me up."
"If this is so, you are probably well informed about all that's going on around here," Paser remarked, raising his eyebrows meaningfully.
Amunemopet nodded, then fastened his gaze on Siamun.
"Indeed I am. And I am happy to meet the esteemed architect and overseer of the royal granaries in person, about whom I've

heard quite a few astounding tales."

"And surely entirely positive ones," Paser added eagerly. "Even Nebamun's critical eye could not have found any fault with our young friend here."

"Of course not," Amunemopet said slowly, eyeing Siamun curiously.

"How are things going down in Nubia?" their host inquired after a short pause.

Siamun let out a deep breath. He was relieved not to be the main subject of the conversation anymore.

The King's Son of Kush drained his cup before he spoke.

"Very well, I'm glad to say. The tribute has been assembled and is waiting to be loaded onto our ships. As soon as His Majesty returns from his campaign, we are going to fill the treasuries and storerooms with Nubia's riches."

Paser beckoned a servant to fill their cups. "It is astonishing how much you have achieved already during your short tenure," he said with an approving nod.

"Thank you, but this praise is Heqanefer's due as much as it is mine," Amunemopet said, putting his hand on the shoulder of his dark-skinned companion. "Without his tireless support I wouldn't have been able to achieve half as much. After all, following my father's untimely death I didn't have much time to acquaint myself with matters of the local administration."

Again, his gaze lingered on Siamun who, this time, met it calmly. Siamun sensed how something akin to familiarity formed between them. Or did he only imagine it? He glanced at the Nubian who had been following the conversation in silence. According to Amunemopet's words he had to be some high-ranking member of the Nubian administration. He appeared to be in his forties, and thus old enough to have served under several previous kings.

"When will you honour me with your visit, Siamun?"

Amunemopet's question lingered a little too long while Siamun thought desperately of an answer.

"The honour is entirely mine," he replied hesitantly. What was he supposed to say? Should he dare accept this invitation?

"With your permission I would love to send for you and Her Highness tomorrow night," his cousin said helpfully.

Rather confused, Siamun muttered his thanks, not at all convinced that this was a good idea. However, seeing Amunemopet's conspiratorial look, his uneasiness lessened somewhat.

"I believe we may have quite a lot to talk about," his cousin said, smiling.

****

"I suspected right from the start that the architect Siamun might be my cousin," Amunemopet explained. "I couldn't be quite sure, though, even when we met at Paser's, because you didn't let anything show. But then I realized that everything I knew about my cousin applied to you, and your resemblance with me wasn't lost on me either, so I thought my suspicion may be right after all."

"I was anxious not to betray my identity because I feared that you might expose me unwillingly."

Amunemopet gave a hearty laugh. "You don't seem to think much of my diplomatic skill, I must say."

Relieved, Siamun joined his laughter. "Yes, this was probably rather stupid of me. I reckon it is the constant fear of being found out that makes me suspicious of almost everything."

During the ensuing silence he let his gaze roam across the unusually extensive garden that stretched out in front of him. There were several ponds, flowerbeds and trees and shrubs as far as the eye could see. It was most apparent that his maternal grandfather Huy, in his day King's Son of Kush under King Tutankhamun, had attached great value to life out of doors. Even his Nubian residence had sported a garden that had been without equal in the whole town, as Amunemopet had just related.

Despite his reservations, Siamun had been unable to decline his cousin's invitation. And he was glad for it. It did him good to talk openly about his family to someone who belonged to it himself. Amunemopet had been born in the second year after Siamun's move to Iunu, thus he was only twenty-one years of age and still unmarried. Although they had never met before – except for their brief encounter the previous night- there was an intimacy between them that was simply astounding. Perhaps there was something in the old saying about blood being thicker than water after all.

Amunemopet stretched himself luxuriously and clasped his hands leisurely behind his head.

"I must make the most out of my time here," he declared. "In a few days' time I'll have to go back to baking hot Nubia."

Siamun was surprised. "Is it really so hot there, even now at the beginning of winter?"

His cousin grimaced. "In winter it's hot, in summer unbearable. You should deem yourself lucky to be here."

Siamun nodded gravely. "That I do, all the more so, since I have finally had the chance to visit the place where my mother grew up."

Amunemopet, too, had turned quite serious. "It must be hard to be brought up in all secrecy, unable to meet one's own relatives or to travel freely."

Siamun reached for his wine cup, but instead of raising it to his lips he wrapped his hands around it and peered thoughtfully into the dark red liquid.

"You can say that again, but I am forever grateful to Meritamun for raising us the way she did, with so much love and affection that she almost made us forget that we were orphans. But ever since I was old enough to learn about my parents, this insatiable yearning awakened, the yearning to get closer to them, to fill in the gaps and get to know them instead of just hearing tales about them. For years on end I was unable even to visit the places that might somehow connect me to them, but now that I am able to catch up on this it feels as if I'm piecing my own past together."

By the look on Amunemopet's young face he could tell how deeply affected he was.

"But isn't it very hard for you to hide your true identity from your own wife?" he asked after a short silence.

Tia had not accompanied her husband for lack of women in Amunemopet's household, and Siamun was admittedly glad she hadn't.

Slowly, he let out a deep breath. "Indeed it is," he replied in a dismal tone of voice. "I must always be careful not to let anything drop that could arouse her suspicion."

His hands began to fiddle around with the cup they were holding, but Siamun himself was quite unaware of its presence.

"Such is my fate," he went on gloomily. "Even if I had married someone else, it wouldn't be much different. I'll never be able to tell anyone the whole truth."

"Haven't you ever thought of taking what is yours?" Amunemopet asked suddenly.

Siamun looked at him in surprise. "You mean, to exert my right on the throne?"

His cousin nodded. "Exactly."

"Impossible!" Siamun exclaimed, shaking his head vigorously. "You know what kind of terrible bloodshed this would involve, and I don't want to give rise to something like that. Besides, I have no support whatsoever."

"I wouldn't say that," Amunemopet replied smoothly. "I daresay you would have more supporters than you'd probably imagine. Not everybody is entirely happy with a ruler who hails from a family of northerners, and a bunch of soldiers at that. This applies most of all to those who would have to suffer from a shift in the balance of power."

"What do you mean by that?" Siamun asked doubtfully.

"Let me explain. Take the two viziers, for example. At the first glance, both of them are allotted equal shares of power and responsibility. However, if you look closer you'll soon find out that Nebamun's influence is far greater than Paser's, because being the vizier of the north and a northerner himself, pharaoh endows him with more power and privileges. In fact, Nebamun has grown so powerful that nobody ever dares to oppose him. As you have experienced yourself, using bribery and coercion he has managed to set up a whole network of submissively dependent officials. Nebamun even dares to meddle in affairs that don't concern him in the least."

Amunemopet paused to drain his cup. Siamun did likewise, then gazed silently at the glittering surface of a nearby fishpond which reflected the rays of the mild afternoon sun. He sensed what his cousin was getting at, and he didn't like it.

"Just look what happened to the presentation of Nubian tribute which used to be carried out here in Waset, Amun's sacred city," Amunemopet continued. "A good part of it used to fill the magazines of that god's great temple before the rest was distributed among other temples and treasuries. This time, however, our fully loaded ships have to proceed to Mennefer, where the official presentation will take place. As is plain to see, this is mainly to ensure that the local treasuries and the storehouses of Ptah get a far greater share than in earlier years. And who will benefit the most? The vizier of the north, who presides over Mennefer's storehouses, and who leaves no stone unturned to increase his already considerable wealth and influence ever more."

Siamun tore his gaze from the water and fastened it on his cousin.

"It is up to pharaoh to put Nebamun in his place," he said firmly. "What do I have to do with all that?

Amunemopet was clearly not deterred. "Pharaoh lets him do as he pleases, because as a matter of fact he is not adverse to his doings. Seti has already started himself to direct much of his attention at the north of the country. In addition to his own ancestral estate he owns a palace situated close to Avaris where he spends much of his time, not to forget the new military base nearby. For me it is only a matter of time that the entire royal residence will be moved northwards. The southern nomes will inevitably lose out on wealth and power which will lead to uprising and turmoil, and ultimately perhaps even to the separation of the Two Lands. And I surely don't have to tell you, Siamun, that in this case we would be an easy prey for all our enemies, foremost the Hittites who can't wait to get their greedy hands on us."

Amunemopet paused and motioned Heqanefer, who had approached them with a respectful greeting, to join them at the table.

Siamun was at a loss what to reply. To some extent, his cousin's reservations were certainly justified, but the only remedy he could see was Seti's undoing and the annihilation of all his followers. And the key element in this plot would be Siamun himself.

"I had no intention of getting involved in these doings when I left Iunu," he said, not wanting to reveal more in Heqanefer's presence.

"I didn't assume` you had," his cousin replied calmly. "But please allow me to elaborate on one more relevant point nevertheless, namely the question of the succession. Our king is still quite young, but even so his health has weakened considerably over the past months. Only few people are aware of it, since Seti does all he can to cover it up. Just like his father before him, he suffers from sudden surges of pain in his chest which also impair his breathing, and he knows full well that he might share his father's fate at any time."

"So what?" Siamun burst out a trifle harshly. "May the gods grant His Majesty a long and prosperous life, but when the time has come for him to join his ancestors, Prince Ramses will be there to take his place, as Maat decrees."

He didn't fail to notice the meaningful glances that passed between the two men, and he already sensed that worse was to come.

"That's exactly where there is yet another problem, and perhaps the gravest one of all."

Siamun just managed to stifle a groan. What now? He almost began to regret having accepted this invitation in the first place.

"The problem I'm speaking of," Amunemopet continued unwaveringly, "is that in truth Ramses isn't Seti's son at all."

Siamun's eyes widened. "What? This sure can't be!"

Amunemopet ignored his objection. "You might imagine that this is a very delicate matter, but it is true nevertheless. Ramses was sired by the overseer of Seti's estate. I can assure you that my knowledge comes from a very reliable source. And now tell me, Siamun, is it in accordance with Maat if Ramses, a bastard, ascends to the throne of the Two Lands? Of course it's not, and even a proclamation of the divine oracle that solely

served the purpose of forcing Seti into acknowledging his alleged son as heir to the throne cannot change this fact."
Extremely upset by this latest revelation, Siamun had been listening in silence.
"And you think that people would give preference to a king whose father's rule is already being frowned upon?" he asked eventually.
"Nobody in their right mind could possibly disapprove of your father's reign," his cousin pointed out. "This is entirely down to the official politics instigated by King Horemheb and continued by his successors, who sought to consolidate their own power by taking the credit for King Tutankhamun's achievements. As you certainly know, Seti carries things even further than his predecessors, and why? Because he is all too aware of the fact that his throne rests on very shaky ground indeed."
A long silence followed his passionate words. Siamun's mind was in turmoil, and there didn't seem to be a way out, except the one he loathed.
"Do you have any idea who this trusted friend of mine really is?" Amunemopet asked after a short, uncomfortable silence, apparently trying to steer the conversation round to a less delicate subject.
Siamun shook his head wearily.
"Heqanefer is Meresankh's uncle," his cousin said, smiling.
Siamun's eyes widened. "Really? Than you must be-"
"Apakure," the Nubian helped him out. "This is what I'm originally called. The majesty of your father bestowed the name Heqanefer on me when he entrusted me with the administration of Wawat in lower Nubia."
"I have heard of you before," Siamun said enthusiastically, hardly shaken by the revelation that this man seemed to know his true parentage, "and I am pleased to meet you in person. If only Meresankh was here; we have always been very close, and

I know she would love to see you."

Heqanefer smiled amiably. "Perhaps one day this wish will come true."

Siamun was amazed how fluently Heqanefer was able to speak, and apart from a slight accent it was only his dark skin colour that betrayed his foreign origins. Judging by his elevated status, he must have done extremely well. However, Siamun couldn't help wondering how he must have felt when he had been forced as a young lad to accept the language and customs of Kemet that were imposed on him by his overlord, the pharaoh. Having been treated like this, wasn't he bound to hold a secret life-long grudge against the oppressors of his people?

A servant appeared, carrying a large bowl filled with figs, grapes and dom-palm nuts. The men helped themselves generously.

"You must know that I am forever grateful for the kindness your venerable father once showed me," Heqanefer said while he was busying himself with one of the nuts.

"What exactly do you mean by that?" Siamun inquired.

The Nubian raised his eyebrows meaningfully and leaned closer to Siamun.

"Do you know where the royal wife Ajala, Meresankh's mother, was buried?"

"I was told she was buried in a shaft tomb in the Place of Truth," Siamun replied, wondering what the Nubian was getting at.

Heqanefer shook his head slowly. "So you haven't heard about it."

"That's no wonder; after all, everything was kept highly secret back then. If you hadn't confided in me, I wouldn't know either."

Amunemopet's mysterious remark confused Siamun even more.

"What is it that I haven't heard about?" he demanded.
Heqanefer looked up from his plate and smiled at him.
"That Ajala's body wasn't in her coffin at all, but was buried in the cemetery belonging to our Nubian village instead."
"But why?" Siamun called out, utterly surprised. "How can this be?"
Having wiped his hands clean, Heqanefer leaned back and fastened his gaze on Siamun's expectant face.
"Let me explain what happened back then," he began. "Our tribe had just received the sad news that Ajala had died in childbirth and was meant to be buried in Waset's royal necropolis. Some members of my tribe, however, disapproved of a burial in Kemet and were adamant that her body be brought back to our village. They wanted my father, who was then leader of the tribe, to demand the handing over of her mortal remains, but he wouldn't hear of it. Father didn't want to put the new-found peace with pharaoh at risk by making inappropriate demands. The dispute threatened to escalate, so I made up my mind that something had to be done. Together with a cousin of mine and a handful of skilled bowmen I secretly left the village and travelled north, hoping to intercept the royal fleet on its way and somehow get hold of Ajala's mummy without anyone knowing in order to take her back to Nubia."
Siamun's eyes must have become very wide indeed, for Heqanefer stopped his narrative and smiled.
"I know, young master, how incredible this must sound, but being the young lads we were back then we truly believed it would work. Anyway, we really did come across the royal fleet. This was at one of pharaoh's rest-houses where the royal entourage had prepared to spend the night. In order to put our daring plan into action, we had to resort to an age-old trick: Our bowmen lit their arrows and set two of the mooring ships

on fire. In doing so, we hoped to create enough confusion to be able to board pharaoh's own ship and remove my sister's body from her coffin unnoticed. But we were discovered and got caught in the act of prising the lid open. My cousin and I were arrested and questioned, whereas all our companions got killed in the ensuing fighting. Both of us had actually forfeit our lives, since we were suspected to be spies in the service of some rebellious Nubian leaders. Your royal father, however, had recognized me from an earlier encounter and realized what we had been up to, without me telling him. He not only agreed to let us go, but also allowed us to take Ajala's body with us. Of course, this had to be done in all secrecy, or else King Tutankhamun's reputation would have greatly suffered. Therefore, my sister's empty coffin was buried in the Place of Truth, while her body was laid to rest in our home country. Thus, I owe not only my life to your venerable father, but also the fact that my tribe could live on in peace. And to you, Siamun, who you are the son of this truly magnanimous king, I pledge everlasting allegiance just as I did to your father. It goes without saying that your own secret is safe with me for as long as you wish."

Siamun had been listening with rapt attention, overwhelmed by these unexpected revelations.

"Who would have thought of that?" he smiled. "It looks like we all have our little secrets. I must say, though, that if I hadn't heard this extraordinary tale from your own mouth, I would hardly believe it to be true. But now I think it's high time that I left. My wife will be expecting me to hear what we were talking about. It's a pity I can't tell her all."

"I hope I haven't been pressing you to hard, Siamun," Amunemopet said as he accompanied his cousin to the entrance gate. "Reaching out for the crown has never been an easy thing to do. I trust you know yourself what to do. All I wanted was to assure you of my unconditional support, should you ever need it."

On the way back, his words resounded in Siamun's confused mind: *I trust you know yourself what to do.*

If only he did.

****

Fascinated, Siamun watched the cumbersome limestone blocks being unloaded from the boat and hauled on to the waiting sledges. Several strong men then grabbed the ropes attached to them and began to pull them along the causeway towards their destination at the far end of the cliff-lined bay. The load was heavy and the distance considerable, and the fact that the causeway sloped slightly but continuously up rendered it all the more difficult. For the workmen it was hard-earned bread, and their half-naked bodies were covered with sweat that gleamed in the brilliant winter sun. But their spirits were high, since pharaoh had decreed that they be well provided for, and the work load was split up between two teams working shifts of four hours each, so that nobody suffered undue exertion. As a result, the overseers didn't have to do much more than spurring the men on with shouts of encouragement. So far there had been no need for them to make use of their whips, and Siamun hoped that it would stay this way.

He left his post near the jetty and walked up to the far end of the building site, keeping well to the side so as not to get into anyone's way. With some satisfaction, he surveyed the walls of the many small rooms that would make up the rear part of the future temple. They had already reached a considerable hight, and Siamun was quite confident that he was able to stick to pharaoh's timeline which gave him roughly eight more months for the completion of the temple's core. Once the season of Peret was over and the days grew longer again, it might well be possible to employ an additional shift of workers, further speeding up the pace at which works progressed.

However, not much was to be seen in the area behind the temple proper, where the monumental subterranean tomb was to be built. All that showed here were a huge rectangular hole and the beginnings of a tunnel which would later provide sole access to the tomb structure that consisted mainly of a large pillared underground hall serving as a fake burial chamber. There was one particular feature, though, that couldn't usually be found in tombs: a rectangular island right in the centre, surrounded by an artificial moat and destined to house the actual coffin of Seti-united-with-Osiris. The completed subterranean hall was then to be covered with heavy sandstone slabs and soil. Later, a low earthen hillock would be all that could be seen on the surface; but until then years would go by, however great Seti's haste might be.

The king seemed to be in a hurry with almost all he did. Works on his real tomb in the Place of Truth were said to be carried out at full stretch. Siamun didn't know the details of its structure, but he had heard it said that it had already reached a length that surpassed that of many other royal tombs by far. Suddenly he remembered Amunemopet's words regarding pharaoh's ill health. Siamun couldn't help wondering if this was the true reason behind Seti's great hurry. He decided to ask Tia at the next opportunity. But dare he speak to her about this other, simply outrageous matter he had become aware of, too? The apparent fact that she and Ramses were only half siblings, the crown prince a bastard?

Siamun's jaw tightened when he thought of the bastard son of a commoner ascending to the throne of the Two Lands. As his cousin had already pointed out, this would be one of the gravest offences against Maat imaginable. But then, Siamun reasoned with himself, it wasn't his duty to put a stop to it. He had to prevent the seeds that Amunemopet's words had planted in his heart from bearing fruit at all cost. His task was here, right in front of him: Pharaoh's vision of the perfect place of worship. This vision had virtually become his own, and he was going to carve it into stone, no matter what.

When he returned to the small royal palace that was attached to the temple of Osiris to join his young wife, he found her to be in very high spirits indeed. The reason became clear as soon as he caught sight of the set of Senet on the table, which indicated that Tia must have dealt her friend Baket a crushing defeat. While the young woman retreated discreetly from the chamber, Tia came rushing towards him and wrapped her arms around his neck.

"Finally," she breathed into his ear. "I missed you so much."

"I don't believe you," Siamun teased, pulling her body close to his. "To me it rather looks like you may have forgotten all about me, engrossed in your game as you were."

"Don't you see how glad I am that you're back?" Tia insisted with mock indignation before she brushed her lips tenderly against his.

"Of course I do," he conceded gently. "I only hope that you haven't got your mind set on another round of Senet, because I'd hardly stand a chance of winning."

The princess smiled mischievously. "Truth be told, I had something entirely else in mind. A sort of game we can both only win."

Siamun couldn't resist the lure of her lustrous dark eyes, even if he had wanted to. Locked in a tight, passionate embrace, they sank down on the bed and abandoned themselves to the pleasure of the moment.

Later that day, he was sitting with Tia in the tiny enclosed garden of the small royal palace adjacent to the temple of Osiris. Darkness had just fallen, and for protection against the chill of the night they had both wrapped up warm. Underneath her cloak Tia had drawn her knees up to her chest and slung her arms around them, as was her habit.

"The way you're sitting there with only your head showing you look exactly like one of those cube-shaped statues depicting royal tutors and their charges," Siamun joked.

Tia smiled. "Right you are, except that the second head popping out of the folds of the tutor's garment is missing."

Siamun looked at her thoughtfully. "Perhaps there's another little head already hiding inside you, who knows?"

"I wish it were true, but unfortunately it isn't," Tia replied with an air of sadness. "I had my bleeding only recently."

Siamun reached out for her and caressed her cheek with the back of his finger. "That's nothing to worry about," he said softly. "We have only just married, and we have a whole lifetime of love and joy before us. Sooner or later we are going to have children, so the gods will. And if not, I don't care. I'll always love you the way I do now, no matter what."

His wife offered him a grateful smile. "I have always wished for a husband who loves me for myself, not only for the sake of children or because of who I am."

"Your wish has been granted."

Tia nodded. "And this is not the only one," she added in a low voice.

"What else have you wished for, if I may ask?"
"I never wanted to become Great Royal Wife, or any royal wife for that matter," she replied firmly.
"Really?" Siamun said, genuinely surprised. "That's quite unusual, isn't it? I always had a notion that little girls dream of nothing but becoming a queen one day."
Tia shook her head despondently. "This may be true for girls who grow up far from the royal court. I for my part have seen and heard things that made me wish never to be forced into the role of a queen."
Siamun watched her raptly. "What do you mean by that?"
His young wife drew a deep breath before she spoke. "I had the chance to observe three Great Royal Wives at very close quarters. The first was Mutnodjemet, with whom we associated because my grandfather was King Horemheb's designated heir, and it was clear that father was going to succeed him in due course. Therefore it was considered good form for me and mother to call often at the palace and pay the queen our respect."
Tia paused to shift her weight slightly.
"It seems that you didn't like Queen Mutnodjemet much," Siamun remarked quietly.
"She was a horrible woman," Tia burst out, her voice full of loathing. "Downright wicked she was, and her thoughts used to centre only on herself. Most of the time, she treated me as if I wasn't even there. It was only once that she took actually notice of me. I still remember that day, although I was just about six or seven years old."
For a moment, Siamun was so surprised that his breath caught in his chest. It was not unknown to him that, prior to her becoming queen, Mutnodjemet had been scheming behind the scenes at his father's court, but he knew next to nothing about her time as Horemheb's Great Royal Wife. What could she have

done to arouse a little girl's hatred?

"It was on the occasion of one of our frequent courtesy visits," Tia continued in a somewhat calmer voice, propping her chin on her drawn-up knees. Her eyes stared into the empty space while her mind conjured up the happenings from the past. "Both my mother and grandmother were engaged in a conversation with Mutnodjemet, whereas I was sitting some way off, playing with my doll. While I busied myself with making all the doll's fake hair into braids, I listened in to their talk. I wasn't particularly interested at first, but then they began to talk about some royal children unknown to me. They were speculating what might have happened to these children, and whether they were still alive or not. Of course I knew that Queen Mutnodjemet didn't have any children of her own, having suffered several miscarriages and stillbirths instead. Thus I concluded that the children in question must have been those of an earlier king. In my childish mind I began to imagine how wonderful it would be if those children were still alive. I thought that maybe they were going to return to the palace one day, where I could play with them. When the women's conversation seemed to have ended, I voiced my thoughts, not knowing what a grave mistake this was. Both mother and grandmother stared at me in dismay, but when I caught sight of Mutnodjemet, I was frightened to death. Sheer hatred had contorted her features so much that to me she looked like one of those vengeful demons I had heard about, and then she hissed at me with her toothless mouth. *No, they're not alive, not one of them, do you hear me? They're all dead, dead like their mother and father, so stop telling lies!* Never before had I encountered such spite and maliciousness. I was so scared that all I could do was nod silently, hoping that she would leave me alone. Fingers trembling, I went on plaiting my doll's hair, although I was hardly able to see through the tears that were brimming in my eyes. Later, mother gave me a thorough scolding, and from then on I hardly dared open my mouth during those dreadful visits."

Siamun sat in silence, deeply upset by Tia's tale. He was convinced that the children in question had been none other than himself and his siblings. So it seemed that King Tutankhamun's children had been taken as dead back then, or at least they had been assumed to be, a fact that was quite convenient for him.

"Now Mutnodjemet is dead herself, and I'm sure the gods have condemned her," he said in a hoarse voice.

Tia nodded. "That's what I hope with all my heart. Apart from Mutnodjemet, neither my mother nor grandmother conveyed a positive impression of queenship to me. Both were ashamed of their non-royal descent and went to great lengths to cover it up. To this avail they even assumed new names upon becoming Great Royal Wives, the way usually only kings do. My grandmother's name changed from Tia into Sit-Re, and mother styles herself Mut-Tuya ever since. Mother is anxious to keep and, if possible, further enhance her elevated status, and I believe she is hardly able to sleep at night until Ramses occupies the throne of the Two Lands."

In a determined manner, she reached for her wine cup and drained it but refused when Siamun made a move to refill it. Tilting her head back, she directed her gaze at the star-studded firmament above her. Siamun's eyes inadvertently followed hers.

"For as long as I can remember, I have felt lonely," she said in a subdued tone of voice. "Father loves me dearly, that I do know. But unfortunately he has never had much time left for me, owing to his high office. And mother... well, she has saved all her love and attention for Ramses, to sum it up. Why she doesn't care for me eludes me. Perhaps it is the fact that she suffered several miscarriages combined with her great ambition that made her focus on her only son. But she hasn't done him a favour, pampering and spoiling him the way she did and still does. Ramses has become so stuck-up that he hardly listens to anyone's advice already. Towards me he has always been indifferent, taking notice of me only when he had to. Mother was adamant that we both be married to each other, like many siblings among the gods have done. What I wanted didn't matter to her, of course, and Ramses might have agreed to marry me for mother's sake. However, father has always disapproved of this unfortunate alliance. He also saved me from the clutches of those ambitious courtiers who only wanted to marry me to better themselves and to gain more influence. For that I am forever grateful to him, since if he hadn't done so, I might not have been able to become your wife."

Their eyes met, and Siamun saw the tears glittering in hers. Pulling her gently towards him, he began to stroke her hair.

"I sensed that you were unhappy when I first saw you, hovering in your litter high above my head," he whispered.

"I'm sure you were much happier with all your siblings," Tia said after a little while.

"Yes, you're probably right," Siamun replied somewhat reluctantly. "Apart from my father, I wanted for nothing."

"I would dearly like to meet your family. What if I came with you for Satet's burial?" Tia asked eagerly.

Siamun hesitated. He hated to disappoint his wife, but he couldn't let this happen either.

"I don't think that's a good idea," he said. "Everyone will be overcome by grief. Maybe some other time would be better."

Tia nodded slowly. "I understand. Then please tell them to come and visit us here in Mennefer. I can't wait to meet the woman who gave birth to the man I love."

Siamun swallowed hard, but the lump in his throat just wouldn't go away.

"Sooner or later you will get to know each other, I'm sure," he muttered in a husky voice.

If not in this world, then in the next, he added to himself.

Chapter Six

Seti was sitting bent over on his folding chair with his arms resting on his knees, peering thoughtfully into his half-full wine cup. The distorted mirror image of his eye staring back at him fascinated and terrified him at the same time.

He pondered the unsettling news that had just been brought to him by a messenger. Now it was vital to make the right decision, or else he and his troops might soon be facing a full-blown war at two fronts.

A few tribes belonging to the audacious Temehiu had dared to emerge from the western desert in order to advance on Kemet's soil and raid several villages. They had plundered, murdered and raped. Having met with no significant resistance, they had been pushing further ahead, wreaking havoc wherever they went. As if this were not enough, these wretched sand-dwellers were also waylaying unsuspecting travellers and merchants, stripping them of all their goods and belongings and often killing them in the process.

Unless Seti put a stop to it soon, the inhabitants of the western delta would not be safe anymore. Besides, hadn't the heqau-khasut, those foreigners hailing from the Asiatic territories, managed to invade Kemet centuries ago and taken control over her for many generations? That shameful episode of foreign domination had shaken the Two Lands to the core and must never repeat itself.

Swift military action was what was called for. But how was he supposed to drive the aggressors back to their homeland? He was far from home, somewhere on the coastline north of Megiddo, as were all his troops. Their mission was far from over yet. Three of the most important seaports –Tyre, Sidon and Byblos- had already bowed to pharaoh's might, but the equally important city of Simyra was still waiting to be dealt with. And, naturally, Seti wasn't going to stop there. He had ambitious plans, and in order to implement them he needed every man he could get; a fact that hadn't been lost on the wretched Temehiu, as had become painfully clear.

Seti's trail of thoughts was interrupted when Mehy appeared in the opening of the tent, asking to be admitted. Seti nodded, then emptied his cup in one go.

"I have made up my mind," he began when his friend had taken a seat opposite him, "that I should give Ramses the opportunity to prove his worth. Therefore I'm going to send word to him that he is to assemble the few remaining troops and leave Mennefer for one of our forts on the edge of the western desert. Once there he is to await the arrival of the enforcement troops provided by me. Together, they can then advance on the homeland of those vile desert dwellers and wipe them out. What do you think?"

Mehy nodded slowly. "How many of our troops do you intend to send on this errand?"

"One division should be enough. We're in sore need of the other three ourselves. After all, we still have to take on Simyra and Amurru."

Mehy stroked his chin, pondering Seti's words.

"Will the prince be up to this task?" he asked eventually, doubt clearly written all over his face.

Seti sighed. "According to his own judgement, Ramses is ready to take on any task. But even if we are being cautious, I believe he might well be able to stand up to a bunch of unorganized fighters like those Temehiu without causing too much harm to his own men. Besides, this is a convenient way of keeping him busy. If I'm honest, ever since we left Mennefer I have no peace of mind at all. I am constantly worrying about what kind of plot he and his ambitious mother might be hatching right now. Mehy, do you think I'm overdoing it?"

His trusted friend returned his inquiring gaze without wavering.

"Being cautious has never been a mistake," he said calmly. "Of course I do hope that your worries turn out to be unfounded, but one never knows."

Seti nodded approvingly, although he didn't fail to glean the distrust from Mehy's diplomatic words. He rose from his chair and stretched his limbs.

"Have the superior commander of the division of Ptah come and see me, along with that messenger so that I can give them my orders," he told his friend. "And then we should march off immediately to make good use of the remaining hours of daylight."

Mehy made a quick bow and took himself off, leaving Seti to ponder his decision once more.

He felt sure that Ramses wasn't going to like it because he wouldn't be the supreme commander of this operation, but Seti wasn't prepared to run any risk. The only strategy Ramses knew was that of straightforward attack. Putting him in sole charge would not just be irresponsible. It would be madness.

****

With tears in her eyes Meresankh cast one last look at the beautiful face mask of Satet's coffin. It was made of precious cedar wood, and its facial features had been marvellously crafted and painted a pale ochre with the eyes and eyebrows being picked out with black lines. Meresankh thought that the wooden mask bore a striking resemblance to her deceased sister, even down to the somewhat haughty expression on its timeless features.

The last rites had been carried out, and the coffin was being lowered gently down the shaft and into the burial chamber, which was equipped with all the goods necessary for an enjoyable afterlife: several storage jars containing dried fruit and pulses, empty wine jars which were thought to ensure the deceased's continuous provision with this most coveted of beverages and finally a few chests with Satet's garments and jewellery.

But the most important item of the whole burial assembly –at least to Meresankh's mind- was the heart scarab which she knew was resting within the layers of bandages right above Satet's own heart. This scarab owed its importance to the fact that its flat surface was inscribed with a magic spell which was meant to prevent the real heart of the deceased from bearing witness on the day of judgement and telling tales of his or her sinful deeds. Meresankh felt sure that Satet's heart might have quite a lot to tell if it was given the opportunity. She wasn't entirely convinced of the efficiency of such magic, though; but then, it could do no harm either.

After the funeral, the family gathered inside to share the customary meal in honour of the deceased. The mood was still dominated by grief, but the tension of the past weeks began to wear off. Losing a close family member in such a terrible way was always a heavy blow. However, deep down Meresankh couldn't help thinking that Satet had blatantly tempted her fate with her unacceptable and careless behaviour, and she felt sure that everyone else secretly shared her view.

Later, when they were sitting in the garden, Meresankh cast an amused glance at her brother.

"I knew when I saw you last time that there was something going on," she said with a twinkle in her eyes. "And lo and behold, my brother goes and marries the princess, of all people. I would have reckoned with almost anything but that. I am sincerely happy for you, Siamun, but I also do hope that your difficulties won't get worse."

Siamun had lowered his eyes, his embarrassment clearly showing on his handsome face. "I simply followed my heart, just as Tia did. We both belong together. This is the only reason for our marriage, and I trust that the gods won't be so cruel as to punish us for our love."

Meritamun put her hand on his in a gesture of comfort. "Don't worry," she said soothingly. "Don't spoil your happiness with fears that hopefully will never come true. Just be careful not to give your secret away, that's all. I am so happy for you, and I wish you all the best from the bottom of my heart."

Siamun smiled and squeezed her hand affectionately. Then his gaze wandered to his two young nephews who were playing boisterously some way off. Meresankh noticed how intently he watched them, his eyes following their every movement. There was a longing in them that hadn't been there before. The longing to have a family of his own.

May your wish be granted, she said to herself. *And may it be for the best.*

Suddenly, Siamun's eyes snapped back to her.

"Actually, Tia wanted to come with me," he announced. "I had a hard time talking her out of it. But now she wants you to visit

us in Mennefer. Tia is so desperate to meet you."
Meritamun sighed. "I would dearly love to get to know her, too. It's only that I'm afraid that someone at court could recognize me."
"You wouldn't have to appear there at all," he replied eagerly. "Just come to stay with us for a few days. What can possibly happen?"
"We'll think about it," Meritamun smiled. "But aren't you bound to spend most of your time in Abedju, anyway?"
Siamun hesitated. "It's true that I have to survey the progress of works in order to make sure everything goes smoothly. But I have come to realize that my foremen are very reliable, so from time to time they can surely take care of this. By the way," he added softly, "I intend to have a memorial chapel erected there for Satet. As I told you already, she was deeply impressed by the sacred atmosphere of this site. Unfortunately this wasn't enough to make her change her ways, but even so I think her Ba might enjoy visiting there, at least occasionally."
Meritamun nodded silently, tears welling up in her eyes once again.
"Do you know by any chance how our army is doing?" Meresankh asked hastily, anxious to distract her foster mother from her grief.
Siamun shrugged. "To date the only thing we know is that our troops have been victorious throughout, Amun be praised, and that they have suffered no significant losses so far. But I will certainly do all I can to find out more."
He had hardly ended when a servant walked up to him and informed him that a royal herald was waiting to see him. Wondering what on earth could have prompted the herald to follow her brother all the way to Iunu in order to convey his message, Meresankh watched Siamun as he made his way to the entrance gate. He soon returned with a rather grave

expression on his face.

"The herald just told me that I am expected to call urgently at the royal palace," Siamun explained. "It appears to be a very pressing matter indeed, though I can't for the life of me imagine what it is about."

"Haven't you asked him for the reason?" Meresankh inquired.

"I have, but the man pretends to know nothing."

"You have to leave for Mennefer?"

Kenamun had just arrived to join them.

Siamun nodded. "Yes, and as quickly as possible, too."

"Take one of my boats," Kenamun offered. "I don't need them for a while, since Meresankh is anxious not to let me out of her sight any time soon. But we'd better hurry; I have yet to put a decent crew together for you."

Siamun smiled gratefully. "Thanks a lot," he said with an affectionate clap on Kenamun's shoulder. Then he turned to face the two women.

"Don't be afraid," he told them. "There are countless possible reasons for this summons. I'll let you know all about it as soon as I can. May the gods be with you."

Picking up his warm cloak from one of the chairs he whirled round to hurry after his brother-in-law.

"And may they also be with you!" Meresankh called out.

While she was watching the two retreating figures, an uneasy feeling began to get hold of her. Of course, Siamun was right, there were plenty of possible reasons. If only it wasn't the one Meresankh feared the most.

****

The vizier received Siamun in the antechamber to the royal audience hall. Clearly, this room was meant to impress the visitor, as could be derived from the particularly lavish decoration. In addition to the sunlight that poured in through the high-set guttered windows it was illuminated by several torches, the halo of which enhanced the brilliance of the gilded surfaces even further.

Apart from Nebamun, only the Great Royal Wife and a royal scribe were present. Tuya eyed her son-in-law appraisingly, but Siamun didn't pay her much heed. He had greeted her with due respect, and that was in his opinion quite enough.

Both the vizier and the queen were sitting enthroned on elaborate cushioned chairs, whereas the scribe had assumed the cross-legged position typical of that profession. For lack of anything in the way of a seat, Siamun was left standing in the centre of the room. Planting his feet firmly on the ground and clasping his hands behind his back, he returned Nebamun's penetrating stare unblinkingly.

"Overseer of the royal building works in the sacred land and the royal granaries in Mennefer," the vizier boomed. "I have summoned you for a very urgent reason indeed. It may have already come to your attention that the Two Lands are under threat from the dwellers in the great western desert. In fact, the situation is so grave that pharaoh, may he live, be prosperous and healthy, has dispatched one of his own divisions to fight those vile rebels back. In addition, His Highness the crown prince has recently left Mennefer at the head of the remaining troops in order to join the division of Ptah and annihilate the wretched Temehiu. Now" –he made a dramatic pause before he continued with an air of even greater importance- "being the overseer of the royal granaries, your task will be to provide our troops with enough grain and fresh water to last them through this campaign."

Siamun nodded curtly. He had indeed heard of the atrocities in the region of the western delta, although admittedly he had been unaware of the true extent of the threat they were facing. "But you should know," Nebamun went on with a gleeful half-smile surrounding his thin lips, "that the dispatch of the goods alone does not suffice. In order to fulfil your duty, you have also to make sure that the delivery arrives safely at its destination. This means that you must either supervise the transport in person, or you can send someone along who owns your trust. Whichever way you choose, the successful outcome of this operation will be entirely your responsibility. You may be granted a number of soldiers for protection, since the western desert is currently an extremely unsafe place to be. The warriors of those wretched Temehiu have set their wicked minds on attacking everyone who comes along, foremost of all merchants and caravans that look promising to them."

Siamun considered briefly, deliberately ignoring the whispered exchanges between the vizier and the Great Royal Wife and the expectant glances they shot at him. He was determined not to do them the favour of showing any signs of distress, if that was what they hoped to see.

"Where exactly are the troops going to be stationed?" he asked in a matter-of-fact way.

"In one or more of our forts along the edge of the western desert," came the vague reply. "It all depends on how successfully our men will be able to fight their way through. However, it is to be expected that in the long run every fort is going to be manned with a certain number of soldiers, whereas the main part of the division is meant to return eventually to the northern territories in order to join His Majesty's troops."

This didn't sound very encouraging. Having to provide several forts which were probably scattered across great distances with goods wasn't an easy task at all. It meant a long and arduous journey through enemy territory. Then a sudden thought struck him. As far as he was aware, all the forts were situated close to the coastline. Siamun decided to give it a try. "Will I have ships at my disposal?" he asked.

"No," Nebamun replied curtly, a distinct note of satisfaction in his voice. "Owing to the dreadful state of affairs we are currently in, we cannot spare any seaworthy boats. You can have as many donkeys and carts as you deem necessary, but the sea route is not an option. You'll have to travel overland."

"How many troops have to be provided, and for how long?" Siamun inquired, quite undeterred.

"We are looking at five thousand men belonging to the division of Ptah along with the troops led by the crown prince numbering roughly one thousand. As to the period of time which is by no means certain, you should reckon with at least two to three months."

Siamun made a slight bow. "Thank you, venerable vizier, this is all the information I need. I assure you that I will fulfil this task to everyone's complete satisfaction."

"I sincerely hope that you will live up to your promise," Nebamun snarled, eyes narrowing. "The lives of thousands of men depend on you. If the supplies don't reach them in time, they will all die of starvation. In this hostile and barren place they have no allies whatsoever to rely on. Should you fail them, your splendid career might suffer a great deal, as I surely needn't tell you."

With a smug look on his face, he dismissed Siamun who was only too glad to take his leave.

Upon exiting the chamber, Siamun nearly collided with a man whom he recognized to be Tiya, the treasurer who had once hoped for the hand of the princess. The sour look on Tiya's face almost made him laugh.

Clearly, I don't have many friends here in the palace, Siamun thought when he made his way to the great entrance gate. But all that counted now was the task at hand. And he had already a vague idea who might be able to help him with tackling it.

****

"Of course you can have some of my ships," Kenamun said. "That's the least I can do for you. How many do you need?"
"Two should be enough, I reckon" Siamun replied. "And not even those was that mean vizier prepared to give me."
Kenamun looked at him thoughtfully. "It's quite impossible that he couldn't spare a few ships. I assume he just wanted to chase you across the desert. Nebamun seems to have set his mind on making things as difficult for you as possible."
"You can say that again," Siamun growled. "And of course he hopes to make me fail at my task that way. He surely didn't anticipate that I would be able to get hold of a few ships myself."
"You mustn't forget, however, that the sea route can be dangerous, too," Kenamun pointed out. "Pirates are known to cruise the waters of the Great Green in large numbers, especially close to the coastline. Therefore I would advise you to take at least one additional ship with you. Apart from that, it is vital to have large supplies of water on board, since those wretched pirates often employ burning arrows when they attack."
"Do you really have to go yourself?"
Meritamun, who had been listening in silence, didn't look

happy at all.

"Yes, mother," Siamun replied gently. "It's not only that I am personally responsible for the positive outcome of this operation. I also hope to meet Panakht."

He watched her anxiously. The struggle within her was mirrored on her face. Meritamun must be torn between the hope of receiving news of her son and the fear for Siamun's safety. Eventually she nodded tentatively.

"How can you be sure that Panakht is among the soldiers you're going to see?" Kenamun asked doubtfully.

"Nebamun was kind enough to tell me that the division in question is that of Ptah, the same Panakht belongs to. Apparently it has been dispatched as a whole, so the chances are high that I might indeed get to see him. I happen to know his commander, so finding him out shouldn't be that difficult." Siamun was careful not to mention the remote possibility that Panakht might have been killed or injured in one of the previous battles. He knew that was exactly what worried everyone most. There had been no sign of life from Panakht so far; but then, knowing him as he did, Siamun didn't reckon he would care to send a message home, anyway.

"When do you intend to leave?" Kenamun inquired.

"In two days' time. I should be able to gather the supplies and all I need by then."

"All right," Kenamun said with a smile. "The day after tomorrow you'll find three seaworthy ships along with their experienced and battle-tried crews waiting for you in the harbour."

Siamun gave him a friendly poke. "Thank you, Kenamun. I knew I could rely on you.

****

There was something soothing about the gentle up-and-down movement of the prow, which even after days hadn't ceased to fascinate Siamun. He was relieved that so far the sea hadn't been rough or even chopped as was usually the case at this time of year, according to the captain. The second month of Peret had just begun, and the air was crisp and chilly, as was to be expected along the northern coastline. But the cold didn't bother Siamun who, like his companions, had had the sense to wrap up warm.

His companions were the ship's crew that had been hastily rounded up by Kenamun and the handful of guards provided by Nebamun. The greater part of the crew consisted of foreigners hailing from the cities dotting the eastern coast, mainly Tyre and Byblos, where Kenamun had hired them during his many voyages. There were about sixty men in total who had been equally distributed among the three ships. Their understanding of Kemet's language was in most cases limited to the curt commands that were shouted at them, hence to his regret Siamun was unable to talk to them. Instead, he listened to the gibberish they called out to each other with great fascination, even if it meant nothing to him.

Only the captain of his boat, a man hailing from Byblos called Abu, was able to speak Siamun's language reasonably well. He was a somewhat short but sturdy fellow, good-natured and likeable, most of the time anyway. Whenever there was some sort of manoeuvre to be performed, however, Abu turned into a true demon who swept across the whole length of the deck like a sandstorm, all the while barking out commands at the top of his voice. As soon as the manoeuvre was carried out, he returned instantly to his former amiable self. Siamun's initial horror at watching these strange performances had long given way to mild amusement.

As every so often, Siamun's gaze flitted across the long row of neatly arranged sacks of grain that was interspersed with numerous large jars. The greater part of the latter was filled with fresh water, while others contained wine coming from the storage rooms of Siamun's family home. Unfortunately, the wine was meant to be consumed by the more privileged members of the army only, for there simply wasn't enough to provide every common soldier with.

Apart from these provisions, the ships were also carrying considerable numbers of weapons and several huge water troughs, the former serving defence purposes in the case of an attack, the latter being a vital necessity for putting out the fires that often accompanied said attacks. However, Siamun hoped fervently that they wouldn't have to use either.

He inadvertently smiled to himself when he remembered the dismayed expression on Nebamun's face when he had personally attended the loading of the boats. He had inspected the small fleet of robust ships rather suspiciously, apparently wondering where on earth Siamun got them from. If Nebamun was as clever as he thought himself to be, he might soon figure out that the boats belonged to Kenamun, who was known to him from earlier trade links. Siamun didn't care if he did. The only thing that really nagged his mind were his worries about Tia. He knew how hard it was for her to be on her own. With Siamun gone and her father still on campaign, Tia had no one to turn to except her unloved mother and a few childhood friends. She had told him that she intended to spend the time of his absence in their private home instead of moving back to the palace, as her mother had suggested.

Siamun let out a deep sigh. He missed his young wife dearly, and he sincerely hoped to return soon to her.

"Aren't we close to one of the forts yet?" he asked Abu, who was standing next to him leaning over the rail, whistling a merry tune.

Abu grinned roguishly. "Growing impatient, master? No worry, we'll soon be there."

Having said that, he pointed to the blurry line to their left that represented the coast.

"I'm sorry to say that I can see nothing of any interest," Siamun told him, shaking his head in disappointment.

"Really, you can't?" Abu sighed. "You landlubbers have no sharp eyes."

"That's quite true," Siamun admitted freely. "Which is exactly why I pin all my hopes on you, Abu."

Abu's grin broadened, and he nodded eagerly.

"I know this coastline like the back of my hand. The first fort is very near. Must head for the coast now."

With that he whirled round, cupped his hands around his mouth and barked so loudly at his crew that Siamun was tempted to cover his ears. A bustle of activity followed during which the great sail was struck, and soon enough the boat listed gently while it described an elegant turn until the prow pointed straight in the direction of the coastal strip. Siamun turned his head and saw the other boats following their example.

The shore which they neared with slowly diminishing speed didn't look any different compared to elsewhere. A narrow sandy beach seemed to merge with the barren desert behind it. Then, finally, Siamun was able to make out the sand-coloured walls of the fort which hardly contrasted with its surroundings. At the first glance, the rather modestly-sized structure consisted mainly of a tall enclosure wall with battlements and towers at the four corners. Siamun strained his eyes to detect any signs of life, but Abu was quicker.

"There are soldiers on towers," the captain announced casually. "They soon come here with boats."

He was right. No sooner had the ships dropped anchor, than several small rowing boats cast off the shore and came swiftly in their direction.

A little later, a number of men climbed aboard, all of whom greeted Siamun enthusiastically. Among them were two troop commanders of the division of Ptah who told him that only a small unit of five hundred men had been stationed here, while the main body of the division was advancing further west.

"Have the troops led by the crown prince already joined your men?" Siamun wanted to know. He didn't fail to notice the meaningful glance that passed between the two men.

"Indeed they have," the senior commander who had introduced himself as Ptahankh replied. "Although I'm sorry to say that it was almost too late for that."

Siamun sucked in a sharp breath. "What do you mean by that?"

"When we arrived at the agreed meeting point," Ptahankh related, "we found that the troops of the crown prince had not been waiting for us. As we were to learn later, His Highness had commanded to launch an attack on a number of enemy warriors whom his scouts had spotted earlier beyond a stretch of hills. Apparently, the crown prince considered them to be easy prey, for instead of marching across the hills he decided to pass through a narrow, drawn-out gorge without having the area searched prior to that. Unfortunately, this was exactly what the wretched Temehiu seemed to have bargained for. Unnoticed by anyone, they had quickly positioned themselves on the tops of the cliffs to either side of the gorge, with some of them awaiting our men at the far end. Once our troops were filing through, rocks and boulders were thrown down from the cliffs, while those about to exit were engaged in fierce fighting.

The better part of them, however, had become trapped inside the gorge, and there was no escape for anyone. Those who were not crushed by the rocks were showered with arrows."

"That's simply terrible," Siamun muttered. Even Abu had fallen remarkably silent.

Ptahankh nodded gravely.

"It was a good thing that we had sent out scouts to comb the area who reported back to us what was happening," he continued. "We made haste and arrived just in time to save what there was to save. Both ends of the gorge were scenes of bitter fighting. However, the vile rebels didn't stand a chance against the overwhelming power of an entire division, and those who didn't take to their heels were killed on the spot."

"How great were the losses on our side?" Siamun asked, still numbed by the horror of what he had just heard.

"Given the gravity of the situation, they stayed within limits, Ptah be praised. About a hundred were killed and as many wounded, some of them seriously. But the thought of what might have happened if we hadn't managed to arrive in time doesn't even bear thinking."

Siamun couldn't agree more. The entire unit might have been wiped out, had it not been for the division of Ptah. He struggled to comprehend how Ramses could have been so careless. Why hadn't he heeded his father's order to wait for the arrival of the support troops? Was he really that desperate to prove himself in battle?

"Amun be praised that the worst didn't happen," Siamun said eventually, and Abu nodded his agreement. "What about your future plans?"

"The main body of the division is on the move further west," Ptahankh explained. "There are two more forts which have to be manned with a number of soldiers before the rest of them will reach their final destination. All of them will have the task of patrolling the area and do away with any enemy warriors they come across."

"Do you happen to know where the unit of the troop commander Urhiye will be stationed?" Siamun asked hopefully. Ptahankh considered briefly. "As far as I know, they will be among those proceeding to the westernmost outpost."

Siamun nodded slowly. "It looks as if we still have a whole lot of work to do," he said, "so we'd better get going. Take your share of the provisions and load them onto your boats. May the gods be with you."

The men didn't think twice. Hurriedly they seized a dozen sacks of grain and as many water jars, then they were gone. The anchors were weighed and the journey continued.

As Ptahankh had already told them, they had to make two more interim stops. The army turned out to be a good way ahead, since at each of the forts they only encountered a few hundred stationary troops. With growing unease Siamun listened to the brief reports of ongoing fierce fighting, hoping fervently that Panakht would be among those who made it to their final destination.

Then the final leg of their journey began. Having left the customary trading routes behind, they hardly spotted any more ships other than their own; but whenever they did, the respective vessel was inspected very thoroughly indeed.

"Do you fear that we might come across pirates?" Siamun asked Abu on one of those rare occasions.

"It's more likely that *they* come across *us*," the captain grinned, amused at his own joke.

"So what?" Siamun returned boldly. "We are forearmed against any kind of threat, aren't we?"

To his surprise, Abu turned quite serious. "Sure, but the

weapons of the Sherdenu are very dangerous," he muttered. "They have terrible swords with straight blades which can skewer a man in the nick of time, and they wear helmets with horns."

Siamun laughed softly. "Well, I'm not afraid of either horns or swords, be they straight or curved. After all, we know how to handle our own weapons, don't we?"

Abu eyed him doubtfully. According to himself, the captain had engaged in more than one fight during his numerous voyages, and he sure looked battle-tried enough. However, it was clear from the look on his face that he didn't have such a high opinion of Siamun's martial skills. Suddenly, Siamun felt the urge to prove him wrong. Besides, he was desperate for a spot of exercise.

"Abu, are there any manoeuvres waiting to be dealt with?"

"No, master," came the surprised reply.

"Then get yourself a sword and a shield; we're starting right now."

With that Siamun strode up to one of the large chests which he knew to contain swords. He took one without hesitation, then he opened another one from which he removed a shield. When he turned round to move back to the middle of the deck, he stopped dead with a start. Abu stood facing him at the ready, armed with a strange round shield and an even stranger sword. How had he got hold of this curious equipment?

The captain grinned apologetically. "Don't be afraid, I'm not one of the Sherdenu. I took these from one who wanted to kill me."

Siamun heaved a sigh of relief, but at the same time the tension within him rose. It had been a long time since his last exercise in close combat, far too long. And even then it had only been a game. Now he had to stand up against a weapon he had never encountered before, and he almost regretted his rush decision.

But then, it was worth a try, and he certainly didn't want to back out. Determined not to make a fool of himself in front of everyone, he tightened his grip on the hilt of his curved sword and moved closer to Abu, eyeing him warily. If he could remember one thing, it was the rule never to let one's opponent out of sight, not even for the fraction of a moment. From the corner of his eye he saw how more and more men drew nearer, keen to watch the unexpected interlude. Soon, a circle of spectators had formed around the two opponents. Abu was first to raise his sword and bring it down in a flash. With a sickening crash it connected with the shield that Siamun had brought up equally fast. The blow hadn't been overly powerful; after all, the two men weren't set on killing each other. However, it had been enough to fire Siamun's enthusiasm even further. He lunged forward, aiming a sideways swipe at Abu who parried it with ease. From then on it rained blows, none too heavy or powerful to be fended off, but allowing one or the other to gain ground, only to lose it again. Soon, the metallic clanking of the connecting blades stopped bothering Siamun, and he began to enjoy himself. With the men around them spurring them on with hoots and cheers, he almost thought himself to be back in the day when he used to play-fight with Panakht.

After a while, Abu began to use the straight blade of his sword more and more in a fashion unknown to Siamun. The jabs that the captain aimed directly at his opponent's body were quick and to the point and -in a real fight- potentially lethal. While Siamun focused on dodging and parrying them as well as he could he realized that the greatest danger that emanated from this weapon –and its greatest potential for the one who held it- was exactly this kind of straight, powerful jab that couldn't be performed with the curved blades of the traditional khepesh-swords used by the people of Kemet, or at least not in the same manner. In fact, this curious weapon appeared to him rather like an oversized dagger, perfect for lethal frontal thrusts. If Siamun wanted to stand a chance, he had to adjust his own technique, and quickly at that. Again and again he aimed swipes and blows at Abu's sword in order to fend off its vicious jabs. Eventually, he succeeded in wrenching it from his opponent's hand with the help of a particularly forceful blow. The weapon fell down on the wooden planks with a muffled clattering sound.

Seeing that the fight was over, the spectators clapped their hands enthusiastically before they took themselves off.

"Well done," Abu exclaimed, pulling his sleeve across his sweaty forehead. "You are in good shape, master. And I see that you have found a way to fight against the swords of the Sherdenu. Maybe this skill will come in useful one day."

Abu couldn't possibly have anticipated how right he was.

It was in the middle of the night when Siamun woke with a start. He couldn't have been asleep for long, for he was still dead tired. Pinching his eyes with one hand, he tried hard to collect his thoughts. Hadn't there just been some sort of violent jerk? And what about all those pattering feet, the shouts and yells that slowly permeated his consciousness? Were they real, or did his mind play some dubious trick on him?

In order to find out, he would have to get up. Siamun rose with some difficulty and, in doing so, caught sight of Abu's bed. It was empty, with the blanket lying in a crumpled heap atop. Feeling decidedly uneasy, Siamun staggered towards the cabin door and opened it a crack. One look outside, and he was wide awake.

Chaos had taken over. The deck was crawling with people. Men were fighting each other with spears, swords, battle-axes and fists. In a few places, fires were burning. What on earth had happened?

Siamun only had to look at the horned helmets of the intruders, their round shields and the straight blades of their swords to know the answer: the fearsome Sherdenu had attacked them! He needed to get hold of a weapon, and quickly at that. But how? Abu was sure to have taken his own weapons with him, so there were none left in the cabin. The storage chests on deck were out of reach. Then a stroke of luck helped him out of his plight.

Only a couple of paces away from him, one of Abu's men dispatched his opponent with a well-aimed blow of his sword just now. The sword of the dying man fell from his hand and slithered across the planks right up to Siamun's feet. All he had to do was stoop down and pick it up. Wrenching the round shield from the Sherden's arm didn't prove quite as easy, though, since it was firmly fastened to his wrist and elbow with two leather strips attached to the back of the shield. Siamun undid the lashes with trembling fingers and fastened the shield to his own left forearm. Grabbing the sword tightly, he scrambled to his feet, and not a moment too soon.

The sinister figure of the attacker planted himself in front of him and tore his sword up. A precious moment passed until Siamun realized that this was his chance, then he plunged his sword deep into the man's entrails just below the edge of his shield. The Sherden let out a dreadful roar like a slaughtered animal and clutched his belly before he collapsed in an ungainly heap.

Siamun withdrew his sword and stared at the corpse in surprise. He could hardly believe how easy it had been to kill this fearsome warrior. But the battle was far from over, and for him it had only just begun.

Not far from him, he spotted two Sherdenu pushing a member

of the crew back against the rail. One of them raised his arm in preparation for the lethal thrust when Siamun jostled him sideways with all the force he could muster, hoping to yank both of them off their feet. The attacker staggered violently but managed to steady himself, now aiming his deadly weapon at Siamun instead. With a desperate blow that ripped through his arm Siamun thwarted his attack, drawing an agonized yell from his opponent; but now the other had drawn back his arm, ready to throw his spear. Siamun doubled over in a bid to dodge the deadly missile as it sailed through the air. A sharp pain in his right shoulder made him cringe, but when he heard the spear clattering to the ground some way off he realized that it could only have grazed him.

Meanwhile, the sailor to whose aid he had jumped had plunged his dagger neatly between the spear thrower's ribs, dispatching him there and then. His companion, whose forearm dangled precariously from a few remaining shreds of skin, suffered the same fate.

His chest heaving with laboured breaths, Siamun straightened up and tried to assess the situation. What he saw in the eerie glow of the fires was very confusing indeed. With all those bodies still engaged in close combat, it was hard to tell who had the upper hand, the Sherdenu with their horned bronze helmets, leather corselets and knee long kilts or Abu's men who were fighting like lions, aided by the small number of guards.

It was only now that Siamun noticed the ships of their attackers which were dimpling on the waves close by. They must have rammed their own earlier on, causing the jerk that had awakened Siamun in the first place, and subsequently enabling the pirates to cover the remaining gap with planks for easy boarding. He also saw that there was ongoing fighting on the other two ships of his fleet, too, although the pirates seemed to have directed most of their attention at Siamun's boat.

Then his gaze fell on a shape crouching next to the stacks of grain sacks. On coming closer, he recognized who it was. Abu was sitting doubled over with his arms wrapped around his body and his face screwed up in pain.

"Abu, what happened to you? Tell me!" Siamun panted, feeling his blood running cold.

By way of an answer the captain removed a blood-smeared hand from his belly. Siamun gasped in horror at the sight of the blood-drenched cloth of his robe. He ordered Abu to lie down flat on his back in order to reduce the blood flow from his wound.

"Let me be," Abu hissed between clenched teeth when Siamun made to help him. "You must take care of yourself. Watch out, there's one behind you!"

Siamun fumbled for his sword and shot up, parrying the vicious blow just in time. Then his attacker collapsed at his feet, an arrow protruding from his back.

Siamun let out a deep breath. His right shoulder hurt terribly, but he was determined not to pay it any heed. Casting wary looks around, he caught sight of two of Abu's men carrying one of the water tubs between them. Apparently they were aiming to put out the flames which were leaping up the ship's mast and threatening to set the great sail on fire. Then, as if they had a mind of their own, his eyes turned from the fire to the sails of the enemy ships.

The thought hit him so hard that it almost hurt. What if they payed those wretched Sherdenu back in kind by setting *their* boats alight? There were arrows strewn everywhere, and just over there was the bow he needed.

In a trice, he had picked up the bow along with a few arrows and hurried after the two sailors who had just reached the mast. He talked to them urgently, trying to make them understand what he planned to do, but they only gaped at him with blank expressions. Then he gestured them to put the water tub down and held one of the arrows into the fire while repeatedly jabbing his finger in the direction of the pirates' ships. Eventually, it dawned on them what he wanted them to do, and they eagerly followed his example. Soon burning arrows hissed through the air, splitting the darkness with their eerie glow and turning the sails of the enemy fleet into giant torches.

Almost instantly the fighting ceased as the Sherdenu stopped dead in their tracks, staring in disbelief and horror at their burning ships. Someone roared a command, and the attackers took to their heels, forgetting all about their opponents. They jumped up the planks, followed by a volley of arrows and spears which caused a good many of them to fall screaming into the water.

It was not until dawn that the full extent of the damage could be assessed. The wooden planks of the deck were blackened in quite a few places, as was the lower part of the mast, but fortunately this was nothing to worry about. Two of the grain sacks had been slit open, presumably by some curious pirate, which had to be stitched up. Far worse, however, was the havoc those scoundrels had wreaked among the crew. The men mourned the deaths of seven of their comrades who would have to be buried in the sand of the desert upon arrival, and many more had suffered more or less severe wounds. The bodies of fifteen Sherdenu were simply thrown overboard, since the boats of the pirates had long gone, along with the blackened remains of their sails.

"With their horns and the sun disc in between, their curious helmets remind me strongly of Hathor's headdress," Siamun told Abu when he sat next to him. "But that's about all they have in common. The Sherdenu have most certainly nothing of Hathor's beguiling charm about them."

Abu started to chuckle, then clutched instantly at his belly, grimacing with pain.

"Have mercy on me, young master," he whimpered. "Please don't make me laugh."

A thorough examination had shown that the captain had been quite lucky in the circumstances. The injury he had suffered wasn't all too deep. Only the flesh had been torn, while his entrails hadn't been affected. Thus, his chances of complete recovery were good, as long as infection didn't set in. The same was true for Siamun and everybody else who had been injured. The spear that had grazed Siamun's shoulder had torn his skin but left the bone unharmed. For lack of raw meat, which was usually put on fresh wounds to promote the healing process, the injuries were treated with honey dressings.

"Setting their sails on fire was a splendid idea," Abu said in a weak voice. "How did you think of that?"

"Actually, the thought occurred to me when I saw how our own sail nearly caught fire," Siamun explained. "Besides, every child knows that a proper fire is one of the most effective means to create a stir."

Of course, he could have told the captain the story of an entire royal fleet under attack he had heard not long ago, in which fire had also played an important part. But now was not the time for lengthy explanations.

Eventually, the anchors were weighted again and the ships set course for their final destination, pharaoh's westernmost outpost, where thousands of troops were looking forward longingly to seeing them.

****

"You came at just the right time, I can tell you." Panakht sighed contentedly while he gently rubbed his stomach. "Our provisions were as good as gone," he went on, "and there is hardly anything worth hunting to be found in this desolate place. Even the fish we speared in the shallows were about as tasty as crocodile dung."

At seeing his disgusted face, Siamun gave a hearty laugh. Abu, who was sprawling on the camp bed next to him, did likewise, only to groan miserably soon after.

"If you want to do old Abu a favour, don't crack any more jokes," Siamun advised his friend.

"I'll try my best," Panakht replied airily, "although it's going to be hard, now that I'm finally back in the mood for a few jests. Besides, we have all had our fair share of scratches, as far as I can tell."

Siamun nodded. "Sure, only that Abu's scratch goes far deeper than mine or the one on your cheek, which doesn't even hamper your good looks. Quite on the contrary, I daresay that from now on you'll be exposed to an even greater female onslaught, if this is at all possible."

"Oh, I have to admit that I'm not quite as hot-blooded anymore as I used to be," Panakht said modestly. "I guess that's because I'm growing old."

Siamun stopped himself from laughing just in time. He didn't want to infect Abu again.

"If you feel so old already, why don't you start to think of marriage?" he suggested in a matter-of-fact voice.

Panakht raised his eyebrows meaningfully. "You're really going about it well, but you won't get me that easily. After all, not everyone goes and marries a princess just like that."

"She doesn't have to be a princess," Siamun objected, slightly irritated. "There are hundreds of nice, decent girls out there who-"

"One of whom *you* ought to have married," Panakht interrupted rather rudely. "In fact, this would have been the most sensible thing for you to do, all the more so, since you-"

"Quiet," Siamun hissed sharply, jerking his head in Abu's direction. The captain had closed his eyes and seemed to have dozed off, but he couldn't be entirely sure.

Just then, two men entered the room that was one of several situated in a single-storey building that accommodated troop commanders and generals. As a matter of course, the largest and most comfortably equipped room served the crown prince and his immediate entourage as temporary abode. The common soldiers, however, had to spend night and day out in the open, with only their clothes and a blanket protecting them from the cold of the night.

Siamun instantly recognized one of the new arrivals. It was the troop commander and Panakht's friend Urhiye, whose high status entitled him to have his own room. Urhiye walked swiftly up to Siamun and greeted him like an old friend. Then he waved around the flat loaves of freshly baked bread he had brought with him.

"Now, doesn't that smell tempting?" he asked with a broad grin on his handsome face. "Can you do with some more, or have you given up already?"

Panakht just groaned and pointed at the remains of a meal on the table in front of him. He and Siamun had shared several loaves with honey, dried fruit and rather stale, but nutritious beer.

"Thank you," Siamun said more politely, "but we can't get

anything down at the moment. Except, perhaps, for a little wine, that is."

"Do you really mean to say you brought wine with you?" Panakht's joyful exclamation woke Abu who tried to sit up but fell back immediately, wincing.

"Slowly, my friend," Urhiye told him. "Take it easy. You'll have to wait some more until you'll be able to do that king of exercise again."

Abu grinned sheepishly. "Thank you for letting me stay here with you."

"Don't mention it," the young troop commander said with an airy wave. "That's the least I can do for you. But now, if you allow me, I'm going to enjoy some of this delicious stuff. By the way," he added, pointing at his companion, "this is my colleague, troop commander Iny."

Iny, a middle-aged man of rather stocky build who had been following their exchange in silence, offered them a friendly nod before he joined Urhiye at the table.

In the meantime, Siamun busied himself with one of the wine jars. He broke the string and removed the mud clod that had tightly sealed its mouth. To the acclaim of everyone present he poured the deep red liquid into a number of cups, which he then presented to his companions. When he made a move to assist Abu with drinking, the captain rejected his help emphatically.

"A good cup of wine is always worth some pain," he explained as he rolled over on his side and reached for the cup.

"Wine from the previous year, I'd say," Panakht announced, smacking his lips. "And most likely from our own vineyards."

"That wasn't hard to tell," Siamun laughed. "Where else could it come from?"

"Well, maybe the honourable vizier was so kind to supply us from his own stock," Panakht suggested with a roguish grin.

"Nebamun?" Siamun scoffed. "That old miser didn't even let me have a single boat, although I know full well that there were quite a few lying idly in the harbour. But no, he wanted to chase me across the desert along with a pack of donkeys. It's just as well that Kenamun helped me out."

Siamun would have loved to say more, but with all the other men around he couldn't very well do this. He had yet to inform Panakht of Satet's death, and Siamun was at a loss when and how to break this terrible news to him.

"It's a good thing he did," Urhiye said between mouthfuls, "or else you would hardly have made it here. Apart from the fact that the terrain is hostile and difficult to cross, the Temehiu would soon have made short work of you. Although I have to admit that the sea route isn't entirely void of danger, either, as you have seen yourself."

Abu was first to break the ensuing silence.

"On my voyages I got mixed up into many a fight," the captain said slowly, "but this one was different because it was the first time that I have seen the fearsome Sherdenu scampering off like rabbits."

Urhiye looked up from his plate in surprise. "Really? How has that come about?"

"This young man here has not only fought like a lion," Abu explained with plain admiration in his voice, "but he also proved to be very inventive. He had the glorious idea to set the enemy ships on fire, so they had no other choice than retreat to save their own skin."

Both Iny and Urhiye looked at Siamun with wide eyes.

"That does sound interesting," the latter said. "Why don't you tell me all about it?"

Now Siamun took over and described the course of the attack in every detail. The men listened with rapt attention.

"Marvellous," Panakht exclaimed when he had finished. "We

ought to remember that; it might come in useful someday, who knows? And to think that all this happened to you only last night, of all times."

"Indeed, we had almost imagined ourselves to be safely at the end of our journey," Siamun said gravely. "However, it was a stroke of luck that I had a good mock fight with old Abu just the previous day. It might not have been enough to turn me into an excellent warrior, but I believe it did help me by strengthening my courage. I assume, though, that all this was nothing compared to the ordeal you went through."

He didn't fail to notice the meaningful glances that passed between the three men.

"You may be right at that," Panakht muttered, lowering his eyes.

Nodding slowly, Urhiye wiped his hands on a damp cloth.

"The Temehiu are very fierce fighters," he said when he had finished, "and their way of fighting is by no means as unsystematic as one might think. This was the most important lesson we learned from the near-disaster in that ravine. I am absolutely convinced that the Temehiu had chosen very carefully to position themselves beyond that stretch of hills. They had noticed the scouts the prince had sent out, and they hoped that the troops would take the quickest and easiest route through the only gorge. Amunemhat, the second commander in charge, advised Ramses against it, but the prince didn't listen to his warnings. I believe he just didn't want to miss what he took for a golden opportunity to gain the glory of a quick victory. Even the fact that his scouts returned unscathed although -according to their own account- they had been well and truly spotted by the enemy didn't make him suspicious. Normally, it would have been in the best interest of the Temehiu to do away with the scouts to keep their own whereabouts secret, but they were up to something else. They wanted the scouts to return and report back what they had found out. This was all part of their devious plan, and Ramses thoroughly fell for it."

He fell silent, and for a few moments no-one spoke while probably everyone's thoughts lingered on the crown prince's gross misjudgement and its disastrous consequences.

"I suppose it's just too much to expect from a fifteen-year-old to assess such a situation correctly," Iny remarked eventually.

"Of course it is, but this should have prompted him all the more to listen to the advice of an experienced commander like Amunemhat," Panakht pointed out.

Urhiye nodded approvingly. "Quite right, and his foremost duty would have been to heed his royal father's command and wait for the arrival of our troops. His Majesty will not be pleased at all by this blatant abuse of his trust, nor will he approve of the way Ramses rid himself of his second in command by dumping him at the first fort so that he had no opportunity to take part in the further advance. It's a good thing that Djedi, the supreme commander of our division, is a man of great intransigence as well as responsibility. Ever since we joined forces with the crown prince, Ramses hasn't dared to challenge his orders."

Siamun listened in silence, feeling no need to comment on Ramses' capabilities or lack thereof. Instead, another intriguing thought occurred to him.

"How is His Majesty getting along in the face of the strain of his campaign? I have heard that his health is quite poor lately."

"What exactly have you heard, and who gave you this information?" Urhiye asked a trifle too quickly.

Somewhat taken aback by the inquisitive tone of his voice, Siamun decided to take the edge off his remark.

"I think I heard one of my fellow architects mention certain problems," he said with a casual shrug of his shoulders, "but he may have been mistaken after all."

"He most certainly was," the troop commander insisted, eyeing Siamun warily. "I can confirm that pharaoh was in good shape all the time until we parted with the army, and I trust that he still is, because otherwise the campaign would have been cut short. But this is not the case. According to the latest reports, His Majesty's troops have successfully conquered the last remaining sea port of Simyra, and are now advancing on Amurru."

"And that's exactly why the crown prince wants his mission over and done with as soon as possible, so that he can turn his attention to more exciting matters," Panakht mumbled. "May His Majesty be given a long life, since I rather wouldn't want to see Ramses on the throne."

Siamun noticed with surprise how Urhiye's eyes narrowed as if in deprecation as he fastened them on Panakht. Didn't he approve of his last words? Did he secretly support the crown prince despite all his criticism?

No sooner had Siamun started to ponder this thought than he dismissed it. He was probably reading too much into something that hadn't been more than a fleeting signal, or he might have been mistaken entirely. As every so often, he must have been carried away by his vivid imagination.

From then on the conversation was mainly about fighting and battle. Each one of Siamun's companions boasted about his feats, be they real or made up, and praised the bravery of his comrades. Particularly Panakht seemed to be in his element.

I was right after all, Siamun couldn't help thinking. *Panakht was born to be a soldier.*

But he wouldn't have liked to swap places with him.

A little later, Urhiye and Iny left the room to look after the soldiers outside. Being troop commanders, it was their duty to ensure the well-being of their men, listen to complaints and settle disputes, while incidents of a more serious nature would have to be reported to the supreme commander of the respective division.

Once they were gone, Siamun watched Panakht's slumped figure thoughtfully. His friend had probably had too much wine, as had Abu, who looked as if he was fast asleep, snoring softly.

"I'm deeply grateful that you have come all the way here in person," Panakht said slowly, raising his head to look at Siamun. "I appreciate it all the more, since you didn't have to do it. You could have stayed behind and sent someone else along in your stead. But you spared no pains or efforts to come and see me, right?"

"Don't mention it," Siamun said warmly. "My efforts have already been rewarded by seeing you alive and well. However, there is something" –he hesitated, groping for the right words to say- "something really terrible I have to tell you."

Panakht's blood-shot eyes widened. "Why so serious? Has anything happened to mother?"

Siamun shook his head while he drew a deep breath. "It's Satet. I'm afraid to say that she has gone to the West."

"Are you mad?" Panakht burst out. "This sure can't be!"

Siamun cast a wary glance at Abu, but fortunately the injured captain went on with his soft snoring. Then he quickly filled Panakht in on all that had happened since the day they had parted in Waset, omitting neither his troubles with the bribed overseer of security forces nor his suspicion against Nebamun.

"I had a bad feeling about Satet, too," Panakht said in a shaky voice when he had ended. "But I'd never have believed that it would come to this."

Then he turned away and started to cry for Satet, his beautiful, proud foster sister. Siamun could do nothing but watch in silence.

"That vile, mangy jackal of a vizier," Panakht exclaimed all of a sudden, clenching his fists. "If I ever get my hands on him, I'm going to skin him alive before I kill him! Then he shall see what good all his power and wealth can do for him!"

Siamun put a soothing hand on his arm. "Forget Nebamun for now," he said quietly. "There is something else. Something I haven't told anybody yet."

With a heavy heart he began to speak of his last encounter with Satet, the grave insult he had hurled at her and how he had been denied the opportunity to apologize.

The ensuing silence seemed to stretch out endlessly. Siamun started to wonder whether Panakht had been listening at all when his friend finally spoke.

"These things happen, and there's nothing you can do about it," Panakht said, resignation

ringing in his voice. "How often have I hurled insults at you when I was angry, regretting whatever I had said soon after. Thankfully I was lucky enough to be able to apologize each time. My heart goes out to you, but I can't help you apart from telling you that you should stop heaping reproaches on yourself. You did well to admonish Satet for her despicable doings, and I understand that your spiteful remark just slipped out somehow. Nobody can blame you for that. You'll just have to live with it."

"But I don't know how," Siamun replied in a strained voice. "I often think that things might have turned out quite different if I hadn't spoken those cursed words. Maybe they affected Satet so deeply that she cared for nothing anymore, turning her into an easy prey for that scoundrel Nebamun."

Panakht shook his head vigorously. "I said stop blaming yourself! Every human being decides his own fate, at least to a certain degree. What goes beyond one's sphere of influence lies in the hands of the gods. Satet was no child. She was a grown woman, fully responsible for her own deeds, who preferred to do whatever she felt like. And she knew full well that her doings were not only reprehensible, but also dangerous. Nobody had the power to change her, not me, not you and not anybody else, for that matter."

Siamun sat in silence as he let Panakht's words sink in. Of course, the truth had been there all along, somewhere at the back of his mind, but it was only due to the blessing of someone else's reassurance that he allowed his guilty feelings to subside, though they may never vanish entirely. Heaving a sigh of relief, he moved closer to his friend, and side by side they both wept for their lost sister one last time.

Meanwhile, darkness had fallen. They didn't know which hour it was, and they didn't care either. Tired and worn out as they were, they flung themselves on their camp beds and drifted off almost immediately.

It was in the dead of night when Siamun suddenly awoke. Opening his eyelids a crack, he realized that the room wasn't shrouded in darkness anymore. Searching for the source of the mild glow that illuminated the better part of it he soon came across a single oil lamp on the table. He also saw that someone was sitting at the table. Surely this had to be Panakht who was sitting bent over on a chair, his head buried in his arms that were resting on the table.

What he saw struck Siamun as odd. What was Panakht doing there? Why wasn't he asleep? Siamun remembered them both having gone to bed at the same time. Curiously, he raised his head ever so slightly and glanced around. Abu was there, fast asleep, but there was no trace of either Urhiye or Iny. Their beds looked as if they hadn't been slept in at all.

But the troop commanders' absence didn't worry him half as much as Panakht's deplorable state did. By now Siamun was wide awake and rose silently. Panakht didn't seem to notice his soft footfall as he walked up to him and responded with a start when Siamun gently touched his shoulder.
"Panakht, what's wrong with you?"
The glassy stare of Panakht's bloodshot eyes confirmed what Siamun had already suspected: he was totally drunk.
"You wanna know what's wrong?" Panakht mumbled with some difficulty. "I'm an utter failure, and I'm sick of everything, that's what's wrong."
Siamun dropped heavily onto the nearest chair. He already had a faint notion of the nature of the problem, but if he wanted to help Panakht out of this mess, he would have to make him talk.
"Was it all that fighting that upset you so much?" he asked tentatively.
Panakht reached for a nearby cup and drank, apparently oblivious of Siamun's question. Then he wrapped his hands around it as if for comfort and stared straight ahead. It wasn't until Siamun had repeated his words that he finally responded.
"Fighting?" Panakht spat in disgust. "That was no fighting. Carnage would be a far more fitting word. It was just-"
His voice faltered, and he hastily drained his cup.
Siamun thought desperately of the right thing to say, but before he could make another attempt Panakht turned to him and opened his mouth to speak. The reek of wine on his breath almost made Siamun back away.
"You know, it wasn't all that bad at first," Panakht said with a thick tongue, yet remarkably fluently, given the state he was in. "On our way to the northern coast we had an early encounter with a bunch of nomads from the tribe of the Shasu. They were no match for us. Then we reached the first sea port, a town named Upi, whose inhabitants surrendered without a fight.

They were probably glad to get rid of the Hittite dominion. On we went towards Sidon, Tyre and Byblos. There was some fighting going on, but not a great deal. Then we were dispatched to the west in order to drive the wretched Temehiu back. The march was really gruelling, but we were in high spirits. Thought we could easily wipe a few savages off the face of the earth, yet the truth was far from it. As you know, we first encountered them in that cursed ravine. It was just sickening. They had plunged boulders of all sizes down on our men, and as a result the ground was drenched with blood and littered with properly messed up bodies. Heads were smashed to a pulp and limbs torn off or wrenched out of their sockets. Just remembering all this makes me want to throw up. After our initial victory more battles followed. Again and again, Temehiu in their hundreds and probably even thousands formed up to fight us. We charioteers had the task of racing towards the enemy and breaching the front line by dashing straight into it. I don't know how many bodies have been crushed beneath my wheels or the hooves of my horses. I have sensed them, though, and I have seen some of them. Rolling across soft bodies and crushing them in the process is just vile, I can tell you. I got regularly sick. To tell the truth, I lost count of the times that I puked right across my own feet."

Panakht broke off and started to retch. Siamun grabbed the next available jar, hoping that it was empty, and shoved it into Panakht's hand, and not a moment too soon. While Panakht was busy throwing up, Siamun snatched his cup from him and went in search of some water. Having opened one of the water skins that usually accompanied troops on their marches and filled the cup with its contents, he returned to Panakht and offered him a drink.

"Now I can finally understand why my father did what he did, for I am just as cowardly as he was," Panakht said bitterly once he had finished.

"How can you say that?" Siamun cried, outraged at Panakht's allusion to the tragic demise of his father, the general and royal fan-bearer Nakht-Min, King Tutankhamun's cousin. "Nobody should be branded a coward only because he is deeply affected by such atrocities. Quite on the contrary, in my opinion someone who doesn't mind these things is a savage brute and hardly better than an animal. Besides, I'm sure you are by far not the only one who suffers."

"There's no-one who is as squeamish as me," Panakht insisted obstinately.

"How do you know?" Siamun objected heatedly. "Of course, nobody wants to admit it, because just like you everybody feels the need to put on a brave face. Panakht," he said in a tone of voice that was as soothing as it was urgent, "you don't have to carry on if you don't want to. No-one can force you to be a soldier. And you are neither a failure nor a coward if you quit the army. Come with me and find yourself something else to do that suits you better."

Panakht raised his head to look at him, but the glimmer of hope in his eyes vanished as soon as it had lit up.

"What sort of occupation can possibly be suitable for me?" he asked in a tired voice.

"For someone like you the possibilities are endless," Siamun said eagerly. "You can read and write, you are educated and bright. You could start out as an ordinary scribe and work your way through the ranks to become someone of truly high standing, for example a royal scribe or an overseer of estates. Or you could-"

"Stop bothering," Panakht said curtly.

Siamun looked at him with utter bewilderment. "But why?" He wondered if his friend's mind was perhaps still clouded with the effects of his heavy drinking after all. But when

Panakht fastened his gaze on him, it wasn't glassy anymore, and when he spoke he appeared to be sober enough.

"I told you not to bother because you should know as well as I do that these things aren't for me. I'm not meant to sit around in offices and mess about with protocols and lists that are as long as one's arm, if not longer."

"Please, just give it a try," Siamun urged.

But to his great disappointment Panakht shook his head despondently.

"No, my friend, this doesn't work out. I'm not like you. I'm different. I need to be out and about, I crave exercise and the excitement of battle. Actually I do love my life as a soldier; it's only the nasty bits that cause me trouble."

"*Only?*" Siamun scoffed a trifle too loudly. "A few moments ago you were absolutely shattered!"

"So what?" Panakht shot back with an off-hand shrug of his shoulders. "Sooner or later I'll somehow manage to get myself used to it."

Siamun stared at him incredulously. He felt sure that Panakht didn't really mean what he said, that he kept the pretence up only because he felt compelled to do so. He was at a loss, didn't know how to help his friend get out of his plight. Where on earth was Urhiye? The troop commander appeared to be quite close to Panakht, so maybe he could straighten things out.

All of a sudden, a very different thought invaded Siamun's mind. He remembered that there had been something he had wanted to ask Panakht all along. With Panakht's mind still clouded with the effects of his excessive drinking, the opportunity he had been waiting for seemed to have arrived. He had heard it said that the drunk always tell the truth. Before he spoke, he strained his ears and listened carefully for footsteps on the other side of the door, but apart from Abu's soft snores there was nothing to be heard. They were safe for the moment.

"Panakht, I need to ask you something," Siamun said in an urgent whisper.

"Hm?"

"Have you ever mentioned anything regarding my parentage in Urhiye's presence, or anybody else's for that matter?"

It took Panakht a few moments to grasp the meaning of this question, but when he did he reacted with utter outrage.

"What?" he cried. "Are you mad? Of course I haven't! Where did you get this ridiculous idea from?"

Siamun was not deterred. He had to be sure.

"What about an accidental slip of your tongue that might have given my father's identity away?" he inquired.

"Wrong again," Panakht replied, irritation tinging his voice. "Now would you please care to tell me why you're asking me all this?"

Siamun hesitated, not knowing whether to speak of the unpleasant thoughts that kept nagging him ever since pharaoh's right to rule had been publicly called into question.

"If you're still so afraid of being found out," Panakht said suddenly, "then I don't understand how you could go and make yourself at home right in the middle of a nest of snakes."

"By that you mean my marriage with Tia, I take it," Siamun returned somewhat sharply.

"Exactly. What on earth did you think you were doing, if you thought anything at all?"

"To put it short," Siamun explained, struggling to keep his calm, "we fell in love with each other and decided to marry. That's all that there is to it."

"You forgot to mention that pharaoh wishes you the best of luck, too," Panakht jeered. "Until he finds out who you really are, that is."

"He won't find out," Siamun said firmly.

Panakht cast a pitiful glance at him while he slowly shook his head.

"How can you be so sure? Just now, you suspected *me* of having given your secret away. But what about *you*? Will you be able to keep your true identity from your wife for all time? What if the wrong thing just slips off your tongue, or the princess starts to poke around in your past, just for the fun of it? And if she happens to stumble upon something revealing, won't she run to her royal father straight away and tell him all about it? And do you really believe" –he paused to lean closer to Siamun until their faces almost touched- "that pharaoh will spare you? You, the only person with a claim to the throne that is stronger than his own?"

Siamun preferred to remain silent.

"He's going to kill you," Panakht said in a hoarse whisper. "Yes, that's exactly what he's going to do. And he will have to do it, even if he doesn't want to. While he is alive, you must not exist."

He let himself fall heavily against the backrest of his chair, his chest heaving with laboured breaths. All that talking seemed to have exhausted him.

Siamun ran his fingers through his short dark hair and drew a deep breath. He still didn't speak, since he felt that there was nothing he could say. Deep down he knew that Panakht was right, but he, Siamun, was determined not to let things get out of hand, if he could help it.

Just then, he heard the telling sound of approaching footsteps, and a moment later Urhiye appeared in the doorway. He stopped short when he caught sight of the two men sitting at the table.

"What, still up so late?" he greeted them.

The cheerful tone of his voice didn't sound genuine. It was quite clear that the troop commander would have preferred to find them sleeping. He seemed to be embarrassed by the fact that his late return had been noticed. Siamun assumed that he might have spent the last hours in one of the other buildings, where the more high-ranking members of the army whiled away their time with the few women who usually accompanied the troops.

But Urhiye wasn't the only one to feel uneasy. Siamun felt as if he had just been caught in the act of doing something forbidden. He hoped fervently that the commander hadn't overheard the last bit of their conversation.

Urhiye wrinkled his nose when he noticed the reek of vomit, and his eyes searched for its source. Siamun rose without a word and discarded the jug along with its smelly contents outside. When he returned, he found Urhiye sitting on the edge of his camp bed, staring thoughtfully at Panakht.

"Would you care to tell me what prompted him to get all drunk?"

Siamun, at whom the question had been addressed, dropped down on his own bed, wondering what to answer. He decided to tell the truth, even if Panakht wasn't going to like it.

Panakht shot him a furious glance, but then resigned himself to listening in silence as Siamun revealed his problems.

"You probably wouldn't believe me if I told you how many others are affected in exactly the same way," the troop commander said once Siamun had ended.

Panakht's head shot up, and he stared at his commander and friend with utter disbelief.

"What do you mean by that?"

"I mean exactly what I just said," Urhiye replied quietly. "I know that the horrors of war upset many a soldier. Commanders and even generals are no exception. However, it doesn't happen often that they admit to it, but nevertheless it's the truth. Take me, for example. I am by no means the born soldier everyone seems to take me for. In fact, I never even wanted to join the army in the first place."

A smile appeared on his lips when he saw the incredulous stares of his companions. Panakht didn't even seem to notice that his mouth had fallen open.

"It's true," Urhiye went on without wavering. "I always had a civil career on my mind. Upon completion of my scribal training I served as a temple scribe in Mennefer's great temple of Ptah. Then, shortly after our good ruler had ascended the throne, I heard that a number of new royal scribes were wanted. Full of confidence I applied for this position straight away. But although I was fully qualified and had the support of the high priest of Ptah, I was rejected. Others were given preference over me, presumably because my Hurrian name was not deemed appropriate."

Urhiye paused and drew a deep breath, seemingly to calm himself down. Siamun hadn't failed to notice the embitterment in his voice, particularly during the latter part of his narrative.

"Take it from me," the troop commander went on. "You people of Kemet accept foreigners only when they adopt all of your customs, speak your language and change their unusual names into something that sounds more agreeable to your ears. I personally do consider Kemet to be my homeland, since it was there that I was born and grew up. I speak your language as fluently as you do, and yet I found that in many respects things proved to be more difficult for me than for others. The main reason for this is the foreign name my parents gave me, and my refusal to change it. Don't get me wrong," he said when Siamun's serious gaze met his, "but this is just the way it is. Anyway, having been refused a decent administrative position on several occasions, I decided to join the army. Surprisingly enough, His Majesty doesn't seem to be averse to supplementing his troops with foreigners. Yes, Panakht, I only became a soldier because I saw no other way of making a decent career. And the same will apply to my little son, once his time has come. In the beginning, I despised warfare just as much as Panakht does, and for the same reasons. Truth be told, I still don't like it, but I have found ways not to let the horrors of war get the better of me. Now I try to keep my distance to all that happens around me, so as not to let anything get under my skin. This is the only sensible advice I can give to you, Panakht. If you don't heed it, you may not be able to carry on being a soldier."

The ensuing silence was only broken by Abu's intermittent snores. Siamun had been watching the commander intently while he spoke. The subliminal resentment that had accompanied his speech had not escaped his attention. It was quite clear that Urhiye harboured some kind of grudge against whoever he blamed for his missed opportunities. Ultimately, it was the king who granted or denied favourable positions to those who applied for them. Thus, Urhiye's grudge centred most likely on Seti himself.

While his gaze lingered on the young commander, Siamun felt himself transported back to the beer house that he had visited on the day of the oracle, along with Panakht and Urhiye. He had been wondering back then how someone who abhorred large crowds was able to enjoy himself in a place packed with people the way Urhiye had apparently done. The more he thought of it, the stronger he became convinced that Urhiye's alleged dislike of large gatherings had been nothing but a feeble excuse. What if the troop commander had served Panakht up with this lie in order to cover up the true reason for his absence from the procession? Had Urhiye had something to do that he didn't want anyone to know of? May he even have been –Siamun shuddered inwardly at the thought- that veiled man who had challenged Seti's legitimacy with his impertinent question? It would appear that Urhiye did have some sort of motive. Could his apparent resentments have driven him to defame the king in front of the divine oracle and the assembled crowd in order to take his revenge on him?

Siamun's heartbeat quickened as he pondered the likelihood of this possibility. However, tempting as it was, he had to admit that the thought was probably too far-fetched to be true. His vivid mind kept conjuring things up that probably wouldn't stand up to close scrutiny. There were certainly countless other reasonable explanations for Urhiye's behaviour, just as there were hundreds of possible candidates for the infamous role of the veiled one. And yet…

Siamun hardly knew what to think anymore. Had Urhiye indeed been the veiled perpetrator, he would expect him to be more cautious than that when it came to revealing his personal opinions. Besides, the despicable act had directly played into the crown prince's hands to whom Urhiye's grudge presumably extended, by all accounts. On the other hand, when he came to think of the troop commander's curious reaction at Panakht's criticism of Ramses, which he now felt sure he had been right about after all…

Stop all that pointless reasoning, Siamun told himself, exasperated. Even with all the latest revelations taken into account, there was probably nothing in his supposition after all. He had to see to it that he got away from here as quickly as possible. As soon as Abu was on the mend, he was going to turn his back on this desolate place. His mission was accomplished, and Panakht would have to get along with the life he had chosen somehow, if he didn't want his help. There was nothing that held Siamun back any longer.

The past hour had been so charged with emotions that Siamun found it difficult to get back to sleep, but when he did, he slept on peacefully into the late morning hours. When he woke he found the chamber empty, apart from Abu. After a refreshing wash he hurried outside, arriving just in time to hear the final part of a belligerent speech Ramses was delivering to his assembled troops. From the height of a pedestal that seemed to have been erected just for this purpose he spurred them on to annihilate yet another squad of Temehiu that had been sighted by the patrol earlier on.

As usual Ramses had assumed all the trappings of a commander of charioteers, the most striking of which was the bell-shaped tasselled bronze helmet on his head. The close-meshed corselet that enveloped his torso for protection had been made from countless tiny leather slings. A knee-length kilt and a pair of fine leather sandals completed his outfit. Siamun had to admit that despite his youth the crown prince cut an impressive figure already. There was an undeniable air of authority about him, and the manner in which he spoke made it difficult for anyone not to fall under his spell.

While Siamun was standing at the periphery of the assembly, his eyes searched for Panakht. Soon enough, he spotted Urhiye who stood close to the prince, and some way off he noticed someone waving madly. He moved in the direction of the flailing arms and was soon greeted by a jovial grin on Panakht's face.

"Have you had a long enough sleep?" he whispered merrily.

"I guess so," Siamun returned not quite as cheerfully, since he still felt the effects of the disturbed night. "How did you manage to get up that early?"

"I'm not bothered by a little lack of sleep," Panakht boasted. "I'm used to that kind of thing. Besides, we weren't woken nearly as early as usual. I guess we were not the only ones who

had a little too much last night."
They spoke as inconspicuously as possible, since anyone caught chatting or failing to pay attention in any other way might be severely reprimanded by one of the commanders.
"Who is that sour-looking fellow next to the prince?" Siamun asked softly.
"That's Djedi, the supreme commander of our division," Panakht explained just as quietly. "I can hardly blame him for wearing that morose look on his face. He sure has his hands full with continuously curbing Ramses' overeagerness in order to keep his troops from further harm; a task nobody envies him for."
Siamun's gaze fell on a row of prisoners who were crouching on the ground just behind the pedestal. Their curious pointed beards and the long curls that dangled from their temples marked them as belonging to the Temehiu. A thick rope wound around their necks and shoulders, attaching them tightly to one another. Additional fetters on their wrists and ankles forced their limbs into positions that looked very agonizing indeed. Right next to the pedestal, to the left, he could make out a second group of captives. Their hands were shackled, too, but in contrast to their unfortunate comrades they were not tied together. They wore excessive jewellery and colourful open-fronted cloaks around their shoulders which set them clearly apart from their fellow prisoners. These few must be some of the tribal leaders of the fearsome Temehiu.
Panakht, who must have followed Siamun's gaze, nudged him sharply.
"You won't believe me," he began in an excited whisper, "when I tell you that those wretched savages actually wear nothing underneath their cloaks."
"Nothing at all?" Siamun whispered back, amazed.
"Not the tiniest scrap of cloth," Panakht confirmed with hardly

suppressed outrage. "The loincloths they're wearing now were pressed on them by us, for reasons of decency."

Siamun couldn't prevent himself from imagining how the Temehiu must have looked in their original outfits. Suddenly, he felt a strong urge to laugh out loud. Panakht's round-eyed expression did one last thing, and Siamun couldn't stop himself anymore. Seeing that several heads turned immediately towards him, he quickly feigned a coughing fit.

In order to distract himself, he let his gaze roam about the courtyard in which he was standing. Along one side of the enclosure wall, make-shift furnaces had been erected which served for baking bread as well as cooking. The irresistible smell of freshly baked loaves wafted towards him, making his mouth water. The women who were not tending to the furnaces were busy grinding grain and making the flour into a soft dough which was also a vital ingredient for brewing beer. All those physically demanding activities were taking their toll on the women, as could be gleaned from their worn-out faces and slow movements. Feeding hundreds of mouths was no easy task.

Meanwhile, Ramses was bringing his speech to a close. Just then, Siamun saw how one of the captives next to him parted his lips and spat out, sending spittle flying straight at the prince's feet. In one bound one of the guards was at his side and dealt him such a forceful blow to the temple that the man was knocked unconscious.

"You see," Ramses boomed, pointing an accusing finger at the unfortunate, "the kind of vile scum we are dealing with. Finish them off whenever you come across them; do it quickly and thoroughly, so that we can turn our attention to more important matters. Together, we shall smite all our enemies. We shall vanquish the Amorites, conquer Kadesh and drive the wretched Hittites back into their goat-ridden mountains where they belong!"

Lifting his arms in a gesture of triumph, he basked in the tremendous applause that followed his passionate words. Swords and daggers were banged against shields, and an ear-deafening cacophony of yells and shouts rang out from a thousand throats.

"They already seem to have forgotten all about the ambush Ramses led them straight into," Siamun told Panakht. He had to repeat his words louder in order to make himself heard above the racket.

Panakht only shrugged his shoulders. "That's the way it is. We soldiers tend to forget very quickly, and perhaps it's a good thing we do."

The troops that had been chosen for the fight assembled in front of the gate while the rest of the crowd dispersed. Panakht was among those who were to stay behind and guard the fort. When the two friends made to go, a strong voice rang out behind them.

"Wait, Siamun!"

Surprised, Siamun turned round to see the crown prince walking briskly up to him. Ramses stopped a few paces off, his greenish eyes watching Siamun intently.

"I need to have a word with you, architect."

With a furtive smile Panakht took himself off, and Siamun followed Ramses in the direction of his waiting chariot.

"How can I assist you, Highness?" Siamun inquired, seeing Ramses' reluctance to come to the point.

"I have been told," Ramses began somewhat hesitantly, "that you have arrived with a whole fleet of ships."

"This is correct, Highness," Siamun replied. "Although I must point out that this fleet consists only of three boats which were kindly given to me by my brother-in-law."

He had put particular stress on the last words to drive the point home that he could always rely on his family.

Mouth set in a tight line, Ramses nodded briefly. He seemed to ponder how to go about whatever it was that he wanted. Siamun was surprised to see how self-conscious the young man appeared to be all of a sudden. Surely it couldn't simply be his presence that had brought this change about. What did Ramses have on his mind?

Eventually the prince spoke. "You see, I want to depart from here as soon as possible in order to reach the north-eastern coast in time for the imminent battles against the Amorites and Kadesh. Therefore I would like to make my way back to Mennefer by boat instead of marching across the desert. Unfortunately I have no ships at my disposal at all."

Interesting, Siamun thought. It was clear that Ramses implied to use one of his boats for his return journey. This surely explained his initial awkwardness. Asking someone else for a favour, and someone of inferior status at that, was not the kind of thing Ramses was used to, and doing so must have been a real effort of will for him.

"Suit yourself, Your Highness," Siamun said with a deferential bow. "It would be my pleasure to greet you on board of one my ships. However, I have to mention that I do not intend to leave until two or three days have passed in order to give my injured captain sufficient time for recovery."

"Is there no other captain to replace him?" Ramses asked, raising his eyebrows.

"Sure there is, Your Highness, but none as reliable as him. Besides, old Abu wouldn't agree at all with someone else being in command."

"So be it," Ramses said curtly while he mounted his chariot. "We will leave as soon as you see fit."

Back inside, Panakht was nearly bursting with curiosity.
"What did your precious brother-in-law want from you?" he asked, looking at Siamun expectantly.
Siamun lowered himself carefully on the edge of his bed.
"To sum it up, he needs a means of transport to bring him back to Mennefer as quickly and conveniently as possible, so that he can join pharaoh's troops in the north sooner rather than later."
Panakht's eyes widened. "Abu, did you hear that?" he called out. "On your way back you will have His Highness the crown prince on board of your ship. How do you like that?"
Abu's incomprehensible mumble was open to interpretation.
"There's no way he's going to come with us," Siamun declared firmly, wrinkling his brow.
Panakht stared at him in surprise.
"What? Why not?"
"First of all, because I can't stand him," Siamun explained. "And secondly, because I don't want to run any unnecessary risks."
"What risk?"
Catching Siamun's meaningful glance, Panakht moved closer. "Do you think he wants to sound you out?" he asked in a low voice.
"That's quite possible," Siamun replied just as quietly. "His apparent desire for a quick and easy journey might as well be an excuse. Perhaps someone has become suspicious, and the prince has been put on my trail in order to find out more. This someone could be pharaoh himself, or the vizier, or anyone else for that matter. I might be mistaken, but you never know."
"Perhaps he just wants to befriend you, now that you're related," Panakht suggested.
Siamun cast him a withering look. "What do you take me for? I'm not such a simpleton. Besides, even if this was true, I can do without his company."

"But how do you intend to go about it?" Panakht asked. "I mean, you can't very well turn him down."

"No, but I thought that maybe you could help me out."

"Me? What is it to do with me?"

Panakht's bewildered expression made Siamun laugh.

"What if you talked Urhiye and possibly Iny into persuading Ramses to extend his stay some more?" Siamun suggested. "It might well appeal to his vanity if they keep telling him how much his presence is needed for things to go smoothly. This shouldn't be all too difficult."

"I see," Panakht said slowly. "Well, given the prince's undeniable fondness of flattery this might work after all. At any rate, I'll give it a try."

Siamun smiled.

"I knew you wouldn't let me down," he said, extending his arm to seal their pact with a handshake. "We will cast off the day after tomorrow, hopefully without Ramses. Abu should be well enough by then to come through the journey. If we keep spoiling him much longer, he'll never be willing to leave. And don't forget, I'm counting on you."

Chapter Seven

Meresankh peeped cautiously through the crack of the door, still struggling to come to terms with what she saw. It surely was a most unusual picture: Pharaoh's daughter sitting by Meritamun's bedside and wiping her face gently with a damp cloth. Although the princess had been doing this for the last five days already, Meresankh hadn't quite brought herself to getting used to it.

"Everything looks alright," she whispered into Taneferet's ear when she turned away from the door. Taneferet nodded with obvious relief, and together they made their way to the kitchen in order to give their instructions for the evening meal. From there they went into the garden where their children were playing boisterously with their new leather balls.

"Mother's health seems to have improved significantly, don't you think?" Taneferet said when they had settled down at a small table.

"I do," Meresankh replied with utter conviction. "Her skin feels hardly hot anymore, and thankfully she even seems to have some of her appetite back."

Then she leaned back and drew a deep breath. "I really feared the worst when she fell ill so suddenly," she said quietly. "Else I wouldn't have sent for you and Siamun. Mother's body was burning with fever, and her talk was all confused. It was downright frightening."

Taneferet smiled wryly. "And then the princess appeared in Siamun's stead."

"I believe it was one of the greatest surprises of my life when all of a sudden Tia and her entourage stood in front of the door," Meresankh related. "I think I just gaped at her, struck dumb, until Tia explained the reason for her coming."

"Truly, it doesn't happen often that a royal princess comes to visit a sick person, and a commoner at that," Taneferet said with a wink.

Meresankh nodded. "Indeed, she has a good heart. Just think how devotedly she tended to mother, hardly leaving her side and tirelessly administering fluid to her. Tia didn't even seem to be afraid that the evil demon that had caused the sickness might enter her own body."

She stooped down to pick up the ball that had landed right by her feet and threw it back to Amunmesse who was grinning apologetically.

"Do you think," Taneferet began hesitantly, "that mother might have said things in her confusion that Tia wasn't meant to hear?"

Meresankh shrugged lightly. "In the beginning I was afraid of that, too. For this reason I tried my best not to leave Tia alone with her. But with the children around this proved impossible. Anyway, I don't believe that she could have made anything of mother's confused mumble."

She fell silent when she caught sight of Tia walking up to them.

"Meritamun has fallen asleep," the princess told them when she joined them at the table. "I believe she is getting better after all."

Meresankh smiled. "Yes, and this is all your due."

Tia laughed softly. "That's not quite true. If I hadn't been around, you would have done the same in my place. Besides, it clearly wasn't her time to go to the West yet."

"You may be right, and yet I am deeply grateful for all you did, Highness…I mean, Tia," Meresankh corrected herself. "I feel that I wouldn't have been quite up to the task if I had been on my own, and Taneferet has only just arrived."

Tia's gaze travelled down and fastened on Meresankh's belly as she spoke.

"Are you sure that you're with child again?"

"Yes. I have missed my bleeding twice already, and there is that annoying feeling of nausea all the time."

"You do look as if you have lost some weight," Taneferet said in a concerned voice. "Do you believe it's going to be a girl this time?"

"I do hope so, but I can't be sure," Meresankh replied. "I have been wishing for a nice little girl for so long. It must be wonderful to have a daughter like Tia. But with Kenamun always on the go, it took me far too long for my liking to get pregnant again."

A maidservant came along carrying a tray laden with refreshments. She filled two cups with wine, carefully pouring it through the strainer. Then she looked inquiringly at Meresankh, who slowly shook her head.

"Thank you, Merit, but I don't feel like it. I'll just have some water."

Taking slow sips from her cup, she crossed her long legs leisurely, wrinkling her nose when Taneferet offered her some of the honeyed cake.

"I know, it's usually one of my favourites, but now I can barely look at it," she said, smiling apologetically.

Then she noticed how Tia was turning her cup awkwardly around, staring at it absent-mindedly.

As if she had felt Meresankh's eyes on her, she suddenly looked up.

"I believe I never was a good daughter myself," she said in a strained voice.

"What do you mean by that?" Meresankh inquired, exchanging

quick glances with Taneferet.

"I never felt anything in the way of love or affection for my mother," Tia explained. "In fact, I always felt somehow uneasy in her company, particularly when we were on our own. But with you it's completely different. I have never met your mother before, yet I am certain that I would have been full of grief, had she indeed passed away. And although it's only a few days that I have come to know you, I feel we're as close as sisters. How can this be?"

The princess looked so forlorn the way she was sitting there, knees drawn up to her chest, that Meresankh felt a pang of pity for her.

"After all that you have told us," she replied, choosing her words carefully so as not to upset Tia even more, "you always felt neglected by your mother. You saw that she cared far more for her son than for you. Thus, it is only natural if you can't bring yourself to loving her. You really shouldn't have a guilty conscience about it."

"What about you? Does Meritamun love all of you equally?" Tia asked raptly.

"Yes," Taneferet replied, "I think I can speak for all of us when I say that she does. None of us has ever complained about feeling neglected, even though we are not all-"

She bit her tongue when Meresankh shot a warning glance at her.

"I do hope that Siamun is already on his way back," Meresankh said quickly in an attempt to steer the conversation round to a different, less awkward topic. "It seems that Kenamun can't wait to have his ships back. Has any of you noticed that he spends most of his time down at the harbour? And today is no exception."

"I don't think it's only the ships he's after," Taneferet remarked. "I rather believe he has become so used to being on the water

that he can't live without the smell of the river anymore."
Everyone laughed, and the three women went on chatting until voices could be heard from inside the house.

"This must be Kenamun," Meresankh said with a wink. "So he was finally able to tear himself away from the water."

Sure enough, her husband appeared in the doorway.

"Have you any need for a guest?" he asked cheerfully. "I brought one along with me."

He stepped aside, and Siamun entered the garden with a wide smile on his face. He stopped short when he caught sight of his wife who in her turn leapt up from her chair so hastily that it nearly toppled over. Siamun's eyes grew wide with surprise, then he was in one bound at Tia's side and pulled her close in a fond embrace.

"Kenamun is a crafty one," Siamun complained good-naturedly when they had all settled down. Even Meritamun had left her sickbed and was sitting in a cushioned armchair, tightly wrapped in a warm blanket.

"When he picked me up at the harbour," Siamun went on, "he only told me about mother's illness and that she was getting better. However, he didn't mention Tia's presence with a single word."

"It was meant as a surprise," Kenamun pointed out with an innocent smile.

"And a surprise it was," Meresankh added. "Siamun's eyes grew so big they nearly popped out of his head."

Her words triggered a burst of laughter. Siamun left his place beside his wife and knelt down next to Meritamun. Pressing her palm against his cheek he whispered "Amun be praised that you haven't succumbed to your dreadful disease, mother."

Meritamun offered him an affectionate smile.

"Indeed, I believe that I was closer to death than life for quite some time. I have been told that your wife cared for me all the time without ever tiring from it, and for that I am forever indebted to her."

She had to cough a few times, then she cleared her throat. "She did it for your sake, Siamun. Tia loves you very much. Make sure that you never make her unhappy."

Tia had bashfully lowered her eyes.

"Coming here after I received word of your terrible illness was the obvious thing to do," she said quietly.

"Maybe for you, but I'm not sure if everybody would have done the same," Meritamun insisted, looking fondly at the princess.

"I haven't told you yet about the crown prince," Siamun said, breaking the ensuing silence.

"He wished to travel back with me in order to be able to join pharaoh's troops in time. But then His Highness suddenly changed his mind, apparently because some of the troop commanders urged him to stay on."

It was clear from the tone of his voice that this turn of events had been quite convenient for him, and Meresankh could guess the reason why.

"Thank god your journey went smoothly," Taneferet said.

Owing to Meritamun's fragile health they had agreed not to mention the vicious pirate attack in her presence.

So Siamun just nodded. "Indeed, and this is particularly true for the return trip, since Abu's yell wasn't quite as loud as usual, which came as a great relief for the crew, I believe."

"He'll soon be his former irrepressible self, you'll see," Kenamun said with a smirk. "That lad is as tough as leather. But tell me, what is going to happen now? Will all the troops leave the western desert to rejoin pharaoh's army?"

"No, not all of them," Siamun explained. "For the time being, the three forts will remain manned with roughly five-hundred

troops each. Their task will be to reinforce the fortifications and patrol the surrounding area. I assume that more forts are going to be built in due course, given the seriousness of the threat that is posed by the Temehiu, and possibly other tribes as well. The remainder of troops amounts to three thousand men, all of whom are expected to march back swiftly and unite with the main body of the army, wherever it may be by then."
Kenamun gave a low whistle.
"That's quite a distance to cross, come to think of it," he said quietly.
Siamun nodded gravely. Meresankh's thoughts went to Panakht who would be among those who had to perform this enormous task.
"May the gods be with Panakht and grant him a safe return, as they did with Siamun," Meritamun muttered.
Meresankh wasn't the only one to join her prayer whole-heartedly.

****

Back at home, Siamun learned that Nebnefer had wanted to see him urgently a few days earlier. According to Wensu, his call must be about a matter of some import. Therefore Siamun decided to go and see his friend as soon as possible. Having shared a light meal with his wife, he explained his plans to her. Tia wasn't delighted at all.
"Do you really have to do this right now? We have only just arrived."
"I know," Siamun replied, "but whatever this is all about, it

seems to be urgent. Besides, I have a bad conscience already for not having visited Nebnefer for quite some time. He'll think that I'm too stuck up to care for him anymore. Don't you want to come with me?"

Tia suppressed a yawn.

"No, I'm far too tired. You go, and I'll have a rest. I can always have a game of Senet with Benret afterwards if it takes you longer. Don't worry about me."

Siamun nodded, smiling. He was glad that Tia had befriended the quiet slave girl. At first, he had been of a mind to send Benret away, so as not to upset his young wife; after all, the girl had been meant to share his bed. But Tia had seen no need for it, since she knew that her mother's ruthless plan had thoroughly failed.

"Alright," Siamun said. "Anyway, I'll do my best not to be long."

Having refreshed himself and changed his clothes, Siamun mounted his litter and let himself be carried to his former living quarters. But the doorkeeper told him that Nebnefer didn't reside there anymore. He had moved to a private house in the vicinity of the Fine District of Pharaoh.

Delighted at this unexpected information, Siamun made his way to the address the doorkeeper had given him. About half an hour later, his litter was lowered in front of a fancy house that was surrounded by a whitewashed enclosure wall.

Now I can only hope that Nebnefer is at home, Siamun thought as he walked up to the entrance.

He was lucky. A manservant answered the door, and a beaming Nebnefer appeared only a moment later to greet him warmly.

"Have you received my message?" Nebnefer asked when they had made themselves comfortable in what appeared to be the reception room of the house.

"Yes, I have," Siamun replied. "But I wanted to see you anyway. Unfortunately, there wasn't enough time left for me to do so prior to my departure."

On Nebnefer's request, he related all that had happened during his adventurous voyage as quickly as possible, since he was eager to learn what had prompted Nebnefer to contact him in the first place.

"It is quite obvious that Nebamun intended to impede the success of your mission by denying you the much needed vessels," Nebnefer mused once Siamun had finished his narrative. "And now he attempts to do the same in Abedju."

Siamun looked at him in surprise. "What do you mean by that?"

Before Nebnefer could answer, his manservant appeared with a wine jug and two cups. He skilfully poured the wine through a strainer to remove any impurities, then left with a deferential bow.

Both men drank thirstily and replaced their cups on the small table next to them.

"To get back to your question," Nebnefer began, "it seems that Nebamun has imposed drastic cuts to the provisions of the workmen in Abedju and Waset."

"What?"

Siamun had his last sip of wine go down the wrong way, and he coughed terribly.

"How can this be?" he exclaimed with utter indignation once he was again able to speak. "And how do you know?"

"I got this bit of information from a very reliable source, namely his own son," Nebnefer explained with a grave expression on his face. "Penre told me shortly after your departure. Once you were gone, his father almost immediately sent a royal herald to Abedju with the written instruction to reduce the workmen's rations of grain and vegetables by half while cutting out their daily portion of meat entirely. And exactly the same applies to the workmen of Ipet-Sut."

"That mangy jackal," Siamun growled between gritted teeth.

"Furthermore, Nebamun has restricted the delivery of tools and all kinds of materials including mortar and ropes," Nebnefer continued. "I reckon that by now there is a shortage of pretty much everything. The vizier justifies these austerity measures by claiming that due to the war on two fronts there are not enough provisions left."

"Do you happen to know if works have come to a stop already?" Siamun asked raptly.

Nebnefer shrugged. "Not yet, according to the latest reports. But it won't take long for this to happen if things don't change quickly."

Siamun forced himself to take a few deep breaths. This was indeed bad news, worse than he could ever have imagined.

"I would have loved to inform you earlier, but you weren't available," Nebnefer added.

"Sure, and that's the way it was meant to be," Siamun hissed furiously. "It looks very much as if Nebamun had planned it all well in advance and only waited until he got me safely out of the way to set to work. He just wants me to fail. He knows full well how precious little time I have to complete the core of the temple, so he grabbed the opportunity to impede the progress of works, hoping them to fall behind schedule and rendering completion on time impossible. At any rate, I am grateful for your concern, Nebnefer. If it weren't for you, god knows when I would have come to know of all this."

"Don't mention it," his friend said warmly. "In fact, I in my turn owe my knowledge to Penre. Unlike his father, he has his heart in the right place."

Siamun rose from his chair. "My dear friend, I thank you for your hospitality, but I have to go now."

"Why the hurry?" Nebnefer asked in surprise.

"I have to see Nebamun and tell him to undo his so-called austerity measures," he said grimly.

"You can do this once you have eaten with us."
"Eat? Thanks for the offer, but I'm sure I wouldn't get anything down at the moment."
Smiling mysteriously, Nebnefer rose too.
"This would be a splendid opportunity to introduce you to Naunakht," he said.
"Naunakht?" Siamun echoed, puzzled. "Who is this?"
"My wife," Nebnefer explained, beaming. "She is Hatiai's sister. That's how I came to know her. We married three months ago."
"I'm delighted to hear that," Siamun said with a friendly slap on his shoulder. "I should have known when I learned of your moving home. This changes everything, of course. I'll stay on to meet her. By the way, congratulations, if somewhat belated."
Nebnefer grinned amiably. "Thank you. And the same for you. Now wait here while I go and instruct the cook."
Siamun sat down again and used the remaining time to have a good look around. The reception room wasn't very spacious, but in terms of decoration it was in no way inferior to those of larger mansions. Its two slender papyrus bud columns were beautifully painted, and the decoration of the floor tiles imitated a watery landscape complete with all sorts of wildlife. Clattering sounds came from the kitchen next door. Soon, the delicious smells of roast meat and cooked vegetables filled the air, causing Siamun's stomach to rumble. It was a good thing that Nebnefer wasn't there to hear.
After a short while Siamun was asked into the dining room where he was greeted by the lady of the house. Naunakht was a pretty girl with a slender figure who, unlike many other young wives, hadn't been lavish with either make-up or perfume, as Siamun noted with contentment. The ensuing conversation proved her to be witty and sensible, and Siamun complimented Nebnefer on the excellent choice he had made.

After the meal Siamun took his leave. He had a strenuous task before him.

****

In the late morning hours of the following day Siamun stood once more in the antechamber to the royal audience hall and waited impatiently for Nebamun to appear. The great man had been unavailable the previous day, so Siamun had postponed his call and used the time to make a few inquiries.
Eventually, the door was flung open and Nebamun made his entrance followed by a small retinue of men, among them the fat treasurer Hormin whom Siamun had encountered before. Of course, the reason for Siamun's visit hadn't been hard to guess, thus Nebamun had prepared himself in every possible way.
To begin with, neither of the two men gave Siamun so much as a single glance. When Nebamun had lowered himself in his elaborate gilded chair, he talked animatedly with Hormin while the scribes settled down on the floor and readied their writing equipment. Then, after what had seemed like an endless time, the vizier finally deigned to address Siamun.
"Royal architect and overseer of the royal granaries at Mennefer, what is your request?"
"Honourable Vizier," Siamun began, "it has recently come to my attention that there is a serious shortfall in the provisions of the royal workmen in both Abedju and Waset."
A smug expression appeared on Nebamun's gaunt face.
"This is indeed the case," he gloated without elaborating further.

Siamun straightened his back, determined not to let his annoyance show.

"May I ask for the reason that prompted these cuts? After all, according to His Majesty's decree the workmen have been granted equally generous rations throughout the whole period of their employment."

Nebamun's eyes narrowed as he fixed Siamun with his stare. "This is correct, and there was no need to remind me. However, there has been a dramatic change in circumstances recently. At the time His Majesty fixed the workmen's rations he knew nothing of the necessity to wage war on two fronts. You should know yourself that the delivery of provisions to the forts along the western coastline has consumed the better part of the available funds. The only viable solution to this problem was to reduce the workmen's rations to the bare essentials."

Siamun was not impressed.

"I appreciate that these measures may have been deemed appropriate as precautions," he said, watching the vizier coldly. "But now there is no justification for this kind of austerity anymore. The provision of our troops stationed at the forts has been secured for several months to come, and the bulk of the royal army are sufficiently provided for by our northern vassals and the recently subdued city ports, hence there is no need for us to support them. Furthermore, the deputy to the overseer of the local treasury assured me that he has no reservations for a renewed increase of the workmen's rations and other essential material."

While he spoke, the furrow between Nebamun's eyebrows had deepened considerably. Evidently the self-confidence Siamun displayed didn't go down well with him at all. Even Hormin had begun to eye him with a mixture of wariness and distaste.

"There was no need to make inquiries behind my back," Nebamun snarled, visibly annoyed. "I could have told you the same. However, there is one thing that must not be overlooked. One can never trust those northern vassals and city states entirely. They change their mind as quickly as the wind. Today they are friend, tomorrow foe. Hence, they cannot be relied on to secure our troops' provisions, and we must be prepared to support them out of the royal coffers sooner or later."

"Should this indeed be the case, it will certainly suffice to implement appropriate measures in due course," Siamun returned calmly. "It will not have escaped your attention, honourable Vizier, how important the royal building projects in Ipet-Sut and Abedju are to His Majesty. This is particularly true for the latter. As I have been entrusted with the supervision of both projects, I bear responsibility for the smooth progress of works as well as the workmen's welfare. Therefore I request that their rations be increased to the amount originally decreed by pharaoh with immediate effect, and that they be sufficiently provided with tools and other essential building materials."

Nebamun looked daggers at him while he slowly opened his mouth to speak.

"And I," he began in a strained voice, "have the duty of governing the Two Lands during His Majesty's absence. In my capacity as deputy to the Lord of the Two Lands I reject your request. Whether you believe it or not, there are no sufficient funds at our disposal to increase the rations of your workmen. The venerable overseer of the royal treasury will be pleased to explain this to you in more detail, should you wish so," he concluded with a pompous wave of his hand towards Hormin who promptly inclined his head with a nasty smirk on his plump face.

Siamun had no intention of listening to his useless explanations that had surely been drummed into his fat head by the vizier. Realizing that Nebamun held the whip hand for now, he decided to try a different approach.

"This will not be necessary," he said coolly. "Be assured that I will find a solution to this problem, one way or other."
Nebamun's eyes narrowed to slits as they fastened on Siamun's face.
"Don't you dare undermine my authority," he hissed with barely restrained fury. "This won't do you any good."
Siamun only raised his chin a little higher in response.
"Keep your threats to yourself, Vizier" he said with unnerving calm. "You can do me no harm, for I'm the one who acts correctly to His Majesty's mind."
Finally losing his temper, Nebamun jumped up from his seat and pounded his gilded staff so vigorously on the floor that poor Hormin cringed. When he spoke, his voice quivered with rage.
"I'm warning you, architect. Don't be so sure of yourself. Your downfall could be just around the corner."
"And you, honourable Vizier," Siamun returned, not caring to conceal his loathing, "should not forget that many a great one has come to grief because of something he least expected."
For a few moments their gazes locked. Then Siamun turned away and left without so much as a backward glance.

****

"I hate to say that Nebamun is right," Tia told him later. "In father's absence he has the power to make decisions in all important matters."
Siamun wasn't at all pleased. Deeply upset, he stomped about the whole length and breadth of the room.

"I know he does all this only to harass me," he complained. "He wants to defame me so greatly that your father will have no choice but to dismiss me from office. And of course he hopes that it will be his own son's turn next. But I shall not let this happen. There must be a way out of this plight."

Tia rose from her chair and blocked Siamun's path, forcing him to stop dead. Wrapping her slender arms around his neck, she looked at him, worried.

"Do try to calm down," she told him.

But Siamun was far too busy to heed her advice. Having gently removed her arms he resumed his restless pacing and thought hard.

"What if I took some more grain from the royal granaries and used it to increase the workmen's rations and pay for everything else that is needed?" he asked hopefully.

Tia shook her head. "I don't think that's a good idea. Knowing Nebamun as I do, he wouldn't be slow to accuse you of misappropriating the crown's property. I have thought of something else that is far better."

Siamun stopped and looked at her in surprise.

"You have? What is it?"

"Maybe I could help you out with my private means," she explained. "I own quite profitable estates close to the town of Akhmim. Crops are grown there as well as grapes, and there is live-stock in considerable numbers as well."

"And do you think that the yield will suffice to sustain an entire army of workmen?" Siamun asked doubtfully.

"Well, I don't know the exact amount of grain that is currently stored in the granaries. I'll have to talk this through with the overseer of my estates. But I do believe that it should be enough to increase rations for quite some time. Besides, the yield of the next harvest can also be used for this purpose. And if we transfer part of the livestock to Abedju, the workmen will even have plenty of fresh meat to eat each day. The transport shouldn't be a problem, since Akhmim is only a day's journey from Abedju."

She squealed in surprise when Siamun scooped her up and whirled her around.

"Tia, it would be simply wonderful if this worked out," he cried after he had carefully lowered back to the ground.

"I don't see why it shouldn't," Tia said confidently. "I alone decide what happens to my private fortune, not Nebamun or anybody else. I can do as I please. I'll send word to the overseer right now so that he can start to work everything out."

She paused, and a mysterious smile appeared on her face. "However, there is one condition."

Siamun's eyebrows shot up. "Which is?"

"This time you must allow me to come with you."

Siamun cupped her face tenderly in both hands.

"That's just what I was about to ask from you."

****

Two days later, Tia's lavishly decorated boat was on its way south. The crisp breeze of the north wind filled the great sail and helped them make good progress upstream. Apart from two bodyguards and a few servants only the overseer of the princess's estate, a somewhat elderly man called Iurudef, travelled with the young couple. According to Tia Iurudef hadn't exactly been thrilled when he first heard of her plans, raising concerns of all kinds. But Tia had been unrelenting, and so he had had no choice but to resign himself to his fate. Even now as he was sitting on a woven mat, his beady eyes darting across the enormous papyrus that was spread out in front of him, he looked not at all happy, although it was hard to tell whether his furrowed brow was a sign of utter concentration or ill humour.

"Is Iurudef always in such a bad mood?" Siamun asked Tia, having settled for the latter possibility.

His young wife giggled.

"I can't tell you. All I know is that he wears this morose look on his face whenever I see him. But then, he is almost always brooding over one list or another, so maybe it's not his fault. He surely must be more likeable in private, or else his wife would hardly put up with him. By the way, what he's doing now is completely unnecessary, since I know for sure that he has already calculated everything down to the last grain, and not just once."

They were standing at the rail and admiring the beauty of the passing landscape while they spoke. The broad strip of fresh green that bordered the riverbanks seemed to go on forever; only every now and then was it broken by clusters of mud-brick houses that huddled together in the shadow of magnificent palm-trees and wide-spreading tamarinds. The tender stalks of the growing crops stood about a hand's breadth high. Peasants were a rare sight, however. Now that they had done their bit ploughing and sowing there was little left for them to do. The soil was still sufficiently saturated with the waters of the inundation, so that there was no need for irrigation yet. But with spring already there and summer just around the corner, this was soon going to change. Then the peasants and their families would have to tend to their fields with bent backs, pulling out weeds, clearing irrigation channels from mud and sand and running water through them without cease.

"How come that you own estates in far-off Akhmim of all places?" Siamun asked suddenly, posing the question that had been nagging him for the past two days.

"Mother hails from there," Tia replied evenly. "Didn't you know? Anyway, she inherited quite extensive estates after her father had gone to the West, since she had only one surviving brother at the time. When he too passed away, she bestowed part of her inheritance on me."

"I had no idea that your mother had connections to this town," Siamun replied truthfully. "Given the huge distance between Akhmim and the delta, how did your parents' marriage come about?"

Tia sighed uncomfortably. "Their marriage was arranged by my grandparents on either side. Both my grandfathers were commanders of troops serving in the same division and had befriended each other. By the way, my maternal grandparents had almost identical names. My grandmother was called Ruia, my grandfather Raia. Perhaps this inspired mother to press me to marry that unbearable upstart Tiya, who knows?"

"Fortunately, she didn't have her way," Siamun replied, gently putting an arm around her shoulders and pulling her close.

Tia looked up at him, smiling affectionately.

"Now mother is busy looking for a suitable bride for Ramses," she said quietly. "Apparently she has set her mind on some girl from within her own extended family. As soon as the campaign is over, she wants to get everything underway."

Siamun lifted an eyebrow. "Then we can only pray that she makes the right choice for her precious son."

"What about you?" Tia asked after a short silence, eliciting a startled look from her husband. "Don't you have any connections with Akhmim?"

"Me? No, how should I?" Siamun replied innocently, trying hard not to sound too baffled. Where did Tia get that idea from? In fact, Siamun had indeed quite close connections with this place, since his paternal grandmother, the illustrious Great Royal Wife Tiye, had hailed from there. But surely Tia didn't know that; after all, his secret was safe as yet, that he could be sure of. Or, could he?

"Why do you ask?" he inquired nevertheless.

"Oh, I don't know, it was just a thought," was her airy reply.

Still somewhat confused, he remained silent. Tia seemed to sense his tension, for she nestled even closer to him.

"This has always been my favourite season," she said dreamily as she fastened her gaze on the opposite riverbank again. "When the nights cease to be long and chilly and the first tender shoots begin to sprout everywhere, it seems as if the whole world awakens to new life. Everything is so fresh and untouched. But when the season of Shemu comes and with it the heat of summer, the spell is broken."

Siamun turned his head to breathe in the enticing scent of her hair.

"I feel quite the same way. Indeed, the season of growth is so special that even the foul smell that emanates from the muddy fields has its appeal."

Tia broke into a peal of laughter, at the sound of which Iurudef looked up in surprise, only to bury himself again in his notes.

"This doesn't sound very romantic, but there is a ring of truth to it," she declared once she had calmed down. "The musty smell is a concomitant which I am perfectly happy to put up with."

Eventually they left their place at the rail and strolled hand in hand towards their cabin.

"How I wish we would be there yet," Siamun muttered thoughtfully. "My poor workmen won't be in very high spirits right now, and that's putting it mildly."

"I have instructed the captain to make haste," Tia replied. "If all goes well, we'll reach Abedju in three days' time. Don't worry too much; soon everything will be sorted out."

Siamun gave her hand an affectionate squeeze.

"I can't tell you how grateful I am for your help. What would I have done without you?"

****

Siamun was almost stifled by the heat when he and Tia reached the foot of the causeway leading up to the temple. He wondered how it could be so sweltering already at this time of year when it was only pleasantly warm elsewhere. This must be due to the stretch of hills that separated the sacred ground from the flood plain and kept the refreshing breeze wafting from the river out.

He was not the only one to suffer as he could see from the beads of sweat on Amunhotep's forehead. The overseer of workmen had bad news for him, and he came straight to the point.

"The men are in very low spirits," he related with obvious contrition, pulling his sleeve across his sweaty forehead. "It's more than a month now that they haven't eaten properly, and they haven't caught so much as a whiff of meat either. How are they supposed to do such demanding work under these circumstances?"

Siamun exchanged quick glances with Tia. Amunhotep's statement confirmed that Nebamun had ordered the cuts immediately after his, Siamun's departure.

"Don't be upset," he said in a soothing tone of voice. "I blame neither you nor the men for this dreadful state of affairs. Everyone knows that heavy physical work can't be done without sufficient sustenance, and meat in particular. Besides, we may not have fallen behind schedule all that much. I'm going to make a thorough assessment later. First of all, I want to have a look at the injured workmen you told me of."

Amunhotep made a slight bow. "Please follow me, I'll show you to them."

He turned on his heel and walked in the direction of a collection of modest houses which nestled against part of the rocky wall that lined the bay. This was where the workmen dwelt during their stay on site. When the young couple entered the village they could hear voices ringing out from inside the houses. There was occasional laughter, too, but the few men they encountered cast them sullen looks.

"They don't appear to be overly friendly," Tia whispered into Siamun's ear.

Siamun nodded. "That's not surprising," he whispered back. "Nebamun may have decreed the cuts to their rations, but in the end they blame me for their misery, since I am their supervisor. But don't worry; I'm going to tell them soon enough whose fault it is."

Meanwhile, the overseer had stopped in front of the door of one of the houses. Turning to Siamun, he stepped aside with a gesture of invitation.

"Perhaps it will be best if you wait here for me," Siamun told Tia in a low voice. "I won't be long."

At first he couldn't see much after he had stepped over the threshold. But then his eyes adjusted to the rather dim light inside, and he could make out low mudbrick benches that stretched along the walls of the only room and were covered with straw and a layer of rather coarse cloth for comfort. As Siamun knew, the men cooked and relieved themselves out in the open, so there was no need for either kitchen or lavatory. His gaze settled briefly on a man who lay stretched out on one of the benches, then it wandered to another who was sitting cross-legged and leaning against the opposite wall. The latter wore a sling around his neck which supported his right arm. Two more occupants were crouching on the floor and whiling their time away with some sort of game. All of them greeted Siamun respectfully, yet their underlying animosity wasn't lost on him.

"Tell me what happened," he demanded, looking at Amunhotep.

"These men were injured in two separate accidents," the overseer explained. "One happened when the workmen were in the process of dragging one of the sledges up the causeway. The rope was worn, and all of a sudden it broke under the strain. The sledge began to rush downhill, and we could only look on as it gained speed and knocked a man over who wasn't quick enough to get out of its way. His legs were crushed underneath the immense weight, and he died in agony an hour later when all blood had left his body. This man here was hit, too, but he was lucky to get away with a broken leg and a few grazes."

Siamun stepped forth and knelt down beside the sprawling man who eyed him warily.

"What's your name?" he asked.

"Nebi," came the curt reply.

"May I have a look at your injured leg?"

Nebi nodded reluctantly. Siamun lifted the coarse sheet of linen that covered the man's lower body. As Amunhotep had said the visible part of the skin was covered with grazes that were in the process of healing. What worried Siamun more was the deep red stain on the bandages that had been tightly wound around the supporting splint.

"Had the broken bone penetrated the skin?" he inquired, pointing at the stain.

"Yes, lord."

"Was the wound appropriately treated with raw meat and honey dressings?"

"No, lord," Nebi replied with a grim smile. "It's a long time that we don't have these things here anymore."

Siamun exhaled sharply. "I understand. But what about the dressing? Why hasn't it been changed? There sure are more than enough bandages to be had in the nearby temple of Osiris."

Nebi preferred not to answer. Mouth set in a tight line, he averted his eyes. Siamun's gaze travelled to Amunhotep in search for help.

The overseer shuffled his feet with embarrassment.

"We tried it, but they told us that we were not entitled to further supplies of any kind. Allegedly this is what you said in your decree."

"What, *me*?" Siamun exclaimed, baffled. It took him a moment to grasp the meaning of Amunhotep's words. So that scoundrel of a vizier had decreed his cuts not in his own, but in Siamun's name. Things were getting worse by the hour.

He drew a deep breath in order to calm himself down.

"I haven't decreed anything of that sort," he declared. "These are all the doings of the northern vizier. I'll make an official statement later," he added with a look at Amunhotep's puzzled face. "Just tell me quickly about this other accident."

The overseer inclined his head.

"As you may know," he began, indicating the man with the sling, "Ptahmose is a very experienced and skilled workman. At the time of the accident he was perched mid-height on one of the ramps running along the outer walls to check out the soundness of the stone blocks. Some way up, another row of blocks was added to the wall. Just when one of them was hauled into place, a neighbouring block became dislodged and came plunging down towards poor Ptahmose, hitting his right shoulder so forcefully that the joint was wrenched out of its socket. We managed to reset it, but apart from that he also suffered a mighty bruise. It borders on a miracle that he wasn't knocked off the ramp altogether."

Siamun knew that Ptahmose had had a lucky escape. The workman could easily have been killed, but he saw no need to voice his thoughts. However, there was one more thing he had to know.

"How could it happen that the block broke loose in the first place?" he demanded sharply. "Wasn't there enough mortar in the gaps?"

"Indeed, this was an additional problem," Amunhotep replied in a meek voice. "Our supplies of mortar were running low, and so we had started to mix it with more water than usual in order to stretch it. Besides, for the past two weeks or so the men may have worked with insufficient quantities, and I am sorry to say that for the same time works progressed at a far slower pace than usual."

"When did they stop working altogether?"

"Immediately after the second incident which happened only a week ago," the overseer explained. "I gave order to put works on hold for the time being."

Siamun nodded his approval. "And it was high time you did. Apart from the fact that due to lack of food the workmen were hardly able to continue working, gruesome accidents like these would have piled up, and the quality of construction would have suffered greatly too. I can assure you that neither me nor Pharaoh, may he live, be healthy and prosperous, wish any of this to happen. And now let's go, Amunhotep. I want to have a look around the site, and afterwards I have to address the men.

And as to you two, may Sekhmet grant you a quick and complete recovery."

With a brief nod he turned and left.

Back outside, Tia came walking up to him, looking at him inquiringly. Siamun shook his head ever so slightly, willing her to be patient.

"Tell the workmen that they are to gather in front of the village in exactly an hour's time," he instructed Amunhotep. "And make sure they all attend. I have an important announcement to make."

With Tia by his side and two guards following in his wake Siamun set out to a thorough inspection of the whole building site. While they walked on he quickly related to her what he had heard in the workmen's hut. Tia was utterly dismayed, but he told her to be patient.

When they arrived at what was going to be the core of the temple they stopped and had a good look around. The gleaming white limestone walls had reached their final height in places so that the draughtsmen and stonemasons could soon set to work decorating them with carved and painted reliefs. On the outside, some of the mud-brick ramps that served as a means of raising hundreds of stone blocks to the higher levels had already been abolished while others were still standing. Inside the various cult chambers, Siamun noticed, to his delight, that quite a few columns could be seen in various stages of completion. Indeed, if works progressed smoothly from now on, he might still be able to meet his deadline.

Tia, too, was impressed.

"Father will be so pleased," she told Siamun.

"I hope he will," he replied, smiling. "Let's have a look at the sanctuaries proper."

The young couple headed towards the large complex that

housed the seven barge shrines which stood out with their amazing vaulted roofs.

"Isn't it a pity that all this beauty is soon going to be plunged into eternal darkness," Tia whispered.

"That's true," Siamun replied, nodding. "But this is the way it's meant to be. Even the two columned forecourts of which almost nothing can be seen yet will only be sparsely lit, once their roofs will be in place."

When they had gazed their fill, they made their way to the rearmost part of the whole complex. The gigantic pit that was to house the subterranean burial chamber had now reached its final size, but within it not much could be seen apart from the outline of a large rectangular ditch that occupied the centre of the bottom.

"Do you see this ditch down there?" Siamun asked, pointing excitedly in its direction. "This is going to be the moat that will in time represent the primeval ocean *Nun* from which emerged the first mound of creation. Thus, the identification of the island in its middle, bearing the sacred sarcophagus with the mythical primeval mound will be made clear, emphasizing its significance as a symbol of rebirth. Of course, the magnificent rectangular pillars that will surround and protect all this have yet to be built. Once the ceiling of granite slabs will be in place, the only access to this hall will be via that tunnel over there, which, by the way has progressed surprisingly. How do you like it?"

"It's going to be simply breathtaking," Tia whispered in awe, "and very mysterious. As mysterious as the creation of the universe itself. When do you think will it be completed?"

Siamun laughed. "It will take at least two or three years to finish this extraordinary project. Then you will have ample opportunity to visit and admire it."

"Along with you," Tia added eagerly.

Noting that the assessed hour was drawing to a close, they slowly made their way back to the settlement of the workmen. They could see from afar that a considerable number had already gathered in front.

"Now they're going to learn who is really responsible for their misery," Siamun said grimly.

A little later, Siamun stepped in front of his assembled workforce. Before he spoke, he carefully surveyed the faces in the front rows. Annoyance, distrust and sheer anger were mirrored in them, but he was determined not to let himself get worked up.

"Men of Kemet", his strong voice rang out, "who have the honour of building one of the most splendid monuments that can be found throughout the Two Lands! I am aware of the difficulties you have been facing for quite some time. Your rations have been reduced drastically, building materials and other vital commodities have not been delivered anymore. You suffered from insufficient sustenance and dreadful accidents happened that could have been avoided, had the management been right. Be assured that those pointless austerity measures have not been imposed by me, and that I deeply regret the tragic events of the recent past."

Siamun paused briefly to assess the effect of his words. He was pleased to see that at least some of the faces were beginning to brighten up.

"I do not want to keep you in the dark about who is really behind the cuts that caused you so much trouble. Shortly after I had set out on my journey to the western coast in order to deliver the much-needed provision to our brave soldiers, it pleased the vizier of the north to alter His Majesty's decree to your disadvantage. According to himself, he did this for fear of being else unable to meet the costs of the war against both the wretched Asiatics in the north and the Temehiu in the west. However, I can assure you that the vizier has blatantly misjudged the situation. The storehouses of the Two Lands are not as empty as the vizier seems to believe. We are very well able to fund our wars and sustain our workforces properly at the same time, without anyone being worse off."

Again he paused. By now, many of the men were nodding their heads approvingly, while others prodded each other and smirked at the ridiculous idea of the Two Lands having fallen into poverty. Siamun was well aware that he was making a laughing stock of Nebamun, and he had no qualms about it. Served him right, that mangy jackal.

"Therefore I am happy to announce," he went on, raising his voice, "that your ordeal is over. From now on, you will want for nothing. For the time being, your rations will be increased with immediate effect with the help of the private funds of Her Highness, the princess. Even tomorrow we expect the first delivery of grain, vegetables, beer and live-stock coming directly from her estates. From now on, there shall be plenty of food for everyone, and you shall also have a decent portion of meat each day. Furthermore, vital supplies like mortar, tools and good strong ropes are already underway. We shall do exactly the same for your colleagues in *Ipet-Sut* who suffered the same fate as you in due course. I am sure that pharaoh, may he live, be prosperous and healthy, will abolish the misguided vizier's decree and put everything right as soon as he returns from his campaign."

Siamun ignored the joyous shouts that rang out here and there, since he felt that there was one more thing left to say.

"Finally, I want to thank you for taking on the strenuous and at times dangerous task of constructing this splendid temple which His Majesty loves more than any other monument in the Two Lands. You will incur his pleasure, and the blessings of all the gods it is dedicated to will be with you, now and for all times!"

A storm of applause and thrilled cheers broke loose when he raised his arms to indicate the end of his speech. Siamun's name was shouted over and over again. At Amunhotep's sign the crowd began to disperse with excited chattering.

Tia, who had been standing some way off, came briskly walking up to him, eyes shining, and congratulated him on his success. "I believe you have won over their hearts once and for all," she said proudly.

Siamun grinned happily. "Yes, and this is all due to you and your generosity."

They linked arms and sauntered leisurely towards the jetty where their ship was waiting.

"You have defeated Nebamun with his own arguments," Tia went on. "I don't think he'll want to pick another quarrel with you anytime soon. From now on, you will be safe from him and his doings."

If only I could be that confident too, Siamun thought uncomfortably, remembering his recent encounter with the vizier. All at once Nebamun's ominous threat sprang back into his mind.

Your downfall could be just around the corner...

Had this been nothing but an empty threat, a vain attempt to scare the man he so obviously despised? Had Nebamun been so confident to bring Siamun finally down with his machinations? Or did he have something entirely else up his sleeve, something far more sinister?

Siamun sincerely hoped that it didn't turn out to be the latter. A any rate, he couldn't very well let his worries show.

"May the gods give that you are right," he said in reply to Tia's words, squeezing her hand reassuringly.

Chapter Eight

The first rays of the morning sun swept over the camp, awakening it to new life. Little by little the men who had spent the night under the starry sky, covering most of the extensive ground up to the makeshift enclosure wall made from shields, left their mats and blankets behind to go about their business. Seti stood in the entrance of his grand tent and watched on as fires were kindled and sleepy men made for the river to wash themselves and water the horses. He had risen early, or, more exactly, he had hardly slept at all. There had been simply too much that was bothering him. Even his attempt to distract himself with the young Amorite girl had been futile.

Today, a decision had to be made whether to break the campaign off and march back home, or to launch an attack on the city of Kadesh.

Seti knew that opinions among his commanders were divided. There were those who favoured retreat, and there were others who threw their weight behind a further attack. As he might have expected, Ramses was among the latter, seeing the conquest of the infamous city-state as the ultimate goal. Admittedly, Kadesh was of immense strategic importance. Whoever held sway over it controlled the corridor that granted the Hittites access to the south. It was most unfortunate that it was them who had the upper hand since more than a decade. Before that, one of those kings whose names were not spoken anymore had conquered the fortress, but it had fallen back into Hittite hands soon after.

In the long run, it was imperative to get Kadesh back, but not now. This campaign had been going on for too long already; the troops were worn out, and recently Seti had begun to suffer from increased chest pains. He needed a thorough rest, or else he might be in for a nasty surprise. And if he loathed anything, it was the thought of having to die in foreign parts.

The discussion of the situation with his generals and, of course, Ramses was about to begin. On Seti's orders, the young Amorite had retreated to the far end of the tent where she sat in silence, ignored by the supreme commanders of the four divisions who had already arrived. Ramses, however, was noticeable only by his absence. The young man had developed the annoying habit of taking his time with almost everything. Perhaps he saw this as a way of gaining importance, as Seti suspected.

Eventually, the crown prince entered and lowered himself immediately on the last vacant chair with a curt nod in his father's direction, not bothering to say anything in the way of an apology for his lateness.

Seti decided to ignore him for now. From the height of his pedestal he let his gaze roam across the men in front of him who looked at him expectantly.

"Now that we are all gathered," he began quietly, "we can start to discuss the situation we find ourselves in. So far, our campaign has proved successful for the most part. The *Temehiu* have been driven back into the desert where they belong, the most important city ports are ours, and we have conquered *Amurru* and *Fenkhu*. Now the question is whether we stop at that and return home, or whether we should launch another attack. In order to answer this question we need to assess the physical capabilities and morale of the men, taking our losses into account. I expect to hear truthful and accurate information on your respective divisions from all of you. Mehy, being the longest-serving supreme commander you are to begin."

Seti didn't fail to notice the dismissive sideways glance that Ramses cast at Mehy when he cleared his throat.

"Majesty, may I begin with the losses that my division has suffered so far. They amount to roughly four hundred men, most of them owing to our rather unfortunate encounter with the Hittites. A further two hundred of my troops have been more or less seriously injured and are in the process of recovery. Generally speaking, their morale appears to be good, although their fighting spirit is not entirely undiminished. My troops are not exactly keen on another encounter with the Hittites, given that they have dealt us a heavy blow once already."

"Hearing you one could think that they downright defeated us," Ramses growled, "when in reality we could have easily won the battle, hadn't we beaten such a hasty retreat."

Ramses' interjection triggered a stern glance from Seti.

"This is not the matter of debate right now, Ramses," he said firmly. "We must keep to the facts. Hori, what do you have to say?"

The burly man who seemed far too big for his folding-chair made a serious face.

"I'm sorry to say that the division of Amun-Re has suffered losses in the region of six hundred men, along with about as many injured troops. One must not forget that my division was the one to be affected worst by the Hittite counter-attack," he added quickly on seeing Seti's dismayed expression. "Apart from that, I would fully endorse Mehy's statement. After all I have heard, my men do not embrace the idea of having to fight the Hittites again any time soon."

Seti nodded in acknowledgment of his words before he

addressed his next commander.

"Tjanefer, it's your turn."

Tjanefer's assessment didn't deviate significantly from those of the previous speakers. Then Seti's worried gaze fastened on Urhiye.

"Urhiye, I know that you have held the position of supreme commander only for a short time, but I trust that you have been able to form an impression of your troops nevertheless."

Seti noticed that Urhiye drew a deep breath before he spoke. Following Djedi's untimely death in the most recent battle, the former troop commander had replaced the unfortunate general only two weeks ago, while Urhiye's friend Panakht had advanced to the position of a troop commander.

"As Your Majesty knows," Urhiye began somewhat hesitantly, "my division has been dramatically reduced in numbers, owing to the manning of the three western forts. Considering the loss of further four to five hundred men only three thousand troops remain. However, most of them are in remarkably good shape, and I would not hesitate to say that they are in high spirits as well. As far as I am concerned, there is nothing that would speak against an attack on Kadesh."

"Really?" Seti raised his eyebrows in surprise. "Your troops have gone through the ordeal of marching through to the western coast and all the way back again. They must be worn down more than anyone else. Besides, I have heard that a considerable number has been wounded, too. How can you be so optimistic under these circumstances?"

"Most among the injured have long since recovered," Urhiye replied calmly. "During the past few days I have been asking around quite a lot. My troops are longing for retaliation against the wretched Hittites. For them, the conquest of Kadesh would be the culmination of this campaign."

Seti's brow furrowed. He still doubted the sincerity of Urhiye's assessment. Why had he entrusted this foreigner with the supreme command over a whole division of troops? It was a good thing that the final decision would be his, Seti's.

"Generals," he began, drawing himself up in his gilded chair, "given the considerable duration of this campaign, the number of battles we have fought and the overall losses I am of a mind to postpone the attack on Kadesh and leave it for the next season. If we go on now, the risk that the Hittites who are continually provided with fresh troops deal us a truly crushing defeat next time is far too great."

"But isn't it even more dangerous when we leave Kadesh and the Hittites to themselves?" Ramses exclaimed heatedly. "If we retreat, we risk losing all that we have achieved so far."

Seti shot a withering glance at the prince. His hands gripped the armrests of his chair tightly when he leaned forward.

"Quite on the contrary," he said sternly, "if we attack Kadesh now, we barely stand a chance against the Hittites who will defend their stronghold to the last man. They will crush us, and then all our efforts will indeed come down to nothing, because they will snatch from us all that we have gained. But if we give us a break and return in a few months' time, refreshed and in even greater numbers, victory shall be ours."

He had spoken with such great authority that even Ramses didn't dare open his mouth again. However, the fleeting look that he cast at Urhiye wasn't lost on Seti. What was that for? Had the two of them joined forces to extract the approval of the advance on Kadesh from him? And if so, why?

Urhiye, who had reciprocated Ramses' glance with an almost imperceptible nod, cleared his throat awkwardly.

"With Your Majesty's permission, I would like to make an additional statement."

Seti wasn't in the least inclined to listen to any more pointless talk, but he felt compelled to grant the commander's request nevertheless.

"Speak," he said in a rather tired voice, leaning himself heavily against his backrest.

Urhiye smoothed a few strands of his unruly light brown hair back. In contrast to his colleagues and comrades he saw apparently no need to shave his head clean.

"As always, Your Majesty speaks with the wisdom of Djehuty and the justice of Maat," he began rather long-windedly. "However, there is one thing I would like to point out. Since time immemorial there have been particularly close ties between the kings of Amurru and the princes of Kadesh. Ties that are not only based on territorial closeness of their neighbouring kingdoms, but were forged and cemented by intermarriage and blood relationship. Both kingdoms assist each other to the best of their abilities, whatever the matter. It is therefore highly likely that the prince of Kadesh –if we give him a free hand- could send support troops to Amurru to help them get rid of our dominance. These troops could be so numerous that our own stationary unit might not be able to withstand the onslaught. And once the Hittites manage to snatch Amurru from us, Fenkhu and the city ports will follow suit."

Urhiye inclined his head to indicate that he had ended.

"Is there anybody else who feels the need to comment on this problem?" Seti asked, looking hard at the men in front of him, all of whom negated his question –all with the exception of Ramses, that was.

An ominous silence ensued during which Seti pondered all the arguments for and against an attack on Kadesh one last time. He was careful not to let any emotions show; his regal composure didn't betray the annoyance he had felt at hearing Urhiye's audacious words in the slightest. When he had finally made his mind up, he nodded briefly at the military scribe who was crouching to his left, reed brush poised above his papyrus. "Hear my decision," his voice boomed. "Although commander Urhiye's reservations cannot be dismissed entirely, it would not be a prudent move on our part to confront the Hittites in our current, rather deplorable state. The danger of suffering a crushing defeat would be too great. According to our scouts, a large number of Hittite troops are stationed in and around the city of Kadesh, and more will come to their aid if we attack. Therefore I give orders to strike camp immediately and prepare for our return home. It is your duty to inform all troop commanders accordingly. This is all for now. You may take your leave."

Seti watched his generals intently as they bowed and made to leave one by one. Obvious relief was mirrored in their faces except for Urhiye, whose expression was open to interpretation. Ramses, who had been scrutinizing his own toes as if he'd never seen them before, was last to rise and make for the tent opening. Just before he exited, he whirled around.

"You just want to get back home as soon as possible, don't you, father?"

His expression was harsh, the tone of his voice accusing.

For the length of a heartbeat their gazes locked. Without waiting for an answer, the prince then turned briskly away and stomped off.

Seti gritted his teeth in an attempt to control his anger. Of course he wanted to go home; who didn't? Only someone as obsessed with the quest for glory as Ramses and perhaps that upstart Urhiye could think of throwing themselves headlong into another battle, contrary to all common sense.

But not with me, Seti thought grimly. *I want to go back and find out more about the supposed connection between the evildoer of Ipet-Sut and you and your precious mother. And I long to see how far works on my new temple have progressed, which is dearer to me than all I have done before.*

****

"I knew it," Siamun rejoiced as he whirled Tia around.
"How can this be?" she asked once she had gotten her breath back. "I only just told you."
Ignoring the curious glances Benret cast at them from across the garden, he caressed his wife's cheek with his finger.
"Remember when we were on our way to Abedju, talking about spring and how it awakens everything to new life? I sensed there and then that new life was beginning to grow inside you, too."
"If this is so, why didn't you tell me straight away?" she teased.
Siamun smiled mysteriously.
"Well, I thought it best to let you go first."
"Which was indeed a sensible thing to do," Tia admitted. Then she cocked her head to one side and looked at him inquiringly.
"We have yet to work out when our little one is due."
"If you have conceived during the third month of *Peret*, it is due to be born at the very end of the inundation season."
Tia wrinkled her nose. "But that's right at the beginning of winter!"
"That doesn't matter at all," her husband assured her. "We will keep it nice and cosy anyway. Tia, my love, I can't tell you how happy I am. Quick, let's go inside. I'm going to write to my family straight away to share the good news with them."
Hand in hand they stepped into the pleasant coolness of the

columned hallway, then made their way up the stairs to the upper storey where the private chambers were located. Having made himself comfortable in the room that served as Siamun's study, he took his writing equipment from a beautifully decorated ebony casket along with a sheet of papyrus.
"If it's alright with you, I'm coming straight to the point," he said eagerly.
"Go on," Tia encouraged him, watching him intently.
When Siamun took up the reed brush, he noticed with astonishment that his hand shook with excitement.

Dear mother, dear Meresankh,
I hope you and the children are all well. I keep praying for mother's complete recovery every day. Hopefully she will feel much better when she hears of the good news I have for you. Today my beloved wife has told me that she is with child, and we are beside ourselves with joy. I hope-"

"Do you believe they will come to see us soon?" Tia asked suddenly.
"I shouldn't think so," he replied without taking his eyes off the letter, "because mother isn't quite up to travelling yet."
"Then perhaps we can go and see them?"
Siamun looked up in surprise, wondering why his wife should be so desperate to see his family just now. He knew the answer as soon as he caught sight of her sitting curled up in her chair, chin propped on her drawn-up knees. Tia wanted to share her joy with someone, and didn't quite know with whom. Her father hadn't returned yet, and her unloved mother would hardly be the person of her choice. Siamun felt the urge to cheer her up.

"Sure, why not?" he said quickly. "That is, if you feel like it at all, given the condition you're in."
To his relief, Tia's features brightened considerably.
"The sooner we go, the better," she announced eagerly. "Once father returns from his campaign, there will be a lot of celebrating and feasting going on, and we might not be available anymore."
Siamun smiled. "Just as you wish. I'd better warn them of our imminent arrival then."

****

"It's a pity you weren't there," Panakht said, leisurely stretching his long legs out in front of him. "You missed all the fun."
He reached lazily for one of the sweet almond pastries on the table next to him.
"My favourites," he sighed contentedly before he took a large bite off it. While he was chewing, he rolled his eyes with pleasure. "I say, that's pure luxury."
Siamun grinned. "You seem to have missed a lot more than I did," he said dryly. "By the way, what exactly was this fun you're talking about?"
"Well, I mean the whole frenzy in the port of Perunefer of course," Panakht explained not very helpfully, wiping his sticky fingers on a cloth. "All those grand ships, dignitaries, courtiers, royal guards, the cheering crowds... We were received like heroes."
"That's what you are, after all," Meritamun pointed out, pride

ringing in her voice.

"Besides, all that so-called frenzy wasn't entirely your due, but also and foremost pharaoh's," Meresankh teased.

"That's just typical," Panakht shot back with mock indignation. "Always good for some deflating remark or other. Anyway, I had hoped to meet you there by the docks, Siamun. And if not there, then at least at your grand home. I had a hard time tracking you down, only to find that nobody was there."

Siamun raised his hands apologetically.

"I'm awfully sorry for that, but you arrived somewhat earlier than expected."

"I hear the princess was here, too?" Panakht inquired.

Siamun nodded. "Yes, but she decided to leave at once when we received word of pharaoh's return. However, having accompanied her to the palace I preferred to come back and stay on some more. You know that I'm not one who enjoys great bustle. Besides, I could feel it in my bones that you would show up here sooner rather than later. What if we both went back to Mennefer together?"

Panakht considered. "I would love to, if mother lets me go."

"But you have only just arrived," Meritamun said with a weak smile. "Give yourself a rest, and then you can accompany Siamun in a few days' time."

"I believe that Ranefer and Amunmesse wouldn't like to see you go either," Meresankh added, tilting her head in the direction of the two boys who were playing nearby, always keeping an eye on Panakht.

"I'm glad they finally left me alone for once," Panakht said, laughing. "From the moment I arrived, they kept pestering me with all kind of questions, particularly about the scar on my face."

"And I bet you knew how to make the most of it," Siamun grinned.

A sly look appeared on Panakht's face. "You can say that again. I told them that a particularly fearsome warrior was about to cut me in half with his giant sword, but I managed to parry the blow so that the lethal blade only grazed my face. The truth is that I have no idea how this scar came about, but please don't tell them."

Meritamun watched her son warily.

"In whatever way it happened, the outcome could have been far worse," she said gravely. "And surely not just this once. A soldier's life always hangs by a single thread. We must deem ourselves lucky that you haven't come to serious harm, Panakht. Therefore I'm going to the temple first thing in the morning to make offerings of thanks."

Panakht, too, had become quite serious.

"Thank you, mother. You are right. During this campaign I have witnessed so many things that are too gruesome to tell. I have seen death and mutilation all around me. Truth be told, I even owe my own promotion to general Djedi's death. Had Urhiye not moved on to take his place, his position wouldn't have become available in the first place."

"But even so it is a great honour that you were picked for this post," Siamun pointed out. "There sure were many contenders to choose from."

Panakht didn't look quite convinced. "This may be true as far as Urhiye is concerned, but I reckon that in my case my friendship to him was the crucial factor."

"Don't be so shy," Siamun said cheerfully, beginning to wonder if Panakht was still as uncomfortable in battle as he had been before. "I'm sure the decision was made with regards to your abilities, too."

During the ensuing silence he saw how Panakht's gaze lingered on Meresankh who –presumably without being aware- had placed a protective hand on her slightly swollen belly.

"So there's soon to be another addition to the family," he said quietly, as if to himself.

"And this is not the only one," Meresankh replied.

Panakht looked up in surprise. "Who else?"

"Ask Siamun."

He fastened his eyes on Siamun's smiling face.

"Tia has fallen pregnant, too. That's why we came here in the first place: to share our joy with you."

"Well, congratulations to you both," Panakht muttered somewhat awkwardly.

"What about you? When do you think about raising a family?" Meresankh inquired.

Panakht didn't answer straight away.

"Maybe sometime in the future," he replied eventually. "But not so soon. Being a soldier and often on campaign, I can't commit myself to family life yet."

"But many of the soldiers are married and have children," Meresankh objected. "And look how often Kenamun is away from home."

There was no reply. Staring hard at the wine cup in his hands, Panakht looked as if he would dearly love to disappear in it. In an attempt to steer the conversation away from the topic that so obviously embarrassed his friend, Siamun started to ask questions about Kenamun's business. They talked for a while, then Panakht excused himself, yawning.

"I'm worried about him," Meritamun said quietly as everyone watched Panakht's retreating back. "Panakht still doesn't have the slightest interest in starting a family. He doesn't seem to realize how important it is to have children to look after him in his old age and to nourish his *Ka* with offerings once he has gone to the West. This is particularly true for someone who leads such a dangerous life as him."

"Leave it to me," Siamun said, putting a comforting hand on

hers. "This is one of the reasons why I asked him to come with me. There are bound to be lots of banquets during the ongoing celebrations, and on one of these occasions Panakht might come across a lady who catches his eye."

When he and Panakht said their farewells to Meritamun, Meresankh and the boys, Siamun suddenly felt as if he had travelled back in time.
"Do you remember the day we both set out for Mennefer?" he told Panakht. "I can hardly believe that this was less than a year ago. Isn't it amazing how much has happened since then, and how profoundly our lives have changed?"
They found themselves a remote spot on deck and settled down. The boat cast off and gained steadily speed, aided by the vigorous strokes of numerous oars.
"You're right," Panakht said slowly. "It is downright terrifying how much we have changed."
There was an edge to his voice that made Siamun feel uneasy. Had it something to do with Panakht's difficulties in dealing with the horrors of war? Casting a curious glance at him, Siamun decided to get to the bottom of the matter.
"Haven't things become somewhat easier for you?" he asked cautiously.
Panakht looked at him with what could best be described as a mixture of pity and disgust.
"Of course not," he retorted. "This is never going to happen. But it's true nevertheless that something has changed. *I* have changed, and not for the best, I'm afraid."
"What do you mean by that?" Siamun asked, puzzled.
Panakht didn't reply for a long time, and Siamun didn't press him for an answer. Eventually, his eye caught Siamun's, and his lips parted.

"I have turned into a savage beast," he burst forth.

Siamun was terrified, not so much by what Panakht had said, but by the ring of utter despair in his voice.

"I have heeded Urhiye's advice," Panakht went on grimly. "On the surface, I don't care anymore when I slay them, mutilate them and rip their bellies open, the way they do with us. At times, I even enjoy myself. But deep below, down here" –his thumb pointed to his heart- "I despise myself for doing so, and I suffer just as much as I did in the beginning. Sometimes I even fear that one of these days I might perish miserably from my pain."

For a few moments, Siamun was shocked into silence. Then he thought feverishly of a way to help his friend.

"I know that we have spoken about this before," he said, choosing his words carefully, "but now I'm asking you again to try and get yourself used to the thought of doing something else for a living. Go and have a look around while you're with me. You can stay as long as you like; there's no need to hurry. And perhaps I might be able to help you in some way or other."

"So, you're going to help me? Are you going to get me some lousy post as errand boy, manservant and the like?"

Taken aback by the scorn in Panakht's voice, Siamun replied nothing.

"Forget it," Panakht went on with a dismissive wave. "You can't help me. You're not in a position to do so. Or can you turn me into someone really high and mighty like, say, a vizier or king's advisor? See, you can't. This is pharaoh's prerogative. The way he can refuse coveted positions to perfectly suitable men at his own discretion as happened to poor Urhiye, he can also present them to those who aren't worthy of them at all. Or do you mean to say that that beastly vizier has deserved his high office?"

"It's not quite like this," Siamun objected heatedly, ignoring Panakht's question. "Even pharaoh is subjected to Maat, and is not allowed to make purely arbitrary decisions. True, it might happen that he misjudges someone's character and appoints the wrong person to some important office; after all, he is not infallible. But still he has to make every effort to surround himself with decent and suitable men."

Panakht pursed his lips scornfully. "You, of course, would do just that if you were king," he scoffed. "You would only choose men of impeccable character and noble descent to serve you. But perhaps you would make an exception when it came to an old good-for-nothing friend like me, wouldn't you?"

Siamun's eyes narrowed as they fastened on Panakht who was watching him like a predator ready to pounce.

"Don't get your hopes up," he said coldly. "You should know by now that I don't have the slightest ambition on the throne, so stop bothering me."

"What a pity," Panakht said quietly. It wasn't quite clear whether his regret was sincere or not.

Then, all of a sudden, he laughed out loud and prodded Siamun boisterously.

"Forget it!" he exclaimed. "I just wanted to wind you up a bit. I didn't mean to spoil your mood. Don't worry, it was nothing but a silly joke."

Siamun smiled reluctantly at him, although Panakht's awkward apology had done nothing to reassure him. He asked himself if taking Panakht with him had been the right thing to do. Be that as it may, there was no point thinking about it now. It was too late for him to change his mind.

Chapter Nine

Seti had propped his chin on the heel of his hand, while he allowed the fingers of his other hand to drum impatiently on the armrest of his throne. With a furrowed brow he watched the man in front of him warily. Seti was well aware of the fact that he wasn't exactly the picture of royal composure and dignity, but he didn't care. After all, this was more of an informal meeting than an official audience.

His good mood had vanished the moment Nebamun had approached him with his request to have a word with him in private. Ever since he had learned of the vizier's inappropriate measures regarding the workmen's rations, he wasn't on good terms with him at all. Seti had made it clear that he didn't approve of his highhanded actions, and that he wasn't going to tolerate similar behaviour in the future. Nebamun had listened to the rebuke with due contrition. Meanwhile, however, he was clearly back to his usual self; and if the smug expression on Nebamun's face was anything to go by, Seti wasn't going to like what he was about to hear.

"Out with it," he said curtly, eager to get it over and done with. "What is it you wanted to tell me in private?"

"It concerns the royal architect Siamun, Majesty," Nebamun replied with an unnerving air of superiority. "Since we know so little about his background, I have taken the liberty of conducting a few inquiries during the past weeks, in order to protect Your Majesty from possible harm."

You have taken a great deal of liberties during my absence, I must say, Seti couldn't help thinking.

"And have the results of your inquiries added to our knowledge about him?" he asked without much interest.

"Indeed they have," Nebamun replied, his complacent smile deepening. "Among much else I have found out that Siamun's alleged father died several years before his birth, and therefore cannot be his true father."

The note of triumph in his voice wasn't lost on Seti who was still all but impressed.

"You will have to go into more detail to convince me of anything. But before you do that, tell me who gave you the information you base your allegation on."

"Well, I consulted the archives that are kept in the house of life of Mennefer's necropolis. They contain evidence that an architect named Neferibre actually did exist. He designed and built some of the tombs for private individuals there. His own tomb is located in the same cemetery."

"I hope you didn't dare disturb his eternal rest in the course of your so-called investigations," Seti interrupted sharply.

"I can assure you that I did no such thing, Your Majesty. That wasn't at all necessary. My consultation of the archive yielded evidence that was as intriguing as it was incriminating. I found out that Neferibre's final and grandest project was a magnificent tomb he started to build for a court lady named Maia. This lady was, as Your Majesty might recall, the wet-nurse and tutor of a king whose name I must unfortunately mention on this occasion: Nebkheperure Tutankhamun. "

Seti wrinkled his forehead while he pondered the information.

"I remember her name, but how does this prove your point?" he asked, feeling himself running out of patience.

"The records show," Nebamun went on unwaveringly, "that a change in the supervision of works on this tomb occurred in year six of that king's reign. A different architect took over, since Neferibre had suddenly died."

Understanding began to dawn on Seti when he did a quick calculation.

"Year six, you said? And Siamun was born only in the third year of that king's successor."

Nebamun nodded vigorously. "Exactly. This means there is a gap of roughly seven years between Neferibre's death and Siamun's birth. Thus, it follows that Neferibre can by no means be his real father, because no man can possibly sire a child years after his death."

"I know that myself," Seti snapped, feeling his irritation rising. "There must be a rational explanation for the discrepancy of the data. It may be simply down to the carelessness of a scribe. This wouldn't be the first time that a scribal error occurred."

"But not in this case, since the date happens to appear twice in exactly the same way," the vizier objected. "This rules out the possibility of an error. Besides, there is more to come."

Nebamun paused, presumably to heighten the tension. Seti could see that he was about to burst with excitement, but he didn't do him the favour of urging him on.

"Having convinced myself that the architect Neferibre could by no account be Siamun's father," Nebamun continued, a trifle deflated, "I then started to look for someone who would fit this role. I began my quest of finding a cue with his alleged family. The woman purported to be his mother is called Meritamun. He has a brother by the name of Panakht and three sisters- Taneferet, Meresankh and Satet. The latter has regrettably died recently."

Seti couldn't contain his growing annoyance any longer.

"I know all that," he snapped. "Get to your point."

Nebamun didn't seem in the least disturbed by Seti's impatience.

"I was just about to do so, Your Majesty. The question is who these people really are. It only takes some basic knowledge of the royal house as it was back in the day to find the answer. I was then myself employed as a scribe of the palace, and I remember there being a king's daughter called Meresankh, whose Nubian mother had died as a result of the difficult birth and who was nurtured by a wet-nurse called Meritamun. Said Meritamun had been the wife of a certain Neferibre and had shortly before given birth to a child whose name I cannot recall. I wouldn't be surprised, however, if it was Taneferet. Furthermore it is known that the king in question later took another wife called Sitiah who was the daughter of Amunhotep called Huy, then King's Son of Kush. This royal wife bore a son who was named Siamun. Half a year later, King Tutankhamun passed away, and his wife vanished without a trace along with the royal children. Rumour has it that she also died in the process of giving birth to yet another child, but the fate of the remaining children has never become clear. To add to the confusion, the royal wet-nurse Meritamun –who by the way had been briefly married to the general Nakht-Min- also disappeared from view."

Nebamun fell silent, a triumphant smile surrounding his thin lips.

Seti had to admit that the vizier had a point. He knew that Nebamun had spoken the truth, and that the correspondence of names was indeed striking. However, there were a few things that didn't quite fit.

"How can it be," he pointed out, "that Siamun has a younger sister who must have been born around the time that the royal wife Sitiah died in childbirth along with the child in her womb?"

"I have to admit that this is somewhat difficult to explain," Nebamun replied, a sly look crossing his face. "But who can tell whether this woman called Satet truly was his sister? One surely cannot trust the word of a man who covers up his own origins. Besides, that alleged sister of his barely resembled him."

Seti stopped short. "How do you know that? Where have you seen her?"

There was a flicker of what appeared to be fear in Nebamun's eyes, but the wily vizier recovered so quickly that Seti thought he might only have imagined it.

"She was introduced to me when Siamun still resided in the quarters of the royal architects. Anyway, it is by no means certain that this woman is –excuse me, *was*- his sister."

Seti sat there motionlessly as he let all the information sink in. What the vizier implied was outrageous. So outrageous that it was downright ridiculous. Siamun, a forgotten prince? Impossible.

All of a sudden, Seti felt an irresistible urge to laugh out loud. In a desperate attempt to fight it, he tightened his grip on the armrests of his chair until his knuckles turned white. Even if this was no formal occasion, a minimum of dignity had to be preserved. Eventually he felt able to address the vizier.

"Do you really mean to say that the royal architect Siamun is identical with the king's son of the same name, and that he has come to claim the throne of the Two Lands for himself?"

"This is was what would suggest itself," Nebamun replied with obvious satisfaction. "What else could he want?"

Seti cast him a stern look. "That's completely outlandish."

Nebamun's eyes widened considerably as he took this devastating verdict in.

"Why?"

He must be very baffled indeed to forget that this word wasn't usually spoken in pharaoh's presence. Seti decided to overlook this accidental slip generously.

"Your conclusion cannot possibly be right," he explained,

"because if it were true, Siamun would have let the best of opportunities slip by."

Seeing Nebamun's blank stare, he decided to elaborate.

"Have I not been far away from home for four whole months, along with the entire army? And hasn't the crown prince been absent, too? How easily could Siamun have made a move to seize power during this time; I'm sure you agree with me on that, Nebamun. Nobody could have stopped him. In addition to that, he could have enlisted the help of the King's Son of Kush, who according to your theory would be a close relative of his. Amunemopet could have provided him with sufficient troops to carry out his coup. But what did Siamun do instead? He proved his loyalty to his sovereign by personally surveying the transport of supplies to the troops in the far west and by adjusting the rations of the royal workforces who were suffering from lack of food owing to your blunder. Is this what one would expect from a usurper with a craving for power?"

Nebamun assumed an aggrieved expression that sat decidedly ill with his harsh features.

"My only intention was to draw Your Majesty's attention to a possibly grave danger. Of course, Your Majesty knows best what to do with the information resulting from my endeavours."

Seti struggled to ignore the subliminal sarcasm in Nebamun's voice.

"I fully appreciate your efforts, vizier," he said. "But I believe that you are seeing conspiracies where there are none. However, I will speak to Siamun nonetheless. I am sure that he can come up with a credible explanation for all this. You may now take your leave, as I believe that enough has been said."

With a rather stiff bow Nebamun turned and made for the door. Seti didn't move while he watched his form disappear from his view.

Having pondered all that he had heard once more, he arrived at the conclusion that Nebamun's allegations were utterly wrong. At least, his deduction that Siamun was indeed identical with his royal namesake was by no means as inescapable as the vizier would have him believe. Seti wasn't that easily prepared to hear anything said against the man he had such a high opinion of.

****

Two weeks after his triumphant return from war, pharaoh decided to show his greatness and power to their best advantage. Part of the spoils of battle –including scores of slaves- were to be presented to the gods in the great temple, along with the Nubian tribute provided by the King's Son of Kush. Naturally, plenty of parades and processions accompanied by musicians and dancers would enhance the colourful picture of this outstanding event. The festive mood had gripped the whole of Mennefer well in advance.
Then, on the first day of the festival proper, Siamun left his home early together with Tia and Panakht to join the celebrations. It was going to be a long day, and Siamun was secretly worried about his pregnant wife. At times, she wasn't well at all, and she would often complain of feeling nauseous. But as it were, Tia insisted on watching the performance at close quarters, so there had been little point to dissuade her from doing so.
Panakht soon parted with the young couple to make his way to

the barracks where he would join the other charioteers who, like him, had been chosen to take part in the parade.

When Siamun and Tia were carried along the streets, their litter bearers had a hard time forcing their way through the throng of people. Even those who were willing to make way for them were often unable to do so for lack of space.
Siamun enjoyed the spectacle thoroughly. Sitting in his swaying seat high above people's heads, he looked into their beaming faces as he passed by them. Many young children were perched on their fathers' shoulders to have a better view, while others were clasping their mothers' hands so as not to get lost in the bustle. The number of merchants lining the streets and extolling their goods at the tops of their voices seemed to have doubled, and as always on such occasions the mouth-watering smell of freshly baked bread came wafting through the air.
It wasn't far to the temple enclosure, and they soon found themselves in the middle of the vast courtyard. More people lined its sides, albeit not ordinary ones. Only the highest dignitaries had the prerogative of witnessing the imminent ceremony at such close quarters.
At the far end of the courtyard, a royal dais bearing three magnificent thrones spanned by a gilded canopy awaited the arrival of the royal family.
Siamun tore his gaze off the glint of gold and took Tia's hand. They had preferred to remain seated in their litters that had been placed not too far off the dais.
"They won't be long now," he told her, watching her anxiously. "Are you sure you're alright?"
Tia offered him a brilliant smile.
"I'm fine, thank you. I even feel a little bit hungry."
Siamun was relieved. Given Tia's condition, this was indeed

good news.

"I'm glad to hear hat. Then all we can do is hope that the ceremony won't take all that long, so that we can have something to eat soon."

The faint murmur of voices outside the temple precinct rose to a chorus of overawed shouts and cheers. This had to be the royal family approaching the temple via the magnificent sphinx-lined alley. Then a reverent silence descended upon the assembly while pharaoh's litter was carried through the entrance gate. Every head remained inclined until he had ascended the royal dais and turned to face his subjects. Two fan-bearers positioned themselves behind the throne in the middle while the crown prince and his mother alighted from their litters and strode up to their thrones using the smaller side ramps.

At pharaoh's sign everyone straightened up, and Siamun caught sight of more litters entering the courtyard. The dignitaries who had accompanied the royal procession framed the dais in a fixed order according to rank. The two viziers clad in their distinctive garbs stood closest to the king, followed by the royal treasurers Hormin and Tiya and the four supreme commanders of troops, among whom Siamun spotted Urhiye. Their eyes met, and the two men offered each other a friendly nod. The southern vizier Paser greeted Siamun in the same way.

When everyone had taken their respective places, all eyes turned to the high priest of Ptah who paid his respects by kissing the royal feet –an extraordinary favour which Seti accepted with calm dignity- before standing next to the throne. As a representative of this temple, the goods about to be presented were as much his due as they were the king's.

Catching Seti's fleeting signal, Nebamun left his place and stepped forth.

"Praise be the mighty ruler of the Two Lands," he boomed in his most peremptory voice, "the good lord Seti Menmaatre who broadens the borders and tramples the foes of the Nine Bows underfoot! Behold the spoils of war His Majesty has brought back with him and the tribute he has imposed on the subdued tribes in order to fill our storehouses and treasuries and satisfy the gods!"

The penetrating sounds of two trumpets announced the beginning of the presentation. The clatter of hooves could be heard, and soon a number of chariots came rolling in, each one pulled by a team of magnificent brown stallions. The five vehicles were manned with a charioteer and a troop commander each. Panakht, who stood in one of them, grinned joyfully at Siamun as he passed by him. A single foot soldier followed in their wake, a long rope in his hand to which a large number of captives were bound. Only the few women among them were allowed to walk free with their frightened children by their sides. All without exception had to grovel in the dust in front of the royal dais, only to be driven into a far corner to await their fate. Whoever was reluctant to comply would soon see reason when he got a taste of the soldier's whip.

Siamun glanced furtively at Tia, sensing her uneasiness at seeing this rather unpleasant spectacle, and put his hand comfortingly on hers.

"Don't worry, it'll soon be over," he assured her, knowing that the overall number of captives wasn't exceedingly great. Most of them were Temehiu; prisoners hailing from the northern territories were few and far between. Even the booty that was now being presented wasn't nearly as bountiful as that resulting from other campaigns. There hadn't been much to be had from the sand-dwellers of the western desert, who, apart from live-stock and weapons, hardly possessed anything worthwhile at all. The rich coastal cities, on the other hand, hadn't been subjected to extensive looting, for they were meant to be strong trade partners as well as providers of manpower and supplies during any future campaigns.

As it turned out, it had been a wise decision to join the presentation of spoils with that of the annual Nubian tribute. Again, it was Nebamun who had the honour of announcing the appearance of the King's Son of Kush. Amunemopet made a grand entrance with high-ranking members of the Nubian administration trailing behind. Siamun was delighted to spot Meresankh's uncle Heqanefer among them.

Amunemopet strode up to the royal dais with great dignity. With the sheer pleated robe above his garb and his stylish wig, the braided strands of which reached far beyond his shoulders, he was an impressive sight despite his youth. Seti acknowledged his deferential bow with a graceful nod. Then Amunemopet turned to face the entrance gate opposite him and raised the tall flail in his right. The procession of Nubians began to file in.

Following what appeared to be a number of lesser officials were dark-skinned men and women clad in their native garbs which consisted of rather skimpy leather kilts for the former and long skirts for the latter. In addition, some of the men had tall ostrich feathers tucked into their headbands and animal skins slung around their torsos. They carried huge trays laden with all precious things imaginable. There were small bags filled with gold dust, ingots made from pure gold for melting and processing into all kinds of jewellery and exquisite pieces of furniture made from ebony and ivory. Elephant and hippopotamus tusks, shields, swords and true masterpieces of gold work representing entire landscapes were among the more spectacular items. By far the greatest stir, however, was caused by the entry of two live giraffes and a leopard on a leash that kept baring its fangs in vicious snarls. Compared to them, the men who were paraded behind with fettered hands hardly got any attention. Anyway, Siamun knew that their bondage had merely symbolic purposes, for there hadn't been a single rebellion in Nubia since the beginning of Seti's reign. Eventually, all the delivered goods formed quite respectable piles in front of the royal dais, while the captives were assembled by the great pylon, ready to be led into the inner sanctuary to be presented to the statue of the god. Later, they were going to be assigned to one of the various temple estates to do tedious field work, or –far worse- condemned to toiling away in remote mines and quarries for the rest of their miserable lives.

Followed by the high priest and Ramses, Seti left his place under the canopy in order to carry out the appropriate ceremonies. Meanwhile, the ritual slaughtering of fattened bulls had begun, as was clear from the faint panic-stricken roars ringing from the temple's slaughter house. Soon, there would be plenty of meat to be had for everyone.

"How do you like the idea of a nice succulent chunk of roast meat?" Siamun asked his wife cheerfully.

"I think I'm not having any," came the rather subdued reply. "My appetite has entirely vanished."

"You've probably been sitting in this uncomfortable chair for too long," Siamun suggested. "You will need to have a good rest if you want to be fit for tonight's feast."

He would have preferred to leave straight away, but owing to etiquette this wasn't possible yet. After what seemed a very long time, Seti and Ramses emerged from the temple and approached their litters. Followed by a long string of dignitaries, the royal family left the temple precinct. Siamun and Tia were finally free to go.

****

When Siamun entered the great banquet hall with Tia by his side, it was already full, almost to its bursting point. He let his gaze quickly roam across the assembled guests. Everyone of some standing was present. However, the actual guest of honour was without any doubt the King's Son of Kush who had been assigned the most coveted seat right in front of the royal pedestal with its as yet empty thrones.

The young couple started to move in that same direction. Those sitting closest to them rose from their chairs and inclined their heads respectfully as they walked by. Men and women alike were dressed in all their finery, with many of them wearing perfumed cones atop their heads. Additionally, most of the ladies had fastened blue or white lotus flowers to their elaborate headdresses, their lovely fragrant blossoms dangling above their foreheads.

On coming closer to the royal dais, Siamun saw somebody's frantic waving. That someone soon turned out to be his cousin Amunemopet.

"Your Highness, venerable overseer of the king's building projects," he said, rising, "I hope that you give me the honour of your presence."

"The honour is all ours," Siamun replied when Tia nodded her agreement.

"May I take the opportunity to introduce my close friend Huni to you?" he said, indicating a man of about thirty years and slight build next to him. "And this is my equally close friend Heqanefer, who is already known to you."

The men exchanged greetings, then everyone sat down. Siamun's gaze fastened on the massive golden collar that was prominently displayed around Amunemopet's neck. This shebiu-collar was part of the gold of honour that had been awarded to him earlier that day.

"You can't exactly call this comfortable," Amunemopet said with a wry smile, pointing at the collar. "But I'm determined not to flag. You know yourself what it's like to have several deben of gold hanging around your neck, don't you, Siamun?"

"I do," Siamun replied, returning his smile. "Enjoy it, you have thoroughly deserved it. Without your Nubian tribute, the presentation of spoils would have been a somewhat meagre affair."

"I know. That's exactly why I was summoned to Mennefer in the first place. By the way, it's not that bad that His Majesty didn't make much booty. Securing the naval trade routes is worth more than any grand raid. And in my opinion he did well to end the campaign when he did."

Siamun nodded emphatically. "That's just what I think. There seem to have been few to approve the continuation of the fighting. To my surprise, Urhiye is said to have been among them, as well as –perhaps not so surprisingly- the crown prince."

Amunemopet raised his eyebrows. "Urhiye? Who is that?"

"Supreme commander of the division of Ptah, and Panakht's close friend," Siamun explained.

"I see. And why does this surprise you?"

"Because the division of Ptah was the one to fight against the Temehiu. Naturally, they must have been the most worn-out troops of all, and yet Panakht told me that Urhiye tried hard to press for an advance on Kadesh."

"This is indeed somewhat strange," his cousin said slowly. "Perhaps he did so to ingratiate himself with the crown prince, what do you think?"

Heqanefer, at whom the question had been addressed,

shrugged his broad shoulders. "Quite possible," he said vaguely. "Things like these are always hard to tell when one is as far off the action as we are."

"You're probably right," Amunemopet sighed. "I say, I do hope that His Majesty is going to make his entrance soon, or else some people might well start to eat their own fingers next."

Siamun had a quick look around. Indeed, most of the bowls containing dried fruit and nuts were empty, and his own stomach rumbled menacingly.

Just then, the double doors in the wall behind the royal dais swung open, and a herald's booming voice proclaimed first pharaoh's names and titles, then those of the crown prince. Barely waiting for him to end, Seti entered and made for his throne, his features set in an inscrutable mask of royal composure. Only the prince followed him; the Great Royal Wife was conspicuous by her absence.

"Why hasn't your mother come too?" Siamun whispered into Tia's ear.

Tia responded with a helpless shrug. "Mother hardly attends together with father anymore. Most of the times, she makes some flimsy excuse or other, but sometimes she can't be bothered to do even that."

Siamun nodded sympathetically. The relationship between Seti and his wife seemed to be worse than he had imagined. In fact, it probably only really existed by name.

As soon as the king and Ramses had settled down on their thrones, the great hall was filled with new life. Servants bustled around, waiting on the guests with wine while others weaved their way in between the tables offering all kinds of delicious food from overflowing trays. Being the guest of honour, Amunemopet was among the first to be served, and he and Siamun helped themselves generously. Even Tia seemed to enjoy the succulent roast beef and duck that were accompanied

by various vegetables and spicy sauces.
Siamun had just finished his meal when Panakht showed up.
"Are you having a good time?" he inquired.
"Of course," Siamun replied cheerfully.
"Someone who doesn't enjoy a feast like this one can't be helped," Amunemopet said, perhaps not coincidentally casting admiring glances at the pretty dancers who were by now swaying gracefully to the sounds of harps, flutes and lyres.
"Don't you want to join us for a while?" he added with a gesture of invitation.
Panakht grinned amiably. "Sure, why not?"
While he pulled a vacant chair closer, he fastened his gaze conspicuously on Tia's friend Baket who had also joined them. The pretty young woman seemed to have caught his entire attention. In fact, Siamun secretly suspected that it had been her who had attracted him in the first place. If this was so, it was good news indeed.
Amunemopet appeared to share his thoughts.
"You wouldn't believe what banquets can be good for," he muttered with a meaningful smile in Siamun's direction.
"Pardon?"
Panakht's blank expression almost made Siamun laugh.
"I said that I feel honoured to meet you in person," Amunemopet explained.
Panakht beamed. "The honour is all mine. By the way, that collar really suits you. Congratulations!"
"Thank you. And I have just heard that you have already risen to the position of troop commander. That's a great achievement indeed."
"Oh, that's nothing special," Panakht said modestly. "To be honest, it was just a stroke of luck."
Amunemopet smiled. "I'm sure you deserved your promotion, just as your friend Urhiye did. Where is he? I would like to

meet him, too."

All of a sudden, an embarrassed look appeared on Panakht's face.

"That's what I'd like to know myself. He was here with me, but then he somehow vanished. I've got no idea where he might be now."

Amunemopet's eyebrows shot up in surprise. "Really? How strange. Well, there's nothing we can do about it, can we? Maybe I'll have more luck some other time." Then his features brightened. "Look who's coming to see us."

Siamun followed his gaze and saw Paser walking up to them. The southern vizier greeted the men joyfully before seating himself on the chair Panakht had just vacated. Siamun wondered briefly why his friend had left all of a sudden without a word, but then his attention was taken up by the ensuing animated conversation that sprang up almost immediately. The mood became more and more relaxed, aided by the free flow of excellent wine. Although Siamun had come to know his companions only recently, he soon felt as if he was with old friends.

"What is he moaning about now?" Paser cried at one point, jerking his head in the direction of the royal dais. Nebamun was standing behind the throne and whispered something into Seti's ear, his gaze fixed on the young men.

"Whatever it is, it clearly doesn't meet with the king's approval," Amunemopet remarked dryly.

Indeed, Seti shook his head indignantly in response.

"Who cares? We southerners ought to be glad if we get any attention at all," Paser joked, making everyone laugh.

Siamun, however, couldn't help remembering what his cousin had told him about the shift of power within the Two Lands. Amunemopet's meaningful glance intensified his uneasiness, but then he pushed these unpleasant thoughts aside. Tonight,

he wouldn't let his good mood be spoilt by anything.
When Tia decided to leave, she wouldn't hear of his offer to come with her.
"Thank you, but I don't think that's a good idea," she said firmly. "Seeing how thoroughly you're enjoying yourself, I'd rather that you stay on. It's been a long time that you have been in such an exuberant mood."
Deep down, Siamun had to agree with her. He would have deeply regretted to leave just now. Having seen Tia to her litter, he returned to the merry company of his new friends.

****

The veiled figure stole silently down the deserted hallway. Over in the great hall the banquet was still in full swing. Those who didn't celebrate themselves were busy waiting on the guests. Therefore it was highly unlikely that anyone would cross his path.
This and the fact that he was very annoyed indeed lulled him into a false sense of security and caused him to lower his guard. He was angry because he hadn't gotten what he had come for.
Deeply engrossed in his gloomy thoughts, he forgot to keep away from the halo of the next torch. Then it all happened so quickly. Someone turned a corner right in front of him and came dashing towards him. He froze.
The next thing he knew was that the person –a servant girl carrying a tray- collided head-on with him. The girl's eyes widened, first in surprise, then in obvious terror. She opened her mouth to scream, but no sound left it, since the forceful blow to

her temple sent her sprawling. The muffled sound of her body connecting with the floor tiles was nearly drowned out by the clattering noise of the tray that followed behind. The sweet cakes and pastries she had presumably snatched from the kitchen to devour them in all secrecy lay scattered all around her.

Unmoved, the veiled one stepped over the limp body and hurried on, faster still than before. If he didn't want to arouse anyone's suspicion, he had to be back in the banquet hall without further delay. That stupid servant girl had seen him in the light of the torch, but it was very unlikely that she would remember anything once she woke up. That was, if she woke at all. And even if she did, she would probably believe she'd encountered some evil demon, given what a superstitious lot these people of Kemet were.

When he was nearing the great hall, he tore his covers off and hurled them into a dark corner. He had to find a way to achieve his goal, or else he would not only miss out on any future rewards, but he would also have to return the handsome advance he had spent long since. If no opportunity arose soon, he would have to resign himself to more waiting, at least until the next campaign. This was decidedly too long.

He straightened his clothes with agitated movements and smoothed his unruly hair down before entering the hall. Now all that counted was to be alert; things were getting far too hot for his liking.

Chapter Ten

Mesmerized, Siamun looked on as the chisel ate away at the soft limestone, sending tiny flakes flying in all directions. The rough outline of the figure to be carved could already be discerned. It was part of a composition that would show Seti kneeling in front of the enthroned Horus-falcon while proffering two sacrificial vessels to the god. In other places, the wall decoration had progressed much further, with some of the reliefs already being painted with bright, vivid colours. Siamun let his gaze roam across the walls as he slowly moved on. Here the king was shown erecting a djed-pillar, there he leaned on a gilded staff while addressing another deity.

All of the representations had two things in common: The high standard to which they had been executed and the stunning liveliness of the figures. Siamun almost expected them to detach themselves from the walls and come towards him at any moment.

He was deeply satisfied with what he had seen so far. The exquisite decoration further enhanced the outstanding beauty of the temple that was soon going to be inaugurated. Presently, the king was travelling the whole country in order to celebrate the harvest festival. According to tradition, he had to cut a few bunches of crops with his own hand as a token of thanks to the gods who had bestowed this bounty on Kemet's people in the first place. It was the second month of Shemu, the harvest season, and so it was high time to begin. Since the crops usually ripened quicker in the south, Seti had first travelled through to the Nubian border. From there, the royal fleet would sail downstream, with frequent stops at every major town where the same ritual had to be performed over and over again. After Seti's return to Mennefer the celebrations for the fourth anniversary of his coronation were waiting to be dealt with. Only then would he finally have time to carry out the consecration ceremonies of his beloved temple.

Siamun stepped outside and walked briskly up to Panakht who was sitting in the shade of a large awning and fanning himself vigorously.
"There you are, at last," he muttered by way of a greeting. "I thought you'd never be able to tear yourself away."
"Admittedly it was quite hard for me to do so," Siamun replied. He dropped gratefully on a folding chair and reached for the water jug Panakht held out for him. "Those representations have something truly fascinating about them," he explained after a few sips. "It is as if an entire new world was being created before one's very eyes."
Panakht pulled a face. "If only the roof was in place already, I might go and have a look around myself."
Siamun laughed. "We can't very well do that, because at this stage the draughtsmen and stonemasons need all the light they can get to see by. If you can't stand the heat, you can either spend your time sitting around in the shade, complaining, or-" he paused for effect and glanced meaningfully at his friend- "you could go back to Mennefer to see your beloved Baket. Perhaps that's what you want all along."
"What are you talking about?" Panakht grumbled, unable to prevent an embarrassed look from appearing on his face.
"I have eyes in my head," Siamun said casually. "Why can't you

just admit that she has impressed you? I've got a feeling that you two might be well-suited to each other. And as far as I can tell Baket is by no means indifferent to you, either."

"Hm, maybe you're right," Panakht mumbled, scratching his head awkwardly. "Anyway, it's not the right time yet."

Siamun shrugged. "Whatever you think."

He let his watchful gaze wander about the temple that lay gleaming like a jewel in the shimmering heat and scrutinized the immaculate white walls that stood a staggering twelve royal cubits high. Siamun felt deep satisfaction at the thought that against all odds he had managed to bring the core of this impressive structure to near completion in time. He had no doubts that the priests would be able to celebrate their cults in one and a half months' time.

Having tired of sitting idly, he placed the water jug on the floor and rose.

Panakht looked up at him in surprise. "Now where are you going?"

"I just want to have another look at the rearmost rooms," Siamun explained.

"If you think you can chase the men up by constantly watching their every move, you're probably mistaken."

"You may be right there, but then it can do no harm either. Won't you come?"

Panakht struggled to suppress a yawn and flung himself on the ground. "Not now. In this terrible heat, every movement is one too many."

Seeing that it was hopeless, Siamun walked off on his own. He ascended the narrow staircase that gave access to the back of the temple and entered a long corridor. To his left, the rooms dedicated to the cults of Sokar and Nefertem were situated. These two deities would play an important role in the ritual resurrection to new life, the main theme of this temple. But

Siamun had other things on his mind, so he turned right at the next corner and traversed the hall of barges which already sported six impressive columns. Works on the decoration of the walls were well underway. In passing, he greeted the overseer of stonemasons Userhat-Hatiai with a friendly nod. On he went in the direction of the seven sanctuaries. Taking a left turn, Siamun entered the corridor leading up to them. He was not at all surprised to encounter several draughtsmen – some of them perched on tall ladders- who were busily drawing the black outlines of more scenes along with their accompanying texts. As was common practice, every available surface was going to be decorated. On the wall to his right, Siamun could make out the names of several deities. Then he cast a fleeting glance at the opposite wall- and stopped dead. Right under the ceiling, the ancient offering formula that would grant Seti perpetual sustenance in all eternity, was written out in black ink. But it were the royal cartouches underneath that had caught his eye. For written inside them were not Seti's names, but those of Kemet's earliest rulers: Meni, Teti, Iti, Ita, Septi, Meribiap, Semsu.

That was how far the draughtsman had gotten. However, the space was vast, and Siamun realized that this was just the beginning of a compilation that would encompass the names of all the kings who had ever held sway over the Two Lands.

A distinct feeling of uneasiness washed all over him. What was the final part of this list going to look like? Would Seti include all of his predecessors, even those whom he usually systematically ignored, and whose monuments he had either destroyed or usurped?

Just then, one of the draughtsmen climbed down his ladder and pored over a large sheet of papyrus that was spread out on the floor. Siamun had failed to notice it before, but he instantly recognized it as what it was.

"Is this your draft. Amunwahsu?" he asked.
The man looked up in surprise. Apparently he had been oblivious of Siamun's presence.
"Yes, lord," he replied with a slight bow.
"I would like to have a look at it, if you don't mind."
"Of course. Suit yourself."
Amunwahsu backed away and lowered himself gingerly onto the bottom rung of his ladder, using the hem of his kilt to wipe his sweat-covered face.
Heart pounding in his ears, Siamun walked over to the papyrus and crouched down. He didn't take it up, for he didn't want anyone to see how his hands were shaking.
It was an inspired and impressive composition. To the far left, he saw a depiction of Seti and Ramses. The king was holding an incense burner in one hand, while the prince was clutching two libation vases symbolizing continuous and eternal offerings to the kings whose names were written in three long rows in front of him.
Siamun's eyes darted across the signs. When he came to the centre of the middle row, he paused and closed his eyes. He had to gather his thoughts in order to brace himself for what he feared to see next. Or rather, what he feared *not* to see, because it might not be there.
It cost him a great effort to open his eyes again and read on. There it was: Menkheperre, Aakheperure, Menkheperure, Nebmaatre-
He swallowed hard, although his mouth had gone as dry as the sand of the red land. Now it would become clear whether Seti had honoured the memory of Siamun's father and great-uncle. Next to Nebmaatre he read: Djoserkheperure Setepenre, followed by Menpehtire and Menmaatre!
Stunned, Siamun stared helplessly at the writing in front of him. How was this possible? Not only one or two royal names

[308]

were missing, but five! Nebmaatre's cartouche ought to be followed by those of Neferkheperure, Semenkhkare, Ankhetkheperure, Nebkheperure and Kheperkheperure. Seti had all of them deliberately omitted, thus denying the very existence of their owners. He intended to condemn them to sinking into eternal oblivion.

To add insult to injury, the third and last row underneath consisted of a constant repetition of Seti's birth and throne names: Son of Re Seti, Lord of the Two Lands Menmaatre, Seti, Menmaatre, Seti...

Of course, Siamun thought grimly, clenching his jaw. This way, Seti made sure that he wasn't going to suffer the same gruesome fate. He ensured himself of eternal existence after death. He whose name exists, exists himself.

The writing swam in front of Siamun's eyes. A watery drop fell on the papyrus. Only then did he realise that his forehead was dripping with sweat. He pulled his sleeve across with an agitated movement and jumped to his feet. He had to get out of here, away from this unspeakable outrage.

It was only when he had left the temple well behind that he stopped. Panting hard, he pressed his hand on his heart that pounded hard against his ribs. If only it would stop beating altogether, he could escape from this deceptive world and leave it all behind! Alas, it didn't do him this favour. Siamun turned to look at the monument he had been building with so much love and devotion. The gleaming white walls had lost all their splendour, were nothing but a pathetic manifestation of human vanity anymore. Disgusted, he turned away and staggered on strangely weak legs towards the awning. Panakht was still sprawling in its shade, whisking the flies away with languid movements. On hearing Siamun's footfall, he raised his head a little.

"What, you're back already?" His voice was full of surprise. "That wasn't what I'd call a very thorough inspection this time. Have you finally had enough, too?"

Siamun replied nothing. Lips pressed together, he dropped heavily to the ground and crossed his legs.

"What's wrong?" Panakht inquired. "Have you met some sort of evil spirit in there?"

"That wretched liar!" Siamun burst forth, punching the ground with his clenched fist in an attempt to vent his indescribable fury.

Startled, Panakht sat up. "Who do you call a liar?"

"Seti."

Panakht's eyes widened with terror. "You call pharaoh a liar? But why? What happened?"

"In there," Siamun hissed, pointing his thumb backwards over his shoulder, "an extensive list is about to be designed, containing the names of all the kings who ever ruled the Two Lands. It will cover an entire wall. And can you guess which names will be missing from it?"

Panakht lowered his eyes, understanding dawning on him. "I can," he said quietly. Then he looked up and fastened his gaze on Siamun. "But how can you be so sure? This list might not be completed yet."

"That's true," Siamun conceded, "works on it have only just started. But I have seen the draft which shows the entire composition. And the names preceding Seti's own are Nebmaatre, Djoserkheperure and Menpehtire!"

Visibly shaken, Panakht fell silent.

"That's an outrage," he then whispered.

"Indeed it is," Siamun cried, quite forgetting himself. "And not only that. It is an offence against Maat herself! How he can do such a thing, is simply beyond me."

"Not so loud," Panakht urged, casting wary glances all around him. "Perhaps we'd better talk about this elsewhere."

Siamun nodded. "Let's go. Anyway, I can't stand the sight of these walls anymore."

They rose, slipped their feet into their sandals and made their way to their temporary dwelling which was a good way off. Although nobody seemed to pay them any heed, they spoke in low voices.

"I suspected from the start that King Akhenaten's name may be omitted from the list," Siamun said." But my father, who instigated the restoration of monuments in the first place, was a fervent worshipper of Amun and reinstated the cults of all the other gods as well. Under his rule, the Two Lands recovered from the havoc Akhenaten had wreaked, and Maat triumphed over chaos once again. His successors gained a great deal from his achievements, particularly Horemheb and, of course, Seti himself. How can Seti then go about erasing my father's name from the memory of his people, along with those of other, rightfully crowned kings?"

"You're right, it clearly is an offence against Maat," Panakht agreed. "But even so..."

He hesitated, apparently groping for the right words. "I mean, this isn't exactly the first time that you are being confronted with the like. You told me yourself how often you have come across usurpations in the past."

"Sure," Siamun admitted, "but this is different. Seti makes a point of honouring most of his predecessors by displaying their names ostentatiously while denying some of them said honour, intending to condemn the latter to dying the second death by obliteration. This is not only an action unworthy of a king, but also by far the gravest assault on Maat and my father's memory I have encountered so far. I am not having this kind of outrage in the very temple I have been building with so much love and care. I must stop the evil from happening before it can mar its perfection, or else I would feel as guilty as if I had committed this crime myself."

Meanwhile, the temple of Osiris had come into view. They headed for the small whitewashed building on its right which they currently shared with the high priest.

Siamun felt Panakht's sideways glance more than he saw it. "What do you intend to do?" his friend asked raptly.

Siamun drew a deep breath before he answered. "I will try to convince Seti of the necessity to amend the list."

"And…you think he's going to do that? Won't he become suspicious and ask himself why this should be so important to you?"

Siamun shrugged. "I'm going to refer to Maat. And perhaps Tia shares my view and helps me to change his mind."

"But she doesn't know your real motive," Panakht pointed out.

"Perhaps she's going to learn it."

"What are you going to do," Panakht said after a short while, "if Seti doesn't give in?"

Siamun walked on in silence, then stopped a few paces off the entrance to their dwelling and turned to look at his friend.

"Time will tell," he said in a grave voice. "At any rate, I'm not willing to tolerate such evil. We're leaving this horrible place tomorrow first thing in the morning. By the beginning of the third month at the latest, pharaoh will be back in Mennefer to prepare himself for the anniversary of his coronation. Then I will have the opportunity to make him explain himself."

****

Seti's forehead was covered with beads of cold sweat. While he drew another laboured breath, his chest heaved painfully in a desperate attempt to pump air into his lungs. It was a blessing that he had had the foresight to take Iuny with him. The experienced physician did whatever he could.

"Your Majesty should try to drink some more," Iuny said, holding out a shallow bowl. Seti nodded reluctantly, allowing him to put it to his lips.

The concoction within exuded a revolting smell, and Seti had to force himself to take a sip. He had no idea what it consisted of, and –truth be told- he didn't even want to know. Iuny swore by his recipe, insisting that this medication was soon going to drive the evil demon from Seti's heart that caused him so much trouble. Seti was inclined to believe him; if he were a demon, he would surely turn and flee from this stuff at the very first opportunity.

Seti drank as much as he could, then sank back onto his headrest, exhausted. He closed his eyes and waited. Did he imagine things, or did the pressure on his chest really lessen somewhat? After a while, he was quite sure that he was right. The pain eased, and his breathing returned to near normal. Seti felt for the gilded wadjet-eye on his chest. Perhaps he owed it to the powerful magic of this amulet rather than Iuny's potion that the dreadful attack was over.

He didn't really care. Feeling dead tired all of a sudden, he drifted off into a long slumber.

When he woke, he barely felt any pain at all. He searched the cabin with his eyes and eventually spotted Iuny, who was slumped in a nearby chair. Seti stirred, and to his surprise the physician jumped up at once.

"How is Your Majesty?" he asked, worry etched on his face.

"Much better," Seti replied. "Your magic potion seems to have done the trick."

"I'm glad to hear that," Iuny replied with a tentative smile. "It is a long-standing recipe that was handed down to me by my father."

Bracing his elbows against the bed, Seti brought himself into a sitting position. Iuny's father had treated his own father, King Ramses, who had also been suffering from increasing chest pain during his final years. However, eventually nothing and nobody had been able to save him.

"How long do I have?" Seti asked bluntly.

"Pardon?" Iuny returned with a blank look on his face.

Seti sighed. "How many more of these dreadful attacks do you think I'm going to survive?"

Iuny threw his hands up in dismay. "May Your Majesty be granted myriads of years on the-"

"I want to hear your honest opinion," Seti said firmly.

The physician lowered his eyes. "Much depends on the way you lead your life, Horus. You need to give yourself a rest more often. Medicine and magic alone do not always suffice to fight Sekhmet's messengers. Your Majesty has been under a lot of pressure lately. First the strenuous campaign, then the long journey to Nubia and now the celebration of the harvest festival… all this has taken its toll, as it was bound to do."

"You're probably right," Seti agreed rather meekly. "But what am I supposed to do? After all, such are a king's duties."

Iuny cleared his throat discreetly. "Perhaps the crown prince ought to take on more of these duties, if I may say so. By now, His Highness should well be able to do so."

Groaning silently, Seti stroked his shaven head before he rose with some difficulty. Iuny was in one bound with him and supported his arm while Seti made for a small table. Before he could reach for the wine jug on it, the physician grabbed another jug and filled the better part of a cup with water. Then he topped it up with a little wine which he diligently poured through a strainer.

"For a while, Your Majesty ought to drink only wine that has been thoroughly watered down," he explained with an apologetic smile.

"I'm beginning to feel like an old man," Seti grumbled, raising the cup to his lips, "when I'm not even forty years of age."

"If the gods will, Your Majesty will overcome this disease and recover completely," Iuny replied diplomatically. "Does Your Majesty want me to get some water and clean linen?"

Seti nodded. "Yes, do that. And there is something else..."

Iuny looked at his king expectantly.

"This matter concerning my ill health has to stay between us, as usual."

"As you wish, Your Majesty."

The physician bowed and left the cabin. Soon after, a servant brought a bowl with water, a towel and a fresh set of clothing. Seti waved him away and dipped his hands into the pleasant coolness of the water.

He didn't have any illusions regarding the observance of secrecy he wished for. He knew that some of the knowledge had been spilled already, but he did his best not to give rise to ever more rumour nonetheless.

Having washed and dressed, Seti felt so good that the memories of what he had gone through a few hours ago began to fade. Only the fear of death that had gripped him still reverberated deep within him. Never before did he experience something that terrible.

Perhaps I should love my tomb more than my temple, he thought miserably when he stepped outside.

His gaze fell on a number of men who whiled away their time lunging around on the deck and chatting. When they caught sight of their king, they leaped to their feet and snapped to attention. Seti knew that they were going to indulge in their idle activities as soon as he passed by, but he didn't care. Since they were travelling downstream, there wasn't much for the ship's crew to do until they were going to moor somewhere. Unmoved, he made his way to the stern. Leaning on the rail, he watched Ramses' boat which was following close behind. Ramses himself, however, was nowhere to be seen. He was probably spending the hours in his cabin, sprawling on his bed and dreaming of Nefertari, his future wife. Being the niece of one of Tuya's cousins, none other than Tuya herself had chosen her to become her son's bride. While on his way, Seti had seized the opportunity to pay the girl's family a visit. He had convinced himself of her suitability for the role of a great royal wife. Nefertari was slightly younger than Ramses, beautiful, well-bred and apparently blessed with a great deal of patience. The latter would certainly come in useful when dealing with her future husband. As to Ramses himself- well, he seemed to have fallen in love with her the moment he clapped eyes on her. He would have dearly loved to take the girl with him straight away, hadn't Seti curbed his enthusiasm. First of all, suitable living quarters had to be prepared for Nefertari and her entourage, and preparations for the wedding ceremony were still underway.

Anyway, Seti wished the two young people luck from the bottom of his heart. Perhaps, he hoped, Nefertari's presence would cause Ramses to develop a greater sense of responsibility, and to take more interest in those kingly duties that were too boring f-or his liking. As Iuny had rightly pointed out, Seti needed to step down on his activities. And only when he knew that Ramses was truly fit for kingship could he go on his journey to the Beautiful West with his mind at ease.

But before that, Seti had to do at least one more thing. He wanted to consecrate his beloved temple in the Sacred Land of Abedju, and he wanted to enrich it to make it economically independent. For this purpose, Seti had gone to great lengths indeed. He had extended his journey and travelled to the Nubian town of Nauri, which was the site of an impressive temple with attached gold mines. Seti had personally made sure that the gold production would be sufficient not only to sustain the staff of his temple, but also to pay for the daily offerings. A small part of the resources, however, was going to be assigned to its builder as a well-deserved life-long income. Siamun had truly worked wonders. Without his ingenuity, the monument wouldn't possess half the splendour it did. As soon as he was back in Mennefer, Seti wanted to work out all the details and record them in a royal decree.

Actually, he had hoped to meet Siamun during his short stay at Abedju, but unfortunately his son-in-law hadn't been present. According to the overseer of workmen, Siamun had left quite hurriedly a few days earlier without giving specific reasons. Seti sincerely hoped that it hadn't been bad news from Tia that had prompted his hasty departure.

By the way, this was another important thing he longed to live to see: the arrival of his first grandchild.

****

Feeling utterly exhausted, Siamun was leaning himself against the door jamb while he looked out into the garden without realizing what he saw. Why he felt so worn out, he couldn't tell.

Since he had done no strenuous activity lately, it must be down to his constant brooding, and to the disturbed nights during which he tossed and turned more than he slept.

All of a sudden, the memory of the last night prior to his fateful departure from Iunu flashed back into his mind. Unable to sleep, he had been standing by the window and staring into the distance, just the way he did now.

The days seemed to stretch endlessly. In the beginning, Siamun had tried to while away the time until pharaoh's return with all sorts of distractions, but without success. Then he had poured out his heart in a letter to his family, but even that hadn't eased the pain he was feeling ever since that cursed last day in Abedju. He thought of ways to prevent the evil he had encountered so unexpectedly from unfolding almost without cease. Until now, the offensive signs existed only on papyrus, what was bad enough in itself. But as long as they were not chiselled into the wall of this sacred temple, all was not lost. Perhaps he would succeed in making pharaoh change his mind and have the list of kings completed after all. As long as there was so much as a glimmer of hope, he wasn't going to make any rash decisions.

However, if the worst came to the worst, Siamun was determined to enlist all the help he could get. He had already instructed Panakht to send someone who owned his trust to Nubia in order to deliver a secret message. Surely it did no harm if Amunemopet began to ready his troops for possible military action. Lately, Siamun often thought of the renewed promise his cousin had given him last time they met. Amunemopet had again assured him of his full support in case he made a move to seize the throne. In addition, he had also promised to win the vizier of the south over in due course. Siamun knew full well that his cousin's motives were not entirely selfless, but unlike before he didn't care anymore.

And this was not the only thing that had changed. To his own dismay, Siamun had become very irritable. He hated himself for it, yet there was nothing he could do about it. He was surprised that Tia hadn't complained yet, since there was no way she shouldn't have noticed. A few times, she had looked at him in a strange, inscrutable manner, but never said anything.

Siamun was ashamed for being so on edge when he should have been a support for his wife in the perilous time of her pregnancy. The tension within him grew with every passing day. Over and over again, he tested his heart to find out what he was prepared to do. To his own surprise, he came to the conclusion that he didn't flinch from the thought of open rebellion anymore. If Seti didn't give in, he had to bear the consequences.

A faint sound put a stop to his gloomy thoughts and made him jump violently. He shot round.

"You gave me a start," he told Tia, trying to keep his voice soft.

"Sorry, I didn't mean to," she replied quietly. Searching his face, she moved closer and took his hands. "You must tell me what troubles you."

Unable to stand her pleading look, he turned his head. "How do you know if something troubles me at all?" he asked, hoping to sound casual.

"I noticed that you aren't quite your usual self ever since you returned from Abedju."

"Then why haven't you asked me before?"

"I thought you might tell me when the time was right."

Siamun withdrew his hands gently and turned away from her. All of a sudden, his heart had grown unimaginably heavy. Chewing on his lip, he thought fervently of an answer. If he told Tia of his fateful discovery, he wouldn't get around telling her the whole truth. And that was something he had been determined to avoid at all cost.

Wondering where that strange metallic taste in his mouth suddenly came from, he pulled the back of his hand across his lips. A thin red line showed him that he must have bitten his lip too hard.

Unable to hold back any longer, he whipped round and looked Tia straight in the eye.

"There is something I never told you about. Something I have hidden from you all the time. But now, I can't keep it from you any longer. You don't know who I am."

"I do know," Tia said quietly.

"No, you don't," Siamun objected in despair. "I have lied to you about my parents. They are not the ones whom I pretended to be."

"That I know, too."

Amazed, Siamun stared at his wife. How could she be so calm? And what did she mean, anyway? She couldn't possibly know.

"I know that in reality you are not only the royal architect Siamun, but also Prince Siamun."

He felt his eyes widen as if they had a life of their own. The ground beneath his feet started to shake as he grasped the meaning of her statement.

"Who...how..." he stammered, unable to utter a single coherent sentence.

Tia helped him out. "You want to know how I found out?"

All Siamun could do was nod in silence. Tia didn't answer straight away. His eyes followed her as she walked slowly up to a chair and sat down. When she eventually spoke, her gaze fastening on nothing in particular, it was as if she recalled some distant memory.

"When you were on your way to the western coast, I received word of Meritamun's illness. As you know, I immediately left for Iunu and cared for her as well as I could. I felt so much affection for the woman who had given birth to my beloved husband. Her fever was extremely high. So high that she was haunted by feverish dreams. During those dreams, Meritamun said many incoherent things which at first meant nothing to me. However, every now and then I could make out a few names, some of which sounded familiar. Neferibre, Maia, Taneferet, Meresankh and of course your name were among them. Later still, she began to repeat certain names more often: Panakht, Nakht-Min, Siamun and Sitiah. Over and over again Sitiah. Naturally, I wondered who these people were. Back in Mennefer, I managed to find out that Sitiah had been the wife of a previous king and General Nakht-Min Meritamun's second husband. This wasn't much information on its own, but it was enough to put everything into perspective."

She paused and directed her gaze at Siamun. "I know that only Panakht and Taneferet are Meritamun's own children. King Tutankhamun and Sitiah are your and Satet's parents, while Meresankh is his daughter by a Nubian wife called Ajala."

Siamun's mouth had become dry like the sand of the desert. Shocked into silence as he was, all he could do was shake his head in disbelief. Then he pulled himself together and made for a nearby chair on which he dropped heavily. His voice was hardly more than a hoarse whisper when he spoke.

"How could you keep your knowledge to yourself for so long without letting anything show?"

"I only did what you were doing for much longer."

Although there hadn't been even a hint of reproach in Tia's voice, Siamun felt the need to defend himself.

"I didn't do it of my own accord," he pointed out, "but because I had no other option. I was forced to cover my true origins up in order to survive. It has never been easy for me, I can tell you. And ever since I got to know you, it became downright unbearable. I thought it would be sheer madness to marry you, but then it just so happened. Your father smoothed the way for us without having the faintest idea whom he entrusted his daughter to." He stopped short when he suddenly recalled Panakht's words. "You haven't told him anything, have you?"

A hurt expression appeared on Tia's face while she pulled her legs close and slung her arms around them. Had she noticed the distrust in his voice?

"Of course not," she replied firmly. "I am well aware that father won't spare you once he finds out, however high his opinion of you might be."

Siamun nodded slowly. "And you?" he asked in a gentle voice. "What did you think when you learned the truth? What did you feel?"

She returned his anxious gaze with a smile. "To me, it came as a pleasant surprise."

"A pleasant surprise?" he echoed, baffled. "But you had just found out that your husband had told everyone a bundle of blatant lies!"

"Sure," Tia said with a light shrug. "But it was easy for me to comprehend why you had done so. Besides…"

"Yes?" Siamun asked raptly.

"Do you remember what I once told you about one of my dreadful visits to Queen Mutnodjemet?"

Siamun wrinkled his brow while he thought hard. "You mean when she offended you with her claim that the royal children were dead?"

"Exactly. Back then, I had refused to believe her. Just imagine my joy when I realized that I had been right after all, and that – to crown it all- I had even married one of those royal children!"

Siamun gave her a tender look. "You can't possibly imagine what a heavy burden has just been lifted off my shoulders. My heart is as light as it has never been before. Ever since I married you, I was consumed by the desire to tell you the truth. Now that my wish has been granted I feel like a whole new person. Tia, my love," he said in a shaky voice as he rose to take her hands, "we have always belonged together. We must never let anything come between us."

He scooped her up, and together they whirled about the room in a sudden burst of happiness. Their embrace was as heartfelt as it had never been before.

The only drop of bitterness in Siamun's overflowing heart was the knowledge that he still hadn't told Tia of his dreadful discovery. This just had to wait some more. This moment of exuberant joy was far too precious to be wasted.

Shortly after nightfall, the young couple were sitting on the flat roof of their house, watching in awe as the stars came out and studded the black firmament with their bright light. All was quiet; both Wensu and Benret had already retired to their rooms. Only Nebu kept them company. The golden-brown tomcat was lying on his side as close to his mistress as possible, rewarding her gentle strokes with low satisfied purrs. Every now and then, when he moved his furry head a little, his green eyes would flare up like stars when the light of the only oil lamp caught in them. It was apparent from the glowing dots all around that they were not the only ones to enjoy the refreshing breeze that followed the heat of the day.

Siamun finally brought himself to telling Tia all about the outrageous discovery in the temple of Abedju that had shaken him so much. There was a long silence after he had ended. Just when he started to wonder whether Tia had been listening at all, she began to speak.

"It is an outrage," she said quietly. "Father knows this as well as we do."

"Do you think he will add the missing names if I ask him to?" Siamun asked hopefully.

As he might have expected, Tia responded with a sad shake of her head. "No, I don't think he will, because if he did, he would shake the very foundations of his own reign."

"But no king should ever base his right to rule on such a blatant lie only because he pleases to do so," Siamun insisted, feeling his anger rise once again. "Even King Akhenaten was a rightfully crowned king, and if the decision was mine, I would include his name in any such list. If some of his deeds were not in accordance with Maat, the gods may judge him as they see fit. It is not your father's due to point his finger at him, particularly when his own actions contradict Maat, nor anyone else's for that matter. And as to my father" –he caught himself and took a deep breath, realizing that he had become too loud- "well, my father should actually be given a special place of honour among the kings, for it was him who instigated the restoration of monuments at the beginning of his reign when he was hardly more than a child. He transferred the royal residence back to Mennefer, and restored the temple of Ipet-Sut to its former glory. It has to be admitted that due to his young age none of these decisions were solely his, but he could easily have undone all his efforts later and returned to the cult of the Aten, had he wished so. Instead, my father dedicated his brief life to the worship of Amun without neglecting any of the other gods and their respective cults. Under his rule, the Two Lands grew strong and rich again, and he even went to such great lengths as to capture the city of Kadesh in order to keep the dreaded Hittites at bay. Now all the thanks he gets is that others credit themselves with his accomplishments, and if this were not bad enough, his name is about to be erased from the records entirely. I simply cannot, and will not, let this happen!"

Tia had been listening in silence, eyes downcast. Siamun sensed nonetheless that she shared his view. He felt bad at taking his frustration out on her, but he was trying to make her understand why he was so upset. In order to calm himself down, he offered her a cup of watered wine before downing one himself.

"You know, Tia," he went on, "you cannot possibly imagine how ashamed I am of myself. Until now, I was desperate to ignore all the wrongs I encountered as well as I could. I simply looked away, telling myself that there was nothing I could do about it, that these things happened at all times. However, in the temples of Ipet-Reset and Ipet-Sut, this proved virtually impossible to do. The onslaught of abominations I was exposed to there was too much to bear. That's why I ran away."

Tia shot him a surprised look. "You ran away? What do you mean by that?"

The gut-wrenching pain Siamun felt at reliving those dreaded memories must have been mirrored in his face, since Tia glanced at him in alarm.

"When I was given the opportunity to supervise works on the temple in Abedju, I believed this to be the solution to all my problems. I felt certain that once I was there, far away from Waset, I would be able to forget, since there was nothing that would constantly remind me of my heritage. But how wrong I was! Now I realize what a fool I was to think I could get away that easily. In the very place I deemed myself to be safe, I stumble across the worst offence that has ever been committed against Maat and the most despicable besmirching of my father's memory. It is as if I had been running around in circles for the past months, only to arrive exactly where I started out."

"Let me speak with father," Tia said in an urgent tone of voice. "If I do it, he is less likely to become suspicious."

Siamun shook his head wearily. "I'd rather you wouldn't. I know that you mean to help me, but I don't want you to get involved in this, if I can help it. It's not good for you, see?"

His gaze lingered on the curve of her slightly swollen belly that showed underneath the thin fabric of her dress.

"I'm going to speak to him myself," he went on. "I just have to. How can I look forward to the birth of my child when I fail to honour my own father's memory? Do you understand me, Tia?"

His wife nodded despondently. Her hand had come to rest limp on Nebu's back. Eager for more caresses, he turned his head and nudged Tia's hand with his nose. Her features brightened as she stooped down to lift the heavy animal onto her lap and started to tickle his tummy.

"At least there is one thing you needn't worry about," she said after a while.

Siamun looked at her inquiringly.

"Your father's tomb seems to be so well-hidden from view that no-one shall ever be able to disturb his eternal rest."

"I do hope you're right, but how can you be so sure?" Siamun asked. "Everyone knows that it has been cut into the bedrock at the heart of the Place of Truth."

Tia shook her head slightly. "At any rate, its exact location seems to be lost. I know this for sure," she insisted when Siamun threw her a doubtful glance, "because I heard it from Queen Mutnodjemet's own mouth. On more than one occasion she complained bitterly about her inability to track King Tutankhamun's tomb down. It seems to have vanished without a trace, and the same is true for the tomb of the royal wife Sitiah."

"So Mutnodjemet had search parties look for my parents' tombs in order to desecrate them," Siamun hissed between gritted teeth. "This just goes to show how great her hatred must have been. Praise be Amun that her spiteful efforts were fruitless. I can hardly believe, though, that she had the temerity to speak openly about it."

"That's quite true," Tia said, nodding gravely. "I believe her malice was only surpassed by her cold-bloodedness. I sincerely hope that Ammit has devoured her evil heart and forever deprived her of the bliss of eternal life."

"I'm sure she got what she deserved," Siamun replied grimly. "The only good that comes from her actions is that I can draw some comfort from the knowledge that her efforts were futile." Leaning over to his wife, he pulled her close and breathed in the enticing scent of her lush hair as she put her head on his shoulder. Suddenly he wished that this moment would last forever.

"Let's not talk about these unpleasant things anymore. Rather than that, we should make the most of our time together." *For as long as we can*, he added in his mind.

Chapter Eleven

It had been a long time since Seti had been in such high spirits. The remainder of his strenuous voyage had passed better than he had expected, and the dreaded pain in his chest hadn't occurred anymore. It looked as if Iuny was right after all. All Seti needed to do was to relax more often. Once he had dealt with the ceremonies of his coronation anniversary and the consecration of his temple, nothing was going to stop him from retreating to his beloved summer residence in the delta. Perhaps he might take Tia and Siamun with him, if they were available. Tuya surely wouldn't accompany him this time, since she was up to the ears in the preparations for Nefertari's arrival and kept sweeping about the palace like a mad demon. Seti didn't mind; he wouldn't miss her company, for sure.

"With Your Majesty's permission, I would like to serve some refreshments," called a voice from the entrance of the royal apartment.

"Do come in, Ptahmai," Seti replied.

Ptahmai appeared carrying a large tray which he placed on a table next to Seti with an elegant move. Seti's brow furrowed as he watched him pouring first water, then a little wine into a cup.

Of course, he should have known that Iuny had given his most trusted servant appropriate instructions, but still it felt like yet another blow to his already wounded pride.

If I'm not careful, everyone will soon see nothing but a frail, sickly man in me, he thought.

Determined not to let his good mood be spoilt, he pushed this gloomy thought away and decided to focus on more pleasant matters.

"Ptahmai, have a herald sent to my daughter. I wish to share the evening meal with her and her husband. And see to it that Mehy is also invited."

"As you wish, your Majesty. Is there anything else I can do?" the servant asked zealously.

"No, that is all."

Ptahmai left with a deferential bow. Seti plucked a few grapes from the bowl on the tray and popped them into his mouth. As he relished their sweet taste, his thoughts wandered to Tia who shared his love for the delicious berries. He had missed his daughter dearly and was longing to see her. It looked as if his fears for her and her child's health had been unfounded after all, but he wanted to make sure that everything was alright nonetheless. He was also eager to see Siamun. His initial fondness for the young man had grown into a deep, ever increasing affection, since his son-in-law had proven to be not only an excellent architect and organiser, but also someone with a sincerity and stoutness of character that nowadays were rarely to be found. In fact, there were times when Seti was even inclined to see in Siamun the son he had been denied.

Just when Seti's neck had touched the ivory headrest. and as he was about to close his eyes for a short nap, Ptahmai's voice rang out once more, announcing the arrival of the royal architect Siamun.

Confused, Seti raised his head. Siamun? Had he already received his message? But why didn't he wait until tonight? Then it occurred to him that the messenger could by no means have made it to Siamun's house yet, let alone Siamun responding to the invitation. He must have come of his own accord.

But what could he want that was so urgent that it apparently brooked no delay?

Seti decided to receive his son-in-law at any rate. The need for sleep he had felt a few moments ago had vanished entirely.

"Don't make him wait outside, but admit him to my room," he instructed Ptahmai.

Seti got up and glanced briefly at the polished surface of his silver mirror. Having decided that he was presentable enough, he walked up to his magnificent throne and lowered himself onto the cushioned seat. Resting his arms on the gilded supports and leaning himself comfortably against the back rest which sported his cartouches, flanked by a pair of falcon wings underneath a double row of uraeus serpents, he waited for Siamun to arrive.

A moment later, the young man entered.

"I hope Your Majesty is well after the long journey," Siamun said after a respectful greeting.

Seti acknowledged his words with a friendly nod. "Thank you, Siamun. It has been a tedious task indeed, and I'm glad that it's over now. I intend to retreat to my summer palace as soon as possible in order to recover from the strain. But first of all, take a seat and tell me how you and Tia are faring."

Siamun sat down on the chair he had indicated. The young man didn't answer straight away, and Seti knew better than to push him. He hadn't failed to notice the curious glances the young man was casting at his surroundings. Seti waited patiently while Siamun's gaze travelled across the painted vultures on the ceiling which were clasping the royal cartouches in their talons and the sheer endless rows of gilded uraeus-serpents carrying sun-discs on their heads along the walls. Clearly overawed, he then took in one piece of sumptuously decorated furniture after the other.

Smiling to himself, Seti watched him intently. Yes, there was no doubt that Siamun was duly impressed by what he saw. And how could he not be? This was just the kind of reaction that could be seen in any of the few privileged visitors who clapped eyes on these sumptuous rooms for the first time.

Eventually, Seti repeated his question.

"Thank you, Tia is well," Siamun replied, eyes snapping back to focus on Seti. "She sends her regards and asks when she might come to visit."

"Why so formal?" Seti asked, surprised. "She knows well that she is always welcome, and the same is true for you. By the way, I have just sent word to you about an invitation for tonight. Apparently you failed to meet the messenger. I was desperate to see you both, and apart from that I also wanted to discuss a few minor details regarding the new temple with you. Now that you're here, it's just as well if we did this straight away."

He fell silent when Ptahmai brought an additional cup and more refreshments.

"I had actually hoped to meet you in Abedju," Seti went on once Ptahmai had taken himself off, "but you had already gone. When I was told that you had left in a hurry, I began to worry about Tia's well-being."

He looked inquiringly at the young man opposite him. Eyes downcast, Siamun sat there motionlessly with his hands wrapped around his full wine cup. Slowly but surely, Seti got a notion that something wasn't quite right. There was definitely something different about Siamun today, something he couldn't put his finger on yet.

"My departure from Abedju was indeed hasty," Siamun said eventually. His voice had a strange edge to it, and he needed to clear his throat before he went on. "But this had nothing to do with Tia. It was for a very different reason that I left, and it is for this same reason that I have come to see you."

Only now did Seti realize that he had failed to ask Siamun what had prompted his visit. If his changed demeanour was anything to go by, the reason had to be grave.

"Tell me what it concerns."

For the first time since his arrival, Siamun looked him straight in the eye. "When I inspected the interior of the new temple on my last day in Abedju, I came across the beginnings of a huge list on the wall of the gallery between the chapels of Sokar and Nefertem on the one and the seven sanctuaries on the other side. Judging by the draft which I happened to see, the sequence of the royal cartouches is incomplete. There is a gap between the cartouches of the kings Amunhotep Nebmaatre and Horemheb Djoserkheperure, in which several names are missing. I suggest that this list be completed before the stonemasons set to work."

There was an awkward silence following these bold words. Seti was at a loss what to say or think. He had been prepared for almost anything but this unexpected criticism on such a delicate matter.

"The list of royal names has been composed after careful consideration," he explained as calmly as possible. "I have sought the advice of the high priests of all major temples to make sure that it corresponds closely to the information contained in their archives. Besides, I have to inform you that you are not entitled to call the accuracy of its contents into question."

"I'm not implying some accidental error," Siamun continued unwaveringly. "I know full well that the omission of names happened on purpose, and I also know the reason why. Since the time Osiris Horemheb ascended to the throne of the Two Lands, the names of his immediate predecessors have been

systematically ignored and their monuments usurped, only because one of them, King Akhenaten Neferkheperure, has brought innovations about that may not have been very fortunate. But what have Osiris Tutankhamun and Osiris Ay done so that their names are being stricken from the records, dooming them to eternal obliteration? Has not in particular-"
"How dare you speak those names?" Seti hissed, digging his fingernails into the polished wood of his armrests. Siamun, however, seemed oblivious to his rising anger.
"Has not, in particular, Osiris Tutankhamun rendered outstanding services to the restoration of all cults, and to the enrichment and stabilization of the Two Lands? Since this is so, why is he being punished by the deliberate obliteration of his name, as if he had never existed?"
Breathing heavily, Seti felt a cold shiver creeping up his spine as he suddenly remembered Nebamun's words. Why hadn't he heeded the vizier's warning? Why hadn't he launched investigations into Siamun's past while he had the chance? Deep down, Seti knew the answer to these questions. Afraid of what he might find out, he had kept putting this unpleasant task off from one day to the other until he had conveniently forgotten all about it. Now that it was too late, he didn't even have the time to regret his negligence.
"Who are you?" Seti asked in a voice that didn't seem to belong to him. He dreaded the answer even before it came.
"I am one who doesn't exist."
The words lingered in the air, mysterious and fateful. For a moment, their gazes locked, and Seti had to exert all his will power to withstand Siamun's cold piercing glance.
"I am the son of a man who does not exist, therefore I do not exist either."
"You are Prince Siamun, son of Osiris Tutankhamun," Seti uttered with great difficulty.

"Indeed I am," Siamun said, unmoved. "And as I can see now, you do know my father after all."

"Of course I do," Seti returned in a strangely hollow voice. "I was a young man of about fifteen years already when your father went to the West."

Seti's thoughts travelled back to the time when both his father and Horemheb had been commanders of the royal chariotry. He had met the young king a few times, and as he conjured his image up in his mind, he realized all of a sudden why Siamun's appearance had struck him as familiar right from the start. Now that he recognized the uncanny resemblance between Siamun's expressive eyes and boldly arched brows and those of his true father, he was at a loss how he could have failed to draw the conclusion that was virtually inescapable,

"I am aware of your father's merits, but I follow the example set by King Horemheb and my own father," Seti pointed out, gradually recovering from his shock. He realized at once how feeble this must sound, but at least his voice had regained some of its former strength. "I will not include the names of the Rebel of Akhetaten and his relatives in my list. They don't deserve to benefit from the prayers and offerings that will be made in honour of my ancestors. Thus is the will of Maat."

Siamun thumped the armrests of his chair so hard that Seti started. "Thus is the will of Maat?" he cried. "This sure can't be true! Maat is the truth, not the lie. I'm not having such a barefaced lie in my temple!"

Seti let out a scornful laugh. "*Your* temple? Are you beginning to warp the truth, too?"

"So you admit it," Siamun exclaimed, triumph ringing in his voice. "How can you go on calling yourself Menmaatre when you so readily distort that very truth yourself? You will incur the wrath of the goddess, and she will forever curse you for your vile actions."

"How dare you talk to me like that, me, the Lord of the Two Lands?" Seti spat, outraged. "I should have you arrested this very instant!"

Then he stopped short as another dreadful thought hit him. "You planned all this right from the start, didn't you?" he went on in a menacing whisper. "You adopted the guise of the gifted architect only to bring yourself close to me, and you married Tia not for love, but to legitimate your rule once you would have seized the throne."

"Nonsense," Siamun snapped coldly. "It's true that I lied about my origins, but that's all. I married Tia solely for love, and because we were meant for each other. My only motive for joining the royal architects was my desire to take part in the most ambitious royal building projects in the Two Lands. I just didn't want my talents to be wasted. I never intended to reach out for the crown. For most of the time, I deliberately ignored all the wrongs around me that were committed in your name. But now, I can't do this anymore. If you don't comply with my wish, Pharaoh, I will try every means to have my own way."

"Never!" Seti shouted, beside himself with fury. "I am the living Horus, and I'd rather die than do anyone's bidding. Do whatever you want and rush towards your ruin, you fool!"

"Well, suit yourself, Majesty," Siamun hissed before he leapt up and stormed out of the room, not wasting another look at Seti.

Pressing one hand on his thumping heart, Seti tried desperately to come to terms with the outcome of this incredible conversation. Actually, if he considered Siamun's point of view, he couldn't reproach him for what he did. Siamun's assertion that he had come with no other intention than designing royal monuments certainly did ring true. He didn't lust for either power or wealth; he was completely absorbed in his work. But now, it seemed that he had stumbled upon something he was unable to reconcile with his filial duties to his royal father. Clearly, this was more than he could take. And regarding that, too, Siamun had admittedly every right to be outraged, since it was every son's foremost duty to celebrate his parents' funerary cult and to care for their Kas in order to keep them from perishing.

However, being a king, Seti couldn't always do as he pleased. His hands were tied, for he had to continue the condemnation of the memories of the rebel kings which had helped to secure an entire new line of kings, or else he might not just loose his credibility, but also jeopardize his own rule. There was no other way out of this plight.

As to Siamun… Being the last male member of the former royal house, he had in fact a greater right on the throne than anybody else, including Seti. He was the bodily son of a rightful king, and he had been officially recognized as King Ay's heir apparent. Strictly speaking, this fact rendered Horemheb's accession unlawful and turned him into a usurper of the throne. Thus, both Seti's and his father's right to rule was called into question, since they derived it solely from Horemheb. And the same applied to Prince Ramses and all future kings that were to spring from this line.

Ramses… Suddenly, Seti's heart rebelled against the thought of this bastard ever wearing the double-crown. It was downright grotesque: Here was a prince of royal blood who was unable to exert his right on the throne, there Tuya's illegitimate offspring who was soon going to be crowned. What if he…

No! Seti scolded himself. The mere thought of it was sheer madness. But even so, he couldn't quite get it out of his mind. What if he appointed Siamun as heir apparent instead of Ramses? He was so much worthier of the crown than this conceited-

"What's going on?"

The shrill female voice pierced his thoughts like a dagger.

Annoyed, Seti looked up and saw Tuya rushing up to him. A very confused-looking Ptahmai followed in her wake.
"What are you talking about?" Seti shot back, irritated.
"I have just heard that Siamun is in truth the son of a previous king," she panted.
"Tell me something I don't know yet," he scoffed. "I heard it from his own mouth just a few moments ago."
Tuya's eyes widened in horror. "What, he was here? And you just let him get away unscathed? He'll come back and kill us all!" she shrieked while she kept tearing at her dishevelled hair.
"Stop that nonsense," Seti snapped. "Do you think I don't know how to defend myself? Siamun can't possibly do any harm. The deplorable rabble of supporters he might have procured will be no match for my guards."
"No, he has to be arrested and executed before it's too late! And Tia must be brought back to the safety of the palace at once, or else anything might happen to her. Oh, what a disaster!"
Seti decided to ignore his wife's hysteric wailing. However, concerning Tia she had a point. Under these circumstances she must not stay on with Siamun. He had to dispatch a number of guards to bring her to the palace at once, whether she was willing to come or not. Only then could he start to think of himself.

****

Yet again, the young woman smoothed the strands of hair back that kept sticking annoyingly to the damp skin of her face. It was certainly no pleasure to be out and about at this time of year. There wasn't even the slightest movement of air, and instead of giving some relief from the heat, the glittering surface of the river seemed to double it by reflecting the unrelenting rays of the sun in the fashion of a mirror. But then, this was by no means a pleasure trip. Quite on the contrary, the occasion couldn't have been graver.
Ever since the arrival of Siamun's letter two days ago, Meresankh had had a long and fierce battle with her heart to decide whether or not she should risk it. Back at home, everyone had been deeply affected by the anguish that could be gleaned from Siamun's written words. But it had been one sentence in particular that had shaken her to the core. It read:

I will not tolerate this outrage, and I will not rest until I have restored my father's memory, no matter what.

Meresankh had sensed at once that Siamun was prepared to do anything. He would stop at nothing, and he certainly wasn't going to give any thought to how much he could lose in the process. Meresankh was just as determined to protect her brother from harm. She had to talk him out of it, had to convince him of the futility of it all. But to do this she had to get to him first.
Knowing that neither Meritamun nor Kenamun would let her go, she had sneaked from the house in the dead of night, just like Satet had done. Naturally, the memory of her sister's dreadful end had immediately haunted her, but she had tried to ignore it. Her heart went out to her foster mother and her husband who would both be dead worried about her once they found her message, but Meresankh couldn't help it. She knew

that they would want Siamun to be safe too, and that was what her venture was all about. In fact, not only his life, but the lives of many other people were at stake; therefore Meresankh had decided, after careful consideration, that this mission was more important than her duties to her family.

Meresankh opened the water skin she had brought along with her and drank thirstily. She longed for the journey to be over, not only because of the strain or the heat, but also to escape from the greedy eyes of the ship's crew that followed her even into the remote corner she had chosen for herself, although she did nothing to provoke their lecherous glances. She hadn't painted her face at all, and her baggy dress revealed nothing of her figure or her swollen belly. However, her natural beauty and the fact that she was travelling on her own were apparently enough to attract unwanted attention.

Meresankh fastened her gaze on the nearby riverbank. She was glad when the looming silhouettes of the Great Pyramids came into view, signalling the end of her journey. As she came inexorably closer to her destination, her heartbeat quickened. If only she wasn't too late.

After she had disembarked from the ship, Meresankh looked out for someone who could show her the way to Siamun's house. She spotted a skinny young lad dressed in nothing more than a grubby kilt who was apparently waiting for a job and walked up to him.

"Do you happen to know the house of the royal architect Siamun?" she asked him straight.

The boy nodded, eyeing her curiously.

"Where do you have your luggage?" he inquired.

"I don't have any. Here, take that," she said, impatiently pressing a piece of copper worth half a deben into his hand.

"Once we're there, you'll get the same again. But now move, I don't have much time."

Eyes shining, the boy stared at the bit of metal on his open palm. Clearly, this was more than he had expected.

"Follow me," he said and trotted off, with Meresankh hurrying after him.

When she stood finally in front of Siamun's house, an uneasy feeling crept all over her, for it looked strangely deserted, lacking any apparent signs of life coming from within as it was. She had to knock on the door several times before it opened a crack. A somewhat elderly man, apparently a servant, stood on the other side and asked her warily what she wanted. She told him in a trembling voice.

It turned out that neither the lord nor the mistress of the house were present. Despaired, Meresankh asked him for their whereabouts and the reason for their absence, but the man was reluctant to speak.

Eventually, she heard the sound of approaching footsteps, and a young woman appeared in the opening, forcing the elderly servant to step aside. The door swung open, and Meresankh was ushered in.

Having closed the door behind her, the pretty young woman introduced herself as Benret. Meresankh had heard of her before.

"Yesterday around noon, the lord of the house went to the palace to meet the king," Benret explained with due haste. "He has not returned yet. And the mistress, Princess Tia, was brought to the palace shortly afterwards."

"She was brought?" Meresankh said, surprised. "Do you mean to say she didn't go of her own free will?"

"Indeed, she didn't want to go," Benret confirmed. "The princess wanted to stay here and wait for her husband's return. But the messenger hadn't come alone. He had brought a number of guards with him who took her away without more ado."

"How simply terrible," Meresankh muttered, dismayed.

So her worst fears had come true after all. It looked very much as if Siamun, following his conversation with pharaoh which had almost certainly gone wrong, had gone to meet his supporters straight away, probably in order to make the final preparations for his imminent rebellion, whatever they looked like. Meresankh had no doubts that Panakht was also involved, since he could provide Siamun with much-needed manpower. Meresankh had no choice but to rush to the royal palace at once. Perhaps it wasn't too late yet. As long as Siamun didn't lay hands on the king, all was not lost.

She thanked Benret and assured her of her master's safe return. Wishing she would really be as confident as she would have the girl believe, she hurried off.

This time, Meresankh was in no need of a guide, since it was almost impossible to miss the great royal palace. At first, the streets she went along lay conspicuously deserted. There was no trace of the milling crowds and merchants who usually filled them with life, and this wasn't a good sign at all. However, as she neared the temple of Ptah, things changed drastically. The vast area between the temple precinct and the palace was crawling with people. Not ordinary ones, but heavily armed soldiers.

The mighty portal of the palace, usually shut tight and well-guarded, stood wide open. As she made her way through it, Meresankh couldn't help noticing the bodies that were sprawling in their own blood. The sight of their slit throats and bellies nearly made her retch, and she rushed on. As was apparent from the unambiguous sounds coming from the main

entrance of the palace proper, fierce fighting was going on there. In addition, the entire front of the building was guarded by soldiers, many of them desperately trying to fend off more rebels. In order to avoid them, Meresankh turned right and came eventually to an unguarded side entrance –presumably used only by servants- which she quickly slipped into.
Inside, she made a few steps, then stopped and tried to get her bearings. The smell of cooked food lingering in the air helped her to realize that she must be somewhere near the kitchens. She forced her heart to recall the layout of the various rooms which she used to roam herself more than twenty years ago. Yes, now she remembered the locations of the audience hall and the royal living quarters. She didn't know where Seti had taken up position, but in all likelihood it was in one of these two places. This meant that Siamun would aim to get there, too. But she had to be quick if she wanted to intercept him in time. Rushing down the columned hallways, Meresankh soon encountered the first unmistakable signs of death and destruction. The further she came, the fiercer the fighting seemed to become. Suddenly, she heard suppressed hissing sounds next to her. Startled, she stopped dead and turned to see what it was. There, in a niche that was partly hidden by a broad column, she spotted several terrified-looking women - presumably servants- crouching on the floor, huddled together in an apparent bid for safety. One of them waved to her frantically, prompting her to join them.
Meresankh only shook her head in silence. She would have dearly loved to do so, but her destination was elsewhere. Lips clamped tightly together, she turned away from them and hurried on.

Chapter Twelve

Siamun had parted with Panakht just a few moments ago. His friend was to storm the palace with his men and besiege the throne room, one of Seti's possible retreats. However, to Siamun's mind it was far more likely that the king was hiding in his own private living quarters. A rear access leading directly to the palace grounds would allow him to flee if his apartments were stormed by the front entrance. But Siamun was determined to cut this route of escape off. To this end, he and his men were marching across the extensive grounds, heading straight for the rear part of the palace.

As Siamun was stomping along, he recalled –not for the first time- his fateful conversation with pharaoh. Seti had made a huge mistake by receiving him in his private bedroom. More than ever, Siamun had seen him as an intruder, someone who by no account belonged there. It was him, Siamun, who belonged, not Seti. Almost twenty-four years ago, Siamun and his family had occupied those very rooms. A small infant, sleeping in his little bed next to his parents. Meresankh had had her bed in an adjoining room. While he had been sitting there, talking with Seti, he had pictured himself living in these sumptuous quarters along with his family. Everything stood so clear in front of his eyes as if it was real. Then, yet another, rather gloomy thought came back to his mind. Meresankh had often told him of the day their father had left for his last, fateful hunt, and how deeply she regretted not to have said good-bye to him. It had been very early in the morning, and five-year-old Meresankh had just awoken. Too lazy to rise yet, she had been

listening to her parents' voices. When she eventually got up, her father had already gone. She never saw him again.
While Siamun had been looking at his surroundings, his disapproval and anger had been continuously rising. At the same time, he had sensed that Seti had taken his intent glances to be signs of awe and admiration. Siamun had seen it in his smug face. Of course, being the conceited fellow that he was, Seti just would think so, not knowing how utterly wrong he was.

Their advance went by and large smoothly. They barely encountered any resistance, and when they did, it was swiftly broken. This probably meant that their plan was working well. Urhiye, whom Panakht had easily won over, was fighting with a large number of men in the front part of the palace, mainly in order to engage as many royal guards as possible into the fight, and to direct everyone's attention away from the rebels' true aim. Siamun had been wondering what had driven the general to join forces with them. Perhaps it was the secret grudge he might still bear against Seti, owing to his ruined scribal career. Or it was something else entirely. In the end, it didn't make any difference. All that mattered was Urhiye's support which had brought them at least two thousand more troops.
At last, the rear part of the palace loomed up before them, and rows of soldiers guarding it were just becoming discernible. As the rebels drew closer, a good number of them detached themselves and advanced on them, brandishing their weapons. The ensuing ferocious fighting didn't last long, since the royal guards were heavily outnumbered by Siamun's men, who seemed to stream from the ground like an endless army of ants. Soon, all of Seti's soldiers were lying in their blood, scattered across the ground, and the same was true for their comrades

who hadn't abandoned their posts by the palace. Dazed by this partial victory, Siamun realized that the way into Seti's private quarters was free. But they had to be quick, since the deed had to be done before the main body of royal troops came to know where the real battle took place.

Siamun entered the narrow hallway leading into Seti's rooms at the head of his men. As he had anticipated, a number of guards were waiting for them on the opposite end, hoping to slay them one by one as they emerged from the corridor. But the rebels had been prepared for this and forced their way in nonetheless with only minor losses. Siamun, too, suffered a deep cut in his right arm. However, having just caught sight of Seti, he paid no heed to either pain or bleeding.

An elite unit of royal body guards formed a protective circle around him, but even so Siamun could see through the gaps that Seti was sitting on the same throne that he had occupied when they had last met.

"Give up!" Seti called out in a stony voice. "You are doomed to failure. Don't make it any worse than it already is."

"I don't think so."

Siamun strode up to the heavily armed guards without hesitation, relying on the backing of his most experienced men who had been sworn to lay down their lives for their future king. Seti's guards brandished their swords, but their attempted attack was immediately thwarted by the rebels who by now filled the whole chamber and threw themselves on their opponents with chilling screams. Instantly, Seti's protective wall dissolved as everyone engaged in fierce fighting. Siamun, however, had his mind set solely on Seti. Desperately, he fought his way past, blindly slashing and slicing away as he went. Then he saw the king leaping up, a look of surprise and horror spreading over his face as he caught sight of the young, blood-smeared warrior whose eyes were ablaze with rage and grim determination. Seti's hand whisked to his sash, and a moment later the blade of an iron dagger flashed in his right.

"You mustn't think that I give up without a fight," Seti hissed as Siamun drew closer.

"I expected nothing else," Siamun replied. "A king is only a true king when he fights to his last breath."

"What do you know of kingship, anyway?" Seti snapped, his voice full of scorn.

"At any rate more than that bastard who is never going to wear the double-crown, if I can help it."

With a howl of fury Seti lunged forth, thrusting his dagger from above. Siamun parried the blow with such force that the weapon fell from Seti's hand and clattered to the ground. For a moment, they both stared at it in disbelief, then Siamun tightened the grip on his khepesh-sword and tore his arm up.

"Siamun, don't!"

From the corner of his eye, he saw a bright figure flying towards him. His eyes widened in horror.

"Tia!" he cried in dismay. "What are you doing here?"

In the nick of time she had reached him and clung to his raised arm. "Siamun, please don't do it!"

"Tia, I must finish this," he panted while trying in vain to shake her off. "Go away and hide somewhere safe!"

In a flash, a royal soldier jumped forth from behind Tia's back, battle-axe raised high above his head. Siamun had trouble parrying the blow, and he felt how the strength drained from his injured arm.

Now I'm done for, was all he could think.

But then an ear-splitting scream came from his attacker's mouth, and Siamun saw the tip of a spear protruding from his belly. The tip disappeared, and some of the blood that gushed from the wound splattered across Tia's white dress, drawing terrified shrieks from her.

"Tia, I told you to get away!"

Siamun saw the axe-thrower collapse at his feet, and he came face to face with Panakht. In his right, his friend was holding the spear he had just retrieved, and his clothes and body were covered with blood that didn't appear to be his. In one bound he was at Siamun's side.

"Didn't I know that you wouldn't be able to see this through?" Panakht hissed into Siamun's face. "Why don't you kill him?"

Siamun stared back at him furiously. "I can't do that, as long as Tia-"

"Oh, come on," Panakht spat in contempt and raised his spear. Drawing his arm back, he took aim at Seti who just stood there, petrified. When Siamun turned back to Panakht, he caught a glimpse of something strange and terrifying in his eyes, something that he had never seen there before and that he instantly recognized as sheer bloodlust.

I have turned into a savage beast.

Panakht's ominous words reverberated in Siamun's heart as he raised his sword and brought it down on Panakht's spear with all the force he could muster before it left his hand. He heard a sharp hiss, and the tip of an arrow bored its way into soft flesh. Siamun's eyes darted in the direction it had come from and met Mehy's cold gaze. Letting out a piercing scream, Panakht reared up before he crumbled and fell sprawling across his own spear. Siamun stared at his dead friend in utter disbelief. Tia went on screaming, louder still than before, and finally Siamun looked up at her. With an expression of utmost terror on her face, she pointed up and behind him. Siamun shot round. He perceived the flashing blade only when it whizzed by him, missing his shoulder only by a hair's breadth. Siamun had clearly felt the gust of air on his cheek. Someone grabbed his injured arm and jerked him so violently that he was yanked off his feet and went down with a muffled cry. Instantly, he could feel the weight of several men on him, pressing him hard on the ground. Siamun struggled for all he was worth to throw them off, but then one of them jammed his knee so forcefully between his shoulder blades that he groaned with pain. His arms were yanked behind his back and tied with coarse rope that cut painfully into the flesh of his wrists. Eventually, the pressure eased, and he was roughly pulled to his feet.

Seti's eyes rested coldly on him. "I told you that it was futile," he said sharply.

"You should be grateful to your daughter," Siamun hissed. "You owe her your life, since I couldn't kill you in front of her."

"How noble of you," Seti replied with a mocking smirk. "Take him away!"

Two men clamped their hands around his arms and gave him a hard shove. Furious with Tia as he was, Siamun felt no pity for her as he saw her writhing on the floor, violent sobs ravaging her body. While he was being dragged towards the entrance, he took in all the mess around him. Numerous dead and injured were scattered all across the chamber. The surviving rebels were fettered and taken away just like him. Then he passed by Urhiye –who by some miracle seemed largely unharmed- and wondered why the general was still walking free. Had he only feigned his allegiance to him after all?

Thinking about it now was futile. Instead, Siamun's heart went out to Panakht. To his friend who had been killed before his very eyes. But at least he had had the mercy of a swift death. The same wouldn't be true for Siamun, whatever his destiny.

Siamun stumbled on, half dragged by his guards. The pain in his right arm was becoming unbearable, since his captor showed no consideration for his injury. Siamun gritted his teeth to prevent any sound of anguish from coming over his lips while he thought gloomily of the pain he would have to endure soon. Rebellion against the king was inevitably punished with one of the most gruesome modes of execution: death either by impalement or by being burned alive. To make matters even worse, the whole family of the perpetrator usually suffered the same fate.

Siamun's heart grew heavy when he realized how many people had lost their lives during this short-lived insurgence, as was apparent from the great number of bodies strewn across the floors of the hallways. While most of them were clearly soldiers, some civilians –presumably servants- had also fallen victim to the fierce fighting. Even a few women were among them. There, right ahead of him, was yet another female body. Her limbs were contorted as a result of her violent death, the front of her white dress drenched with blood. Upon coming closer, Siamun realized that there was something strangely familiar about her, despite the glassy stare of her wide eyes. This surely wasn't-

No! his heart screamed in anguish. This mustn't be her, not Meresankh, his beautiful dear sister! His legs faltered as he stood there staring down on her, unable to tear his gaze off the beloved face. He wanted to sink down beside her, but the guards yanked him to his feet and urged him on.

Tears stung in Siamun's eyes, and he didn't hold them back. Why? Why did Meresankh have to die such a horrible death? He didn't ask what she had come here for. He knew it, anyway. He should never have written that confounded letter.

Meresankh had come to save him from harm, that he knew as surely as if she had told him herself. And in doing so, she had rushed headlong towards her own ruin. What would become of her family, her young sons? Who would take care of a decent burial for her?

His trail of thoughts was interrupted when they stopped in front of a door. Siamun was roughly pushed into the tiny room behind it. When his eyes became used to the rather dim light that filtered in through a single guttered window slit, he could see that apart from a single reed mat on the naked floor it was bare of any furnishing.

One of the guards undid the rope around his wrists. "This is where you will be staying until the day of your final judgement, traitor," he snarled. "And don't waste your time thinking of escape. You are under strict surveillance, and this door will be guarded day and night."

With that, they both left, slamming the door shut behind them. Several bolts were shot into place, but no receding footsteps were to be heard.

Exhausted, Siamun leaned his back against the wall and slid slowly to the ground, burying his face in his hands.

Siamun the traitor.

Only an hour ago, all had been possible. He had been on the verge of becoming King Siamun, but then the tables had turned against him. Now, he was condemned to sitting around in this wretched hole and waiting for his death sentence. If only Tia hadn't turned up…

But whatever had happened, it didn't matter anymore. He had to see her one last time before he embarked on his journey to the Beautiful West. That was, if she wanted to see him at all. Him, the rebel Siamun. They had to become reconciled, and he had to tell his wife something very important. Something that might have spared him all this trouble, had it been applied to him.

****

For the first time after what had seemed like an eternity, Siamun was about to leave his prison cell. How much time had passed exactly since he had been captured, he wasn't able to tell. In the beginning, he had tried to keep track of the days, but at some point he had gotten into a muddle and lost count. However, if he was asked to give a rough estimate, it would be about three weeks. Three long weeks, amounting to a whole month, during which he had been aimlessly pacing to and fro between these narrow walls, feeling like a wild animal trapped in a cage. Three endless weeks of reflecting on the sense and nonsense of his attempted rebellion.

Was he responsible for Panakht's death? *No*, he told himself. Panakht had joined his cause of his own free will, and Mehy's arrow would have found its target anyway. Wrestling the spear from Panakht's hand hadn't made any difference. But had his venture had any prospect of success to start with? *Yes*, was Siamun's answer. If only he had been able to do away with Seti, everything else would have been child's play. He would have had all the support of his cousin's Nubian troops, as well as that of a good part of the regular army. Amunemopet, Heqanefer and Paser were sure to be his staunch allies, and many more high-ranking courtiers would have become his loyal servants. Now, of course, none of this was valid anymore. Following his utter failure, nobody would want to be involved with him anymore. And Siamun wasn't going to drag anyone into this mess, as long as he could help it. He had been questioned three times in this wretched hole, each time by the supreme supervisor of Mennefer's security forces Neferhotep. The very man, of all people, whom Pashedu had accused of having been corrupted by Nebamun. At least Siamun had been spared another unpleasant encounter with that fat, good-for-nothing Bakenkhensu. In the presence of two scribes and several heavily armed guards Neferhotep had interrogated Siamun until he had felt like being turned inside out. It had come as a great relief, though, that he hadn't been subjected to the vicious beatings that usually accompanied such interrogations. Perhaps this meant that Seti had preserved at least some of the respect he had once had for his gifted architect. Be that as it may, with the exception of his communication with Amunemopet Siamun hadn't held anything back, not even his express intention to kill the king.

Now that he was on his way to his trial, Siamun thought wearily that he would have to go through all this one more time. And he had little doubts that his worst enemy was going to be in charge of his interrogation.

He was led into the audience chamber with his hands still tied behind his back. Blinded by the bright light streaming in through numerous good-sized windows, he squeezed his eyes shut. When he dared to open them again, blinking, he was greeted by a silent wall of men whose hostile stares he felt more than he saw. They were seated on a drawn-out pedestal that ran along the entire opposite wall. In its centre, the royal dais with Seti sitting enthroned underneath a gilded canopy loomed up menacingly. Siamun caught a glimpse of his stone-faced expression before he was forced to throw himself down and kiss the floor in front of him. Having done so, Siamun still had to remain in a kneeling position with his head bowed. The two guards who had brought him here didn't leave his side. Then a man rose from his elaborate chair next to the throne and descended from the pedestal, imperiously pounding his gilded staff on the ground with each of his steps. The sly look on his face was just the way Siamun remembered it, and his close-set eyes were ablaze with old and renewed hatred. His thin lips stretched briefly into a gleeful smirk before he opened his mouth.

"Rebel Sekhamun!"

Bewildered, Siamun cast a furtive look at Nebamun. Had he been mistaken, or had he really just been called Sekhamun? Then he recalled the long-standing custom of warping the names of evildoers in order to give them a ridiculous or outrageous meaning. In his case, Siamun, *the son of Amun*, had just been turned into Sekhamun, *one whom Amun doesn't hear.* Siamun decided to ignore this additional humiliation. After all, they couldn't really change his name. In the next world, he would certainly be Siamun again.

"Rebel Sekhamun," Nebamun repeated in a booming voice, "you have been brought before this venerable tribunal because you are accused of the most abominable crime imaginable. You have tried to murder our good ruler, the Lord of the Two Lands Menmaatre Seti, after you had wormed yourself into his Majesty's confidence using foul means. You have attempted to usurp the throne and seize power in order to throw the Two Lands into turmoil. To this avail, you have conspired with your accomplices to storm the palace and-"

"If this is so, why are my accomplices not here with me?" Siamun cut in boldly.

Nebamun banged his staff so forcefully on the ground that the air reverberated with the sound.

"Hold your impertinent tongue!" he thundered. "You are in no position to ask any questions. You only speak when you're asked to do so, is that understood?"

Siamun clenched his jaw and lowered his head.

"You and your accomplices," the vizier resumed, "conspired to force your way into the king's living quarters in order to kill him. It is only due to the intervention of the gods that your evil plan was thwarted. All this has been sufficiently proven, and you have admitted to having instigated this ill-fated rebellion.

However, until now you have refused to expose all of your accomplices. This is your last chance to make amends. If you comply, pharaoh –may he live, be prosperous and healthy- might grant you the favour of a slightly less agonizing death than you would face otherwise."

"You do know them already," Siamun said firmly without raising his head. "My only accomplices were the troop commanders Panakht and Urhiye, nobody else."

"That's impossible," Nebamun objected. "There must have been more people involved in this than you admit."

"I'm telling the truth," Siamun insisted. "My only collaborators were Panakht and Urhiye, whose help I had enlisted to gain the support of their troops."

"You're lying," the vizier spat with undisguised contempt. From the sound of his footfall and the pounding of his staff it was evident that he was now agitatedly pacing to and fro. "You must have had greater support than that, or else you wouldn't have been able to exert power, had your despicable plan worked. What about the King's Son of Kush, who happens to be your maternal cousin? Look at me when you answer my question!"

Siamun raised his eyes reluctantly. "He knew nothing of my plans," he replied, hoping that his communication with Amunemopet had indeed remained undetected. "I am telling you the truth. I had no other accomplices."

Stopping dead, Nebamun bored his eyes into Siamun's as if willing them to penetrate his heart. "Is it pure coincidence then that I have received reports of increased massing of troops just behind the Nubian border? Were these troops not meant for you?"

Siamun didn't answer straight away. He felt an irresistible urge to nurse his aching knees. When he tried to shift his weight a little, two strong hands pressed instantly down hard on his shoulders.

"I don't know anything about those troops," Siamun said eventually, not caring to conceal his growing irritation. "Why don't you ask the King's Son of Kush himself? He should know."

"Be careful," Nebamun snarled, eyes narrowing to slits. "I'm not having any of your cheek. You may have forfeit your life anyway, but just think of how many different ways there are to die, some more gruesome than others."

He shot one last menacing look at Siamun before he turned to approach the royal throne. He spoke with Seti, briefly and in hushed tones, before he addressed the man sitting to his left whom Siamun only now recognized to be Paser. The man who would have sworn allegiance to him, had his rebellion been successful. Their eyes met, and Paser averted his gaze hastily and with a shame-faced expression.

While Nebamun was busy consulting more members of the tribunal, Siamun let his gaze roam across the whole assembly. Almost everyone of some standing had gathered to witness this trial, among them the treasurers Hormin and Tiya and several supreme troop commanders, Urhiye's colleagues. Only one particular face was missing. The one face Siamun had expected to see more than any other. Prince Ramses was not present. How could this be? The crown prince was one of the most important men in the Two Lands, second only to pharaoh. Had Seti prevented him from attending? Had he feared that Siamun might avenge himself on him by exposing Ramses' true parentage in front of everyone?

Then Nebamun's cutting voice penetrated his thoughts.

"Rebel Sekhamun, behold the verdict of this venerable tribunal presided by pharaoh –may he live, be prosperous and healthy! You have been found guilty of the attempted murder of the king, rebellion against the crown and the incitement of others hereto. Your punishment will be death by execution, and the same will apply to your immediate family. The exact method of execution will be chosen by pharaoh –may he live, be prosperous and healthy-, as will the way in which your body will be destroyed. In addition, your wretched name will be erased wherever it appears. It will be stricken from the records, so that it will be as if you had never existed. Should it become absolutely necessary to mention you in the future, you shall only be referred to as the vile rebel Sekhamun. This is the fate of those who commit such outrageous crimes. May Ammit devour your sinful heart and feast on your entrails, and may your Ba forever wander about restlessly, deprived of prayer and sustenance."

"And the same to you!"

The sound of Siamun's bold voice reverberated from the walls and lingered in the air during the ensuing shocked silence. He had raised his head defiantly and straightened his shoulders as well as he could.

Nebamun stood still, transfixed. His eyes bulged while his mouth opened and closed in silence like that of a fish on dry land.

"May Ammit devour both your heart and entrails, so that my dead sister's Ba may be appeased at last. Apart from that, I have one more wish. I need to speak with Princess Tia before I die."

The stunned silence seemed to stretch endlessly. Everyone present appeared to hold their breath.

Nebamun was first to recover. "How dare you-"

"His wish is granted," a firm voice rang out.

It was the first time Seti had spoken out loud. Nebamun shot round and stared at him incredulously.

"This trial is over," Seti went on, cutting Nebamun's imminent protest short. "The execution will be carried out tomorrow. Take the perpetrator away from here!"

At least he hadn't called him Sekhamun. For a brief moment, the gazes of the two men who were unable to co-exist met. To his surprise, Siamun saw no triumph in Seti's eyes, not even the slightest hint of satisfaction. Instead, it was resignation that was mirrored in them.

Instantly, Siamun lost any fear of his imminent death. It would only put an end to a life he wouldn't have been able to continue as before, anyway. Finally he was going to be freed from the burden of his heritage that had been weighing on him for as long as he could think. Seti, on the other hand, had to carry on, had to watch how Tuya's bastard son shared his throne in due course. But worst of all, Seti would get to sample the bitter taste of loneliness. There was no-one left to give him unconditional love and support. Not even Tia, who would see him with very different eyes from now on, since he was not only her father anymore, but also the murderer of her beloved husband. And Seti knew this all too well. That was the deep sorrow that had spoken from his eyes.

Siamun was roughly pulled to his feet and taken away. He did not resist. He was ready to face his destiny.

****

They hadn't thrown him back into that wretched hole of a prison-cell. Instead, they had locked him in a bright, fairly comfortable looking room. There was a simple bed, two chairs and even a small table which would be of no need to him anymore. Siamun sank down on the edge of the bed and propped his head on his hands. How he was supposed to get over the last remaining time of his life, he just didn't know. He didn't want to lose himself in gloomy thoughts again. He almost wished that his death sentence would have been carried out on the spot.

The sharp sound of a bolt being shot back rang out. Startled, he sat upright and stiffened. He hadn't been aware of approaching footsteps. His eyes darted to the door as it opened with a slight grating noise. In came an armed guard, followed by a second one. Had his bold wish for a swift death already been granted? It was only when the two men stepped aside to make way for a dainty figure that he knew what was happening. So Seti had kept his promise after all. Tia had come to say her good-byes to him.

She made a few tentative steps, then stood self-consciously in the middle of the room, barely looking at him. Siamun didn't really know what to do or say, either. The recent happenings seemed to have driven an invisible wedge between them.

No, things couldn't stay like this. They had to talk in order to calm the troubled waters, and he had to give his wife some vital advice. Otherwise, he wouldn't be ready to leave this world behind.

Siamun got up from the bed and lowered himself onto one of the chairs. "Come," he said in a gentle voice, eyes fastened on Tia's face. She complied with his wish with obvious relief. They turned their backs on the two guards who had by now positioned themselves on either side of the closed door. This way the young couple could delude themselves that they spent their last remaining time alone with each other.

Siamun cleared his throat rather awkwardly. "I assume that you have come here of your own accord."

He realized how stiff this must sound, but he couldn't think of anything better to start with.

"Yes, I wanted to see you at all cost," she replied, still somewhat shyly. "It is... I wanted to explain it all to you."

She hesitated, and Siamun gave her an encouraging nod.

"I know that it's all my fault that you ended up the way you did," she went on in an unsteady voice. "Believe me, I didn't want things to turn out like that. I only didn't want you to die, neither you nor father."

"How did you come to be there in the first place?" Siamun asked a trifle sharply. He felt like reliving those dreadful moments yet again.

"On the day you left for the palace and I waited for your return in vain," Tia answered with unmistakable reproach in her voice, "father's guards came and took me away. I was brought to the palace where I was made to stay in my former apartments. Father told me everything about his meeting with you. I feigned surprise, since I couldn't very well tell him that I knew your secret all along. I explained to him that I didn't at all mind you being a royal prince, and that you posed no danger to me or anyone else. Then father told me something that astounded me very much indeed."

"What was it?" Siamun asked raptly.

For the first time, Tia raised her eyes and looked straight at him. "Father said that he had been toying with the thought of designating you heir apparent in Ramses' stead, or even appoint you straight away to be his co-regent. To his mind, you are far worthier of the crown than Ramses. But when he considered the consequences such a move would inevitably have, he abandoned the idea. It seems impossible to reconcile two factions that are so far apart. Chaos and bloodshed on an unimaginable scale would follow."

Tia broke off and drew a few deep breaths before she carried on. "I asked father what he intended to do. Avoiding an answer, he only told me to stay in my apartments which I was not to leave under any circumstances. I was left alone with Baket and a handful of guards for my protection. When the fighting broke out the next day, Baket helped me to slip away unseen and to steal to father's chambers. At first, he was furious with me, but then he ordered me to hide in an adjoining room and stay put, since it had become too dangerous for me to return. There I was, dead worried and trembling with fear. Then I heard how the rebels stormed in, and I dared to open the door and peer through the crack. I saw you and father standing there, about to kill each other. This was when I couldn't take it anymore and rushed to you. You know the rest."

Siamun had been listening with rapt attention, determined not to reveal the state of turmoil he was in. Could it really be true that Seti had considered sharing his throne with him? As enticing as this thought was, Seti had done well to abandon it quickly. The ensuing unrest would surely have been far worse than the fighting that had merely lasted a few hours.

"There's still something you haven't told me yet," he said eventually, putting his hand soothingly on hers. "What did you feel when you saw me and your father engaged in fighting? Whom did you want to save?"

He was determined not to be angry with Tia, no matter what her answer would be like.

"I was desperate to save you both," she muttered in despair. "I thought of a way to stop this madness. I knew that you wouldn't kill father in my presence. And then I screamed to save you from the lethal blow that nearly split you in two."

Siamun nodded thoughtfully. "Initially I took your screams to be for something else. When I finally realized the truth it was almost too late."

Tia opened her mouth to speak, then hesitated.

"Is there something else I should know?" he asked gently.

"Do you know who wielded the sword that nearly killed you?"

"No. Presumably one of the royal soldiers," Siamun said with a light shrug, although he had already a notion that this would be too easy. Who could it have been? Ramses, perhaps?

"It was General Urhiye."

"What?" It took him a moment to grasp the consequences this statement had. "*He* tried to kill me? Are you sure?"

Tia nodded vigorously. "Yes, absolutely sure. I saw him with my own eyes, didn't I? That's probably why he's now getting away unscathed."

This, of course, explained it all. Urhiye was pardoned because he had attempted to kill the leader of the rebels. So he had switched sides in the very last moment after all. This man was a mystery to him. It seemed that he didn't know his own preferences. Siamun had sensed from the start that something wasn't quite right about him. If he had been a spy in pharaoh's service, he might have given them away the moment he was made part of the plot. But if this was so, ought Seti not to have been better prepared? No, it looked rather like Urhiye had changed his mind spontaneously and on his own initiative.

"Father has assured me," Tia resumed, "that Meritamun, Taneferet and the children will not be punished, as they are not your blood relatives. And Meresankh-"

She broke off, sobbing.

"I know," Siamun said in a voice that suddenly cracked with emotion. He had failed them all so badly. "I saw her lying in her own blood when I was taken away. She died for my sake. I'm absolutely certain that she wanted to dissuade me from my plan. Can you take care of her burial?"

"Of course," Tia said, wiping away her tears. "I spotted her among the few bodies of women who had been brought into the house of life. I had such a shock when I saw her! But I promise you that she will be given a decent burial near her family's home."

Siamun nodded. "I'm very grateful for this. Unfortunately,

things will be quite different for Panakht and me."

She looked at him with utter bewilderment. With a desperate sob she flung herself into his arms. A clanking noise made Siamun look up. One of the guards had moved closer.

"Your Highness, according to my orders I have to bring you back to your rooms now."

"Just a moment, please."

Siamun glanced at him imploringly. The man hesitated, then nodded reluctantly and retreated to the door.

"Tia, my love," Siamun whispered into her hair, relishing its unforgettable scent. If only he could take it with him. "I know that you will soon belong to someone else. Don't tell me who it is."

"I'll never belong to anybody else except you," she burst forth in a choked voice.

"I wanted to ask something of you," Siamun continued with a heavy heart. "I want you to promise me that you're never going to tell our little one whose child it is. Let it grow up in the belief that it has been sired by the man you're going to marry. This will make things much easier, and it might spare everyone a lot of trouble. Will you do this for me?"

Tia nodded wearily, unable to speak.

"Unfortunately, everlasting happiness wasn't ours to be. In the end, the difficulties arising from our different backgrounds got the better of us. I should have known from the start, but I preferred to ignore the warning voice of my heart. I had fallen in love too deeply to heed it. But don't worry, we shall meet again in the Fields of Reeds, should I pass my final judgement. Until then, it will suffice if you don't curse my name."

"I will always hold you dear, and your name will be kept safe in the depths of my heart," she whispered.

The guard by the door shuffled his feet impatiently. "Highness, you really need to go back now," he urged. "You have been

staying longer already than you were allowed to."
Siamun heaved a heavy sigh. "He's right, Tia. Go on, now!"
A choked cry rang from Tia's chest when he freed himself from her embrace. Carefully avoiding her eyes, he leapt up from his chair and flung himself face-down on the bed, burying his face in his arm. The door swung open, then was slammed shut again and bolted. The sound of the receding footsteps tore his heart to shreds.

Death itself couldn't possibly be any worse.

****

Siamun was waiting. There wasn't anything else for him to do but wait. He was sitting cross-legged on his bed, although his aching knees reminded him that he had remained in this position far too long. He didn't feel like moving. What good would it be, anyway? Why would someone facing death move at all? Strictly speaking, even every breath he took was pointless, but Siamun hadn't been able to stop himself from breathing.

His heart refused to dwell on the past any longer. Therefore he tried to focus on the hour or hours that remained of his life. The only uncertainty that was left was the exact way in which he was going to die. Siamun was very afraid of the agonizing deaths on the stake and in the fire. Would Seti have mercy on him and grant him an easier death? And what was going to happen to his mortal remains? If they were going to be burned or fed to the crocodiles, he wouldn't stand a chance of enjoying any kind of afterlife. But then, there was perhaps a remote chance that the gods might show some understanding rather than condemning him to eternal non-existence. Maybe they were on his side. They had to be. Hadn't they urged him to go and seize the throne in the first place? Thus, all may not be lost. As long as there was so much as a glimmer of hope, he wasn't going to tumble into the bottomless abyss of despair.

Anyway, he would soon know for certain. It couldn't be long now.

All of a sudden, a subtle noise penetrated his mind. A sound that repeated itself at equal intervals, over and over again. It must have been there all the time, but he seemed to have been too preoccupied with himself to notice it. It was the soft, steady dripping of a water-clock.

Why would there be a clock in here? Was it to remind him of his imminent death that came closer with every drip? Presumably, this room wasn't meant for prisoners at all. It looked rather as if it belonged to some higher-ranking servant; perhaps it had been vacated for the sole purpose of allowing Tia to meet him in more pleasant surroundings than that gloomy hole would have been.

Be that as it may, the sound of the dripping water transported him instantly back to that night preceding his departure from Iunu. Strangely enough, his heart didn't refuse to linger on that particular memory. Could it really be only a year that he had left so full of hope and confidence? He remembered how the hours had been dragging on endlessly, yet at the same time they had flown by far too quickly for his liking. Exactly the way he felt now. Time hardly seemed to pass at all, but on the other hand the precious last moments of his life slipped inexorably away from him, the way tiny drops of water slip through one's fingers.

Why, oh why hadn't he listened to the warning voice of his heart back then? Had it not been loud enough?

No, he had to admit to himself, it hadn't been because of that. Even if his heart had screamed its warning out loud or hurled it right into his face, he wouldn't have paid it any heed.
Indeed, Siamun thought gloomily, *man is a creature with a peculiar nature: Driven by insatiable curiosity, he sets out to challenge his fate, and he won't rest until he finds out for himself what the future holds for him. It has always been this way, and this way it will always be.*

When he heard footsteps approaching his door, he was both relieved and terrified. They were coming for him at last. Perhaps they would let him know beforehand in which manner he was going to die. *Amun, don't let it be the stake or the fire!* The bolts were shot back one by one and the door swung open. Someone entered the chamber with measured steps, balancing a rather large vessel made from dark blue faience on the tray he carried. Siamun's gaze lingered on it before it travelled to the man's face. It was young with a hooked nose. Ramses.
"Greetings, Prince Sekhamun," he said merrily, placing the tray on the table with a sweeping movement. His tone of voice was just as mocking as his stiff bow. "You will be pleased to hear that my royal father –may he live, be prosperous and healthy- has decided to grant you the favour of an easy death by your own hand –quite undeservedly so, if you ask me. This beautiful vessel-" he jerked his head in the direction of the cup- "contains a concoction that will take you to the next world in a not overly agonizing manner. However, what expects you there might be far worse. But in the end this is entirely your fault. Did you really have to go wild because of such trifles?"
The young man shot him a reproving glance. For a moment, Siamun felt like a dim-witted pupil who gets his well-deserved rebuke.

"I wouldn't call the outrage committed by His Majesty trifles," he said quietly. The relief he had felt at the prospect of a fairly quick death by poison was now superseded by renewed anger which he struggled to restrain. "And I know he is going to pay dearly for it, once his time has come."

"How dare you slander the Lord of the Two Lands even now, in the face of death?" Ramses demanded, glaring at him.

Siamun was not impressed. "If pharaoh fails to comply with the laws of Maat, he ought to be prepared to face accusations as well as the wrath of the gods. But let's not go on about this. More than enough has been said already, and I have grown weary of it all. Are you going to pass me that vessel, or shall I get it myself?"

Ramses' brows knitted together. "You don't seem to fully appreciate the honour that is being accorded to you," he complained, sounding genuinely hurt. "The future ruler of the Two Lands is standing right in front of you, and it is from his hand that you will receive the elixir that will bring your miserable life to a close. What's more, I will personally witness your death, which might become a lot easier thanks to my noble presence."

Conceited fellow, Siamun thought in disgust. If Ramses was that stuck-up already, what was he going to be like once he wore the double-crown? May the gods have mercy on the Two Lands.

"To be honest, I am rather surprised to see you here, of all people," Siamun said indifferently.

The prince, who was by now sitting on the edge of the table, leaned forward, his eyes boring into Siamun's. "Whom did you expect, if not me?" he whispered. "Nebamun perhaps?"

When Siamun didn't reply, he carried on in a conspiratorial tone, as if sharing a secret with him, "Unfortunately, the vizier wasn't available. But he asked me to give you this."

With an air of importance Ramses reached into his sash.

Whatever he withdrew from it was concealed in his closed fist. Then he dropped a small object onto the palm of Siamun's outstretched hand. Siamun knew what it was even before he looked at it. On his palm sat a ring made from pure silver, delicately crafted and adorned with gems of turquoise and lapis lazuli. It was the ring Satet had been fiddling with when he had last seen her alive. Closing his fingers around it, he felt a wave of renewed grief surging up within him. However, owing to Ramses' curious glances, he was determined not to let his despair show.

"I knew that Nebamun had my sister killed all along," he said with a calm that surprised him. "At the end of my trial I cursed him for what he did. I'm absolutely certain that Ammit will devour his wicked heart on the spot."

"Maybe, but what will happen to your own heart?" Ramses said, jabbing an accusing finger at Siamun. "You have nearly committed the most hideous crime there is. Don't you think your heart will be fed to the great devouress, too?"

Siamun chose to ignore this spiteful question. Mesmerized, he watched as Ramses ran his finger playfully along the rim of the vessel with the lethal poison in it. Suddenly, a very different thought leapt into his mind.

"By the way, where were you on that day?" he asked. "Why didn't you come to your father's aid when he was under attack?"

"Not that it would concern you," the prince replied coolly, watching Siamun out of narrowed eyes, "but I was with my mother, protecting her from harm, if you must know."

Siamun raised his eyebrows meaningfully. "Really? Well, consider yourself lucky that your sister interfered and prevented me from killing the king, and that Urhiye betrayed me in the end."

At the mention of the troop commander's name Ramses'

expression darkened considerably.

"Urhiye, that worthless fellow," he scoffed. "Can't do anything properly."

Surprised, Siamun pricked up his ears. "You mean, because he failed to prevent the storming of the palace?" he inquired.

"No, not that," Ramses said, shaking his head impatiently. "I see that you still don't get it. Well, I won't leave you in the dark. Since you will be dead in about an hour's time, I might as well tell you."

He paused while he pushed one of the chairs closer to the bed on which Siamun was still sitting in the same position, but not feeling any pain or discomfort anymore. Casting a weary glance at the closed door, Ramses sat down heavily and brought his face uncomfortably close to Siamun's.

"Urhiye hasn't been in my father's service," he whispered. "He worked for me and the Great Royal Wife. You know, my royal father seems to be very reluctant to share his throne with me, and I'm running out of patience. According to our plan, Urhiye was supposed to assist us to do away with pharaoh as inconspicuously as possible in order to smooth my way to the throne. That was why he was adamant that the campaign be continued at all cost. The prospects of father having a fatal attack due to over-exertion would have been good, weakened as his health is. In addition, an opportunity might have arisen to have him killed during battle or some sort of ambush. But no, my stubborn father had to break the campaign off without paying us any heed. Little later, mother and I learned of your true identity. We were overjoyed when Nebamun told us, since my royal father was at the point of finding out about that affair with the oracle. Mother and I hoped that he was going to see you as the instigator, once he came to learn who you were. But as you know, the truth was far from it. So besotted was father with you that he didn't even bother to get to the bottom of things. However, knowing you to be a man of principle and honour, we were confident that sooner or later you were going to get yourself into a proper mess. And, lo and behold, we didn't have to wait long. Your naïve friend Panakht wasted no time running to Urhiye, of all people, and letting him in on your plot, and it goes without saying that Urhiye shared his knowledge with us straight away. Naturally, we did nothing to intervene, since this was the golden opportunity we had hoped for. Urhiye was instructed to play his part as a zealous rebel as well as he could. On the day of the attack, he was to be close to you, smoothing you the way into father's apartments and seeing to it that you would get to kill him. Then, he was supposed to do away with you. Our devious plan almost worked, but then my stupid sister showed up and spoiled it all, preventing not only his death, but yours as well."

Ramses took a deep breath and leaned back, but didn't take his eyes off Siamun's face. "As it turned out, we got rid of you after all. At some point, I'm sure we'll find a way of dealing with my royal father, too."

Siamun struggled to take it all in. What kind of evil machinations had come to light, thought up by those closest to pharaoh! If that was what the life of a king looked like, he should deem himself lucky that his rebellion had been unsuccessful.

Then, yet another intriguing thought crossed his mind, and he watched Ramses with rapt attention as he spoke. "Was it perhaps Urhiye who helped you to achieve your appointment as heir apparent with his memorable performance during the oracle?"

Now, it was Ramses' turn to be surprised. "How do you know it was him?"

"I noticed back then that there were a few things about him that didn't quite make sense," Siamun explained casually. "But I rather assumed that he was acting of his own accord. Now I know that everything must have been meticulously planned by you and your precious mother. So meticulously that the perpetrator was never caught."

"You can say that again," Ramses agreed with a smug grin on his face. "We truly excelled ourselves."

Growing serious again, he rose from his chair. "It was nice chatting with you, Prince Sekhamun, but I can't go on like that. Time flies, and I still haven't done what I came here for." Shaking his head in mock dismay, he turned round and approached the table. He picked the deep blue vessel up with both hands and held it gingerly out for Siamun, so as not to spill a drop of the precious concoction.

"Here, drink!"

Siamun stared at the cup in Ramses' hands. All of a sudden, he was overcome by an insatiable desire to live. He wanted to see the sun, the rays of which were streaming in through the guttered windows. He wanted to the watch the playing children whose bright laughter rang out not far away. He wanted to be present when his own child was born, wanted to love it and raise it together with Tia.

The longing died down almost as soon as it had awakened. As far as he was concerned, all this belonged to the past, and that was just the way it was meant to be.

Siamun braced himself for the inevitable. He reached for the vessel and wrapped his hands around it. Trying hard to ignore the astringent odour exuding from it, he put it to his lips and drank.

****

The hollow echo of his footsteps had a downright eerie effect. The temple lay deserted. Seti had sent all his so-called friends away. He wanted to be alone when he took his leave from this sacred place which he wasn't going to see for quite some time. And he needed to have his peace when he remembered the one who had created this wonderful structure for him.

Seti wasted no time looking at the magnificent reliefs that adorned the walls around him. Instead, he headed straight for one particular spot.

There it was, the gallery with the list of kings. Seti stopped a few paces away and took in what he saw. The composition was one of outstanding beauty. It was perfect, flawless and – seemingly- without fault.

But then he stepped closer, and his eyes went in search of the names on the far right preceding his own. He lifted his arm, and his finger stroked gently across the narrow gap between two particular cartouches, as if in doing so it could heal the wound that had been ripped open just here.

Seti mourned for Siamun the way he would have mourned the death of his own son. He bore no grudge against the man who had tried to kill him. It hadn't been his fault. The grotesque situation they had both found themselves in hadn't allowed them to exist peacefully next to each other.

Seti also grieved for Tia and the broken bond of love that had once connected them. Siamun's death had changed their relationship profoundly. They were not the same anymore. They had drifted apart, were unable to talk to each other the way they used to. It hadn't mattered whom he had married her to. Seti knew that she wasn't going to be happy with Tija. In fact, Tia would have preferred not to marry at all, but her child needed a father.

When Seti had advised her to never reveal the true identity of its father, she had coldly replied that Siamun had already asked the same of her. This had been very prudent of him. Siamun would have been an excellent ruler, had he been given the chance to prove himself.

Seti's hand dropped limply to his side, but his eyes were still glued to the cartouches of the Kings Nebmaatre and Djoserkheperure. His heart screamed in protest of the blatant lie that was hidden in between them. Now, Seti recognized it as what it truly was: a pathetic and perhaps ultimately futile attempt to amend the past. And he couldn't fight the feeling that despite all his efforts, the names he was so desperately trying to erase from the memory of mankind were going to be spoken again some time or another–perhaps, even more so than his own.

Author's Note

Dear Reader,

when I came towards the end of my first novel "Tutankhamun and the Daughter of the Moon", I decided quite spontaneously that the story should be continued with Siamun, Tutankhamun's fictitious son, as the new protagonist. The first book ends with the demise of Siamun's parents and the disappearance of the orphaned infant and his siblings from view. The thought of what might happen if the royal prince grew into a young man and reappeared on the scene during the rule of a new dynasty of kings was intriguing. What kind of difficulties would he have to face? How would he cope with the burden of his royal heritage?

These and many other questions gave eventually rise to the present story which strives to give insight into the rather unusual situation of pharaonic Egypt at the beginning of the nineteenth dynasty. In the interest of greater authenticity I have refrained from employing the Greek forms of personal and place names wherever possible -although many of these may sound more familiar to modern ears than their ancient Egyptian counterparts-, since they were definitely not in use at the time in which this story is set. Likewise, I have avoided the use of ordinal numbers in connection with royal names, as this method was unknown to the ancient Egyptians. Instead, I have added the unique throne name every king assumed on the occasion of his coronation to their personal names, just the way it would have been done back then.

Regarding Seti's little family, only the existence of one wife – the Great Royal Wife Mut-Tuya- and two children can be gleaned from the archaeological records with certainty. The royal Princess Tia and her husband Tija (whose names are spelled in exactly the same way when written with hieroglyphs, but may have been pronounced in different ways) are well known from their shared tomb in Saqqara and other sources. The exact time of their marriage is not known. It is often assumed that they must have been wed prior to Seti's accession to the throne, since upon becoming a royal princess Tia wouldn't have married a commoner. However, there is no proof for this assumption, nor is the reasoning behind it compelling. In this story, Tia is married to the treasurer at the beginning of Seti's fourth regnal year, which is still fairly early in Seti's reign.

Scientific investigations into the state of Seti's well-preserved mummy have yielded evidence of arteriosclerosis, while his age at death has been established as probably his mid-forties. Therefore it can be assumed that the king suffered from *angina pectoris* for some, perhaps even considerable time prior to his death which may have been brought about by the same ailment, although other causes cannot be dismissed.

Seti's only known son was Ramses, who was later to become Ramses II "the Great". Earlier assumptions regarding the existence of a second, older son have now been proven wrong, as has the existence of another daughter called Henutmire, who was in all likelihood Seti's granddaughter.

The same is true for the quite popular assumption that Ramses was only second in line to the throne, which was founded on representations adorning the north wall of the famous hypostyle hall at Karnak temple. It has long been recognized that some of them had been altered in antiquity, with Ramses' depictions replacing someone else's. This other person was long taken for another royal prince, Ramses' older brother. However, more recent investigations have provided irrefutable evidence for the true identity of this mysterious person: a troop commander named Mehy. Mehy must have been very close to the king, judging by the fact that he was accorded the extraordinary honour of being depicted right behind the royal chariot. Some Egyptologists even suggest that Mehy may have been the designated heir apparent prior to Ramses. While this is debatable, it is clear that at some point Ramses saw the need to erase Mehy's depictions and replace them with his own. What might have prompted this course of action? Had Seti really given preference to his troop commander over his own son, and if so, why?

When I was looking for a rational explanation for Seti's apparent reservations, the first thought that came spontaneously to my mind was that Seti might have doubted his paternity, thus being reluctant to appoint Ramses heir apparent. While I do acknowledge that there might be a number of other possible reasons, or that there might not be anything in it at all for that matter, I decided to make Ramses Tuya's illegitimate son, solely because this adds an interesting twist to the story. I would like to stress that by no means did I want to make a point here, or even establish a new historical fact. However, one should bear in mind that adultery has always been an issue, and one supposedly royal offspring or other might well have been illegitimate. The often cited strong facial resemblance between Seti I and Ramses II is highly debatable and cannot prove a father-son relationship in itself, because much depends on what the spectator wants to see.

My characterization of Prince Ramses is largely based on what we know about him during his time as king. A certain stance of self-importance that surpasses by far what would be expected of a king may be gleaned from written records such as the epic description of the battle of Kadesh and the listings of his numerous offspring. His false assessment of the situation at the outset of this battle in his fifth regnal year may suggest that –at least in his younger years- Ramses was prone to making rash decisions without heeding his advisors' warnings. Despite such shortcomings, however, he has definitely secured his place in history owing to his extremely long and eventful reign, a fact that is mirrored in the overwhelming number of publications on Ramses the Great.

I have endeavoured to create an independent story that can be read on its own, even though the protagonist and several other characters spring from an earlier book. However, should this story leave you keen to find out –among much else- how it all came about that Siamun was forced to grow up in hiding, you may wish to treat yourself to the novel "Tutankhamun and the Daughter of the Moon", available on Amazon, a sample of which can be found on the following pages.

Monika Mangal

November 2016

Preview: Tutankhamun and the Daughter of the Moon

By Monika Mangal

Prologue

He was a prisoner.
He had committed no crime, nor had he done any wrong. And yet his freedom had been taken away from him.
Constantly guarded by heavily armed men who followed him on each of the few steps he was allowed to take.
The fact that these men belonged to his personal guard who were sworn to protect him with their own lives didn't make it any better.
That was the way it had to be, he was told, due to the upheavals of recent times, and because he had become too precious to run the risk of losing him.
Gone were the times when he had been able to roam the vast grounds of the palace together with his friends and his faithful dog Kenu, and sometimes, in a favourable moment, to even venture beyond the palace walls.
Gone were also the times when he had had to copy never ending texts and to do complicated sums under Sennedjem's watchful eye, together with the others: first of all Nakht-Min, then Turi and Paser. And Sitiah.

Now the cramped room, which had always been far too hot and stuffy, appeared to him as desirable as the Fields of the Blessed. And just as unattainable.

But deep in his heart the fighting spirit was beginning to stir. Sooner or later he would succeed in loosening the shackles which had been forced upon him, even if he may never be able to throw them off entirely.

He would not surrender.

Not ever.

Chapter One - Year 1

"Sitiah!" Taemwadjsi's voice was tinged with her growing impatience. "Where are you, we really have to go now!"
"Don't worry, mother, I won't be long! I just have to find my second earring!" a clear voice rang from the inside of the house.
Taemwadjsi sighed. She decided to give her daughter just a little more time. It came in useful that she always took those little delays into account whenever she planned to go out.
Her daughter was a dear, lovely girl, but with her rather careless ways and her love for extensive strolls in the garden her demeanor more resembled that of a boy. And of course Sitiah was not overly keen on tidiness, as Taemwadjsi had just noticed once again. How would Sitiah ever be able to manage a large household and oversee the servants if she did not change her ways soon?
Taemwadjsi stopped herself from dwelling on these worrying thoughts. Now was not the time.
She knew that the proficient Nubian servant Karma, who always took good care of Sitiah, had already started to hunt for the missing earring. She would not rest until she had found it. Taemwadjsi could only hope that it would not take all that long.
Her daughter finally appeared in the courtyard, complete with two earrings.
"Sorry, Mother, but I had to see to Nofret first", she explained. "Do I look smart?"
Taemwadjsi sighed. There had surely been no need to see to the cat, who was always well cared for. But then she smiled.

"Yes, darling, you really do look pretty," she said in response to Sitiah's question.

The girl who was almost nine years old and quite tall for her age was certainly a pretty sight. Her immaculate white dress was made of the finest pleated linen, and a dark blue sash wound around her narrow waist. A broad flexible collar which consisted of countless coloured glass inlays and a pair of fine leather sandals completed her outfit.

Karma had carefully woven glittering glass pearls into a few strands of Sitiah's luscious black hair which fell thick and heavy onto her back and framed her heart-shaped face.

On her arms she wore a few ivory bangles which her father had brought from Nubia along with the precious earrings; golden discs with dangling strands of tiny beads. The girl wore no make-up, apart from a thin line of black Kohl which bordered her large almond-shaped eyes.

Taemwadjsi's outfit resembled that of her daughter, only her dress was a pale yellow and she wore a heavy elaborate wig. She had applied green Malachit to her eyelids and her lips were tinted red.

"Now we should really go, or we shall not arrive in time to greet your father when he leaves the palace."

They mounted their litters which were then each lifted up by four muscular Nubian slaves. Placing the carrying poles gently onto their shoulders they set off, heading towards the royal palace.

While they were on their way Taemwadjsi's thoughts trailed back to the early stages of her husband's impressive career, which had resulted in todays appointment to the office of a King's Son of Kush, an office second in importance only to that of the vizier. Under the previous rulers Amunhotep, her husband, who was usually called by his nickname Huy, had already excelled as a "Brave one of His Majesty's cavalry" and as an "Ambassador to all foreign lands". He had then become secretary to Merimose, the King's Son of Kush at the time. Huy had done his job so well that he was also given the lucrative office of "Overseer of all cattle in the land of Kush" shortly after. Now, finally, the new ruler was about to make him King's Son of Kush himself, and he would also be granted the title of an "Overseer of the gold lands of the Lord of the Two Lands". She couldn't be more proud of him.

The only disadvantage was that Huy's place of work was far from her home town of Waset. He had spent much time in Nubia, and she had visited him several times. She had not liked the country much, and abhorred its extremely hot climate, but she definitely appreciated the high social status she enjoyed there.

During that time her two sons Turi and Paser, who were respectively six and eight years older than Sitiah, had taken part in the lessons of the *Kap*, the palace school attended by princes and the sons of high dignitaries. Later, they had taken up their respective duties as King's Herold and Overseer of the Chariotry.

For quite some time Sitiah had joined the lessons of the *Kap* as well. This had been her father's express wish, for he wanted to make sure that not only his sons, but also his bright daughter would receive the best education possible.

In Taemwadjsi's opinion this had been quite unnecessary, since as a girl Sitiah would never pursue a career of her own, anyway. She just had to find a well-off husband who would take good care of her, and to become an effective "Lady of the House". And for that purpose she did not need to be literate. A position as a singer or dancer in one of the temples would be more appropriate for her. Besides, the interaction with so many boys in the *Kap* had certainly not contributed to Sitiah becoming more lady-like. But Huy did not share her concerns at all.

Taemwadjsi's thoughts came to a sudden halt when her litter was gently set on the ground. She was amazed to see that they had already arrived at the royal palace. She had hardly noticed the bustling crowds in the streets of the thriving city as she was carried along. Taemwadjsi was grateful that even two months into his reign the new Pharaoh still resided in Waset, sparing them the long journey to Mennefer in the north of the country, where the royal court would soon move.

They dismounted their litters and looked around. The wide open space in front of the palace was full of people, many of whom belonged to their own household. A small group of men stood some way off, and one of them greeted them with a friendly smile.

Taemwadjsi nodded politely, and Sitiah became curious. "Who are these men?" she asked.

"The one who greeted me is called Penniut, one of your father's most trusted colleagues. From now on he will be his deputy for the land of Wawat."

"What is Wawat, and who are the others?" her daughter demanded.

"Wawat is the northern part of the land of Nubia, Kush the southern part. Your father will have his residence in Wawat."

"Residence?" Sitiah's eyes widened with excitement. "Will he live in a real palace?"

Her mother laughed. "Well, it won't be quite as impressive as the king's palace, but at any rate it'll be a grand and spacious house. And to answer the rest of your question, the men are all members of Nubia's administration, but I do not know all their names."

Everyone now glanced expectantly at the great gate of the palace. Sitiah could feel that it would not take long for them to open. To while away the time she let her eyes travel over the vast facade of the palace wall that stretched along as far as she could see. She took in every detail of the many niches and the high flagpoles mounted in each of them. The bold colours of the merrily fluttering flags were in sharp contrast to the deep blue of the sky.

Not a sound was to be heard from the inside of the palace.

****

A large crowd of courtiers dressed in splendid white garments had gathered in the audience chamber, intently following the proceedings in front of them. At the opposite end of the hall the glint of gold which beamed off the broad double row of uraeus serpents surmounting the royal canopy caught the eye. Underneath, elevated on the throne dais, sat the Good Ruler, the Lord of the Two Lands, King Tutankhaten Nebkheperure. Wearing the Blue Crown and clutching crook and flail, the insignia of his royal power, his feet rested on an elaborate foot stool decorated with nine bound captives. He watched the ceremony with dignified interest, or so it seemed. In reality he longed for it to be over. Not because his cube-shaped throne virtually lacked a backrest and was therefore rather uncomfortable to sit on, nor because of the pungent scent of sweet perfume which rose from the courtiers and surrounded him in thick swaths, but for reasons which ran much deeper. During his short reign Tutankhaten had already presided over several investitures of various officials. He did not actively take part in the procedures, which were usually carried out by the highest members of the royal court, most often his uncle Ay.

This had nothing to do with his very young age, but rather with the extraordinary importance of his own person. Even the highest dignitary was not allowed to receive his seal of office directly from the king's own hand.

Today's investiture was carried out by Maya, the new Overseer of the Treasury. This might have been due to the immense economic importance that was attached to the office of the King's Son of Kush. He was responsible for the constant and ever increasing flow of precious raw materials into Kemet, especially gold.

"A seal it is from the king, may he live, be prosperous and healthy, who commends to you the land from Nekhen to Napata!" Maya announced just now, presenting Huy with the golden seal of office. In return Huy praised the king's greatness with a rehearsed tribute, which all the other courtiers soon joined.

But Tutankhaten was hardly aware of their words, for he thought fervently of a way to deliver the tiny scrap of papyrus which he had carefully hidden in his broad sash to its recipient. He had already devised some kind of plan, which he had to unfortunately share with somebody else. Pahwah, a member of his personal guard, was a young man he knew he could trust. Tutankhaten had already told Pahwah what he had to do: hand the papyrus over to Huy's young daughter, in a manner as unsuspecting as possible. It had to be done in secrecy, without anyone knowing.

This was no easy task, the young king had to admit. But Pahwah would just have to think of something, and Tutankhaten himself would have to see to it that Pahwah could come close enough to the girl in order to carry out his task without giving the game away. Tutankhaten assumed that Huy would want to visit the temple straight away once he was finished here. If so, he would certainly take his family with him. That was their chance, but only if his assumption was right. He would have to gather his guard quickly and follow Huy on his way. Tutankhaten suddenly saw the funny side of his thoughts, and stopped himself from chuckling just in time. Here he was, presiding over his court in all his splendour, but all the while worrying about nothing but a tiny scrap of papyrus.

Then he heaved a sigh of relief. *Finally,* he thought, when Huy bowed down deeply before him. The ceremony was over at last. And now for the temple.

With a graceful nod he allowed his new King's Son of Kush to leave his presence.

****

After what seemed a very long time, Sitiah heard voices from beyond the great gate, accompanied by merry shouts, laughter and clapping. The enormous door leaves were pulled back by invisible hands, and out stepped the newly invested King's Son of Kush, followed by his two sons and several courtiers. Huy instantly spotted Sitiah and her mother, and approached them with a broad smile on his face.

Sitiah would have loved to rush up to him and throw her arms around his neck, but she remembered what her mother had told her. She had to behave more like a lady.

So she waited until her father had reached them and handed her one of the two bunches of pretty flowers, still smiling. He gave her a quick hug, then he turned to his wife.

"Congratulations, dear husband," Taemwadjsi said, moved. "I am so proud of you."

"And I am just as proud of you," he declared. "I know well that you dislike many things about the land of Kush, and yet you try to put up with them for my sake. I have really worked hard, of course, but without your support I would never had come so far. May my new office be a blessing for us all! Besides, I am really looking forward to the grand reception at home."

Sitiah looked enquiringly at her father. "Whom do we expect?"

"Someone's being nosy again," her older brother Paser tutted.

"And for whom have you dressed up like this, anyway?" Turi teased, pulling gently at one of her beaded strands of hair.

Sitiah scowled. "You do not quite look like stable boys either!" she shot back.

This made everybody laugh. Indeed, according to the occasion the two young men were dressed in their finest garments and even wore fashionable wigs, just like their father.

Sitiah looked at her father lovingly. That was what she liked about him most: his radiant smile and the many tiny wrinkles that formed at the corners of his warm brown eyes. She was relieved to see that even the importance of his new office did not prevent him from smiling, as she had secretly feared.

"Now we must leave for the temple, or we shall be late for our own reception," Huy declared with a wink.

He instructed one of his servants to bring his chariot which was his favorite means of travel. During his wait he was surrounded by more people all congratulating him on his success. Eventually the group of men whom Taemwadjsi had introduced as Huy's colleagues approached them.

"Greetings, noble King's Son of Kush who is to be praised! May the blessings of the gods be with you and your family, and may our efforts in the land of Kush be crowned by success!"

Huy and Penniut embraced each other warmly.

"Thank you," Huy replied. "We will get along well, that's for sure."

After he had exchanged a few words with the other men he mounted his chariot. Nodding briefly he took up the reins, and the magnificent brown stallions fell into a trot. Paser and Turi followed him in their own chariots, while Sitiah and her mother mounted their litters.

They soon reached the nearby temple of Ipet-Sut. Huy, who had been awaiting them, led his family through the first of the towering pylons. The offerings consisting of different kinds of bread, fruit and flowers were carried by servants who then arranged them neatly on a nearby offering table. A bald priest started incantations while another burned incense. The sweet smelling fumes tickled Sitiah's nose, and she was glad to leave the temple.

In the first courtyard she and her mother waited for the men to catch up with them. Soon Sitiah was so absorbed by the colourful paintings on the surface of the great pylon that she was hardly aware of the sound of approaching horses. But then her attention suddenly snapped to the chariots rolling into the courtyard.

The exquisiteness of the three chariots and the fact that they were accompanied by a staggering number of guards led her to the conclusion that this had to be a very important person indeed. In fact, it could be no other than the king himself, who was surrounded by a wall of guards as soon as he dismounted from his chariot.

Her heart began to beat faster. She had just managed to catch a glimpse of him. She had so wished to see him, but now her knees grew weak and all courage left her.

Someone pulled at her sleeve, and Sitiah remembered to move back and bow down as the etiquette required.

The group of men were moving towards the temple, but all of a sudden she heard the sound of steps very close by. Surprised, she lifted her head and saw one of the king's guards approaching her, carefully avoiding to look at her. Sitiah's eyes widened when his hand touched hers, apparently trying to put something into it. Startled, she closed her fingers around whatever it was and hid it hastily under her sash.

The man just looked on and kept going, leaving Sitiah very confused indeed.

Just now, through a gap in the ring of guards, her gaze fell on the king who had slowed down his steps, looking intently at her. She tried hard to ignore the Blue Crown he wore with its protecting vulture and cobra and focused on the familiar face instead. One by one she took in its features: the boldly arched eyebrows, the expressive dark eyes outlined with Kohl, the strikingly slim nose and the firm chin.

Then their eyes met, and Sitiah instantly felt that the invisible bond between them had not been broken. Tutankhaten seemed to feel the same, and a smile so slight that it was hardly perceptible lay on his full lips. Sitiah knew well that no one was supposed to stare at the king in such an inappropriate manner, but she just couldn't help it.

Eventually he had advanced so far that he had to tear his gaze from her. Sitiah saw him and his followers disappear under the huge doorway of the pylon.

The spell was broken, and all of a sudden Sitiah remembered the tiny object which had come into her possession so unexpectedly. She was eager to uncover its secret.

****

End of preview